The Longest Siege

The Longest Siege
Port Hudson, Louisiana, 1863

RUSSELL W. BLOUNT, JR.

McFarland & Company, Inc., Publishers
Jefferson, North Carolina

LIBRARY OF CONGRESS CATALOGUING-IN-PUBLICATION DATA

Names: Blount, Russell W., Jr., 1946– author.
Title: The Longest Siege : Port Hudson, Louisiana,
1863 / Russell W. Blount, Jr.
Other titles: Port Hudson, Louisiana, 1863
Description: Jefferson, North Carolina :
McFarland & Company, Inc., Publishers, 2021 |
Includes bibliographical references and index.
Identifiers: LCCN 2021034528 | ISBN 9781476684116 (paperback : acid free paper) ∞
ISBN 9781476643366 (ebook)
Subjects: LCSH: Port Hudson (La.)—History—Siege, 1863.
| BISAC: HISTORY / Military / United States
Classification: LCC E475.42 .B56 2021 | DDC 973.7/34—dc23
LC record available at https://lccn.loc.gov/2021034528

BRITISH LIBRARY CATALOGUING DATA ARE AVAILABLE

ISBN (print) 978-1-4766-8411-6
ISBN (ebook) 978-1-4766-4336-6

© 2021 Russell W. Blount, Jr. All rights reserved

*No part of this book may be reproduced or transmitted in any form
or by any means, electronic or mechanical, including photocopying
or recording, or by any information storage and retrieval system,
without permission in writing from the publisher.*

Cover image: Admiral Farragut's fleet engaging
the rebel batteries at Port Hudson, March 14, 1863;
map of Port Hudson (Library of Congress).

Printed in the United States of America

*McFarland & Company, Inc., Publishers
Box 611, Jefferson, North Carolina 28640
www.mcfarlandpub.com*

For Mark and John,
young men with a love for history

Table of Contents

Acknowledgments	ix
Preface	1
CHAPTER ONE: Changes in Commands	7
CHAPTER TWO: A Natural Stronghold	22
CHAPTER THREE: "The Very Earth Trembled"	34
CHAPTER FOUR: "The Enemy Are Coming"	48
CHAPTER FIVE: A Miserable Loss	60
CHAPTER SIX: "Death Was Always with Us"	76
CHAPTER SEVEN: "This Day of Blood"	94
CHAPTER EIGHT: Unspeakably Dreadful Days	107
CHAPTER NINE: The Whisky Charge	119
CHAPTER TEN: Submission	132
Epilogue	145
Appendix A. The Port Hudson Garrison: Organizations Paroled at Port Hudson, July 10, 1863	157
Appendix B. Organization of the Union Troops at Port Hudson (Nineteenth Army Corps), as of May 31, 1863, Major General Nathaniel P. Banks, Commanding	159
Chapter Notes	163
Bibliography	175
Index	181

Acknowledgments

In the research, writing and publication of this book, I am indebted to a number of people who gave of their time, work and advice. While there are some whom I've met or communicated with, there are others I know only through their words, written in books and articles, which were based on their tireless efforts in researching and telling the stories of the past. They are the historians, both past and present. For those historic writers such as John D. Winters, Edward Cunningham and Lawrence Lee Hewitt, who have contributed to both the literature of both Port Hudson and the Mississippi Valley Campaign, I am most grateful. Their narratives are excellent examples of historical research. Some of the historians I have relied on are well-known in Civil War literature. But there are others whom the reader will understandably not recognize. Those were the actual participants in the event, who made valuable contributions to this work through their memoirs, letters and diaries. Although they were not acclaimed and, for the most part, long forgotten, they, too, were historians, who should be acknowledged as such. We are fortunate that following the war a number of them had their recollections published in books, unit histories, personal memoirs, and diaries. For me, their accounts were indispensable in lending depth and perspective to the Port Hudson story. Thankfully, because of our current electronic age, most of those narratives are now archived on the Internet and readily available.

As with my previous books about specific battles, I've always felt obligated to walk the ground where the event took place before trying to describe it to the reader. While it's true that Mother Nature is always changing her landscapes, it's also true that what remains of those sites is important for us to preserve and maintain for historical posterity. The state of Louisiana should be commended for the job of doing that at Port Hudson. It's unfortunate that the town itself is no longer there. Much of it was destroyed in the daily cannonading of the siege, and what little remained slowly disappeared when the Mississippi River nudged its course away from the ruins. However, the land surrounding the once bustling town of

Port Hudson still remains. Yet it's something of a paradox, both magnificent and eerie—"lovely, dark, and deep," as Robert Frost once put it. Standing beneath the canopy of those trees, I could imagine being in one of nature's most beautiful cathedrals, though one that's haunted by a violent past. That said, I would like to give a special thank-you to Interpretive Ranger Marvin Steinback at the Port Hudson State Historic Site, who guided me through those preserved areas of the battlefield where men began killing each other in the spring of 1863. Along the way, he freely offered valuable explanations for matters which I would have, otherwise, never known. I'm also grateful to Marvin for providing me with access to the photographs from the historic collection at Port Hudson.

Although I write at home in my basement office, a reclusive refuge I fondly refer to as "the Bunker," much of my research is done at the Local History and Genealogy branch of the Public Library in Mobile. In that regard, I owe a great debt to Elizabeth Theris-Boone, known to the library's patrons as "Lizzy," and her staff of archivists, Valerie Ellis and Denisha Logan. They provided me with access to indispensable sources of information, such as the U.S. government's *War of the Rebellion: A Compilation of the Union and Confederate Armies,* containing copious volumes of every pertinent scrap of paper produced by both armies during the war. While the Official Records, as they're commonly called, are probably the most essential documents housed in the Mobile library, so, too, are many others, such as the the fifty-two-volume compilation set of *Southern Historical Papers*; a complete set of the *Rebellion Record: A Diary of American Events*; the series entitled *Battles and Leaders of the Civil War*; together with numerous periodicals such as the *Louisiana Historical Quarterly, Louisiana History, Alabama Historical Quarterly* and *Alabama Review.*

For reasons that would be of no interest to the reader, this book was difficult to write. Suffice it to say that a book does not miraculously leap forth between its covers. This one was no exception. It required the effort of many competent and diligent people. For that reason, I owe a special debt of gratitude to the editorial staff at McFarland, not only for agreeing to publish this book but for their tireless efforts to make it better. From the very beginning and throughout the entire process, they showed great patience, gently prodding me onward, always with the right blend of encouragement, faith, and constructive suggestions. Specifically, many thanks to McFarland's resourceful editors David Alff and Charlie Perdue.

Last, but under no circumstances least, I thank my family. To my lovely wife, Elaine, I have once again found myself indebted to her. Although she disclaims any expertise on the Civil War, she read and reread every page of the manuscript, offering grammatical suggestions and corrections, no doubt intent on saving me from embarrassment when it passed under the cold, clinical eye of a copy editor. She also took on the tedious task of indexing. And to my son, Russell III, or Trip, as we call him, go my sincere thanks. As with all my previous books, he expended much time and effort in dealing with the photographs and permissions. He is truly a young man of unrivaled loyalty and will. To both Trip and Elaine go my everlasting love and thanks.

To these and all who shared in the making of this book, I extend my profound thanks for their contributions, which hopefully made this a better book. As to any remaining faults or errors, I accept full responsibility.

The enemy are coming, but mark you,
many a one will get to hell before he does to Port Hudson.
—Franklin Gardner

Preface

In the middle of July 1863, one week after the surrender of Port Hudson, the *Imperial*, a cargo boat from St. Louis, sailed without escort into the port of New Orleans and unloaded its freight. Ordinarily, this would have been an everyday, uneventful sight in such a large port except for the fact that it marked the first time in two and a half years that the Mississippi River was open for commerce all the way from the state of Minnesota to the Gulf of Mexico. It also marked the end of a prolonged struggle by the Union to gain complete control of this all-important waterway, which split the Southern Confederacy in two. The news renewed the spirit of the people of the North, especially Abraham Lincoln, who gratefully remarked: "The Father of Waters again goes unvexed to the sea." Conversely, this was a devastating blow to the South, preventing their armies from receiving food and supplies from the bountiful supply that flowed from the severed western regions.

Accomplishing this was the most decisive and critical undertaking by the Union armies during the American Civil War. Thus the campaign was long, harsh and critical, extending up and down the Mississippi River Valley, furiously raging through places in Missouri like Belmont and New Madrid, sweeping across Tennessee at Forts Henry and Donelson, Shiloh and Memphis, into Mississippi past the bluffs of the river town of Vicksburg, and engulfing Louisiana from New Orleans to Baton Rouge, and finally to Port Hudson. Along the way, a multitude of soldiers, wearing both the blue and gray, would lose their lives in the fight for possession of America's largest and most magnificent river.

By late 1862, the Confederacy had lost control of most of this vitally important waterway. What remained under their command was a 110-mile crow's-flight stretch of the lower Mississippi River. Following its winding meanders, however, that distance would dramatically increase to about three hundred miles. Commanding this length of the Mississippi insured the blockage of Union traffic to and from New Orleans. Adding to the importance of the geography within this last segment of the river still under Confederate control was the convergence of the Red River, the supply artery from the west. So, there's little wonder why the Confederate government was determined to hold on to and protect this last span of the

River from falling into Union hands. To insure against this happening, they established two mighty fortresses anchoring each end: Vicksburg on the north and Port Hudson on the south.

Volumes of literature now exist on the events surrounding the much larger fortress at Vicksburg. But, for the most part, Port Hudson has not been so well advertised. Typically, it appears in the historical accounts of Vicksburg as a sort of sideshow, hidden or neglected in the shadow of the greater contest. However, the two bastions were bonded together in the defense of the river, and the Union would have to take both of them to insure their objective. But it's also true that the ultimate fate of each of them depended on the survival of the other. This is the story of the smaller garrison at Port Hudson and the lengthy and determined stand made there by the Confederate defenders. Although their tenacious resistance did not affect the outcome of the war, it played an important role in the struggle for the Mississippi River. The struggle to take Port Hudson continued for seven long weeks, and required the exertion and sacrifice of a great many Union troops, who would have otherwise been deployed against Vicksburg. That alone delayed the Union's victory there, and prolonged a war considered by many to be the most cruel and desperate chapter in America's history.

Over the years, a few excellent historical works which specifically focused on the Port Hudson Campaign have appeared in Civil War literature. Many of these are cited in my bibliography and acknowledgments. Most of these accounts detailed the fighting, day by day, throughout the siege. After becoming interested in this important incident in history, I felt the story deserved a retelling. Moreover, I decided to approach it in a different manner, which may not be apparent from the title or the table of contents. First, I felt it would be worthwhile to give an account of the political, economic and military circumstances leading up to actual event. That, I hoped, would give the reader at least some appreciation of the enormous stakes involved in the contest for control of the Mississippi River and, by extension, the entire Mississippi Valley. Beyond that, I intended to present a more accurate portrayal of the characters, primarily the commanders, who displayed the best and the worst traits of leadership. Perhaps in no other campaign could one find men in authority with such a wide variety of the human persona: brilliance, ineptitude, valor, cowardice, tenacity, indecision, humility and arrogance were all present during this campaign. Finally, without neglecting the important battle pieces, I wanted to re-create more of the common soldiers' experience, both blue and gray, as they endured the horror and miseries associated with the unique tactic of warfare known as the siege.

The siege, of course, is an ancient military practice which has been used by armies for centuries, dating back to Old Testament days. Typically, it follows certain procedures, and often has far deadlier results than a single grand battle. By definition, it requires that the enemy position be surrounded or blockaded, and then compelled to surrender by every method of war and external pressure that the besiegers could bring to bear. Because those being besieged had no means of receiving food and supplies for a prolonged period of time, starvation was the most persuasive force. From 70 AD when Titus Flavius and his Roman legions besieged Jerusalem to the German siege of Leningrad during World War II, extreme hunger has played a crucial role in forcing surrenders. In the cases of both Jerusalem and Leningrad, the starvation was so severe that it led to cannibalism. That aside, armies also employed other methods to expedite the submission of an enemy stronghold. Those were, of course, more deadly and diabolical than the slow, agonizing process of starvation. Through the years, weapons and methods used in sieges have been refined. Early weapons such as giant catapults were eventually replaced by artillery barrages and bombings. By the time of the Civil War, cannons and mortars of all sizes were employed to reduce the surrounded bastion to rubble, and the digging of approach trenches and tunnels had become the preferred maneuver of advancing against the enemy fortifications. Apart from the physical components of a siege, there was always a constant, grinding, psychological strain, which soldiers on both sides were forced to endure. They were fraught with the nerve-racking, never-ending threats of death from sniper fire, cannonades, and the diseases which festered within such close living conditions.

Without question, Port Hudson was a classic example of a siege, and is believed to be the most prolonged one of the American Civil War. During the course of writing this book, I had the opportunity of being guided over much of the ground that has been preserved around the site, which gave me a better understanding of what made this siege so difficult and long-lasting. While it presented a sort of primordial beauty, the terrain surrounding the place was one of the worst imaginable in which to fight. Then again, wars have always seemed to be capricious in choosing the stages upon which they will perform their tragedies. The land was, and still is, interspersed with creeks, vine-clogged, chocolate swamps, forest lands chopped up with steep ridges and deep ravines. Here and there, farm fields offered better movement but little protection from the flying projectiles. The great Mississippi River bordered one of its sides, where Union gunboats prowled its waters. The enclosure was completed by the breastworks of the Union army, strung out in a giant semicircle and anchored on each side by the river. Within this confinement, the town of Port Hudson and its fortifications were both surrounded and blockaded. Here, all the components of a siege were present: the battles and skirmishes, the incessant shelling and sniper fire, the diggings, the filth, sickness and disease, starvation, and the constant tension created by this sort of warfare.

This book tells the story of men at war, fighting under these conditions. They were the common soldiers who came from all kinds of backgrounds and walks of life. Among them were the Louisiana Native Guards who, for obvious reasons, fought on the Union side. At Port Hudson, they were the first all-black volunteer regiment to participate in a major Civil War battle. They were certainly a unique outfit. Recruited mainly in New Orleans, a cosmopolitan city with less bigotry than the rest of the "Old South," many of those black soldiers were free men. In the First regiment of the Louisiana Native Guards, all of the men were free, and most had backgrounds as skilled laborers, such as barbers, cobblers, carpenters or bricklayers. A few were educated, owned businesses, and were prosperous. Many of these black men were made line officers, although the higher field officers were white. The Second and Third Regiments, however, were mainly former slaves. Yet all of them were aware of the question that confronted them: Would they fight when engaged in actual battle? Because most of the high-ranking officers, such as Banks and his predecessor Butler, were skeptical of their willingness to fight and their military value, black soldiers often found themselves assigned to menial tasks like guard duty, or performing labor that was shunned by the white soldiers and referred to as fatigue duty, such as digging trenches, making roads, or hauling supplies. At Port Hudson, however, they were given their first opportunity to prove that they would meet the challenge of battle and fight.

I should mention here that precious little exists in the way of primary materials for black soldiers, such as letters and diaries. Even in the Louisiana Native Guards, most were ex-slaves and entered the service without being able to read or write. History depends on such firsthand documents, and without them there is a very empty pocket of silence: the voices of the black soldiers. Since no primary accounts of their experience at Port Hudson were available to me, I was, for the most part, compelled to rely on reports penned by white officers who led the black regiments, or the testimonies of rank-and-file white soldiers. Fortunately, there have been several recent histories that authenticated and complemented those accounts, such as Noah Andre Trudeau's *Like Men of War* and James Hollandsworth's *Louisiana Native Guards*, which are well-researched and excellent accounts of the black military experience in the Civil War.

On the other hand, there is no scarcity of firsthand documents written by white soldiers. A mountain of reports, diaries, letters and memoirs are available to plow through. They provide a valuable insight into the thoughts and feelings of the common soldiers. But more importantly, at least for me, they give us a glimpse of why these men fought, suffered and died. For those who enlisted, their primary reason seemed to be the notion that war would somehow be a romantic adventure, a popular opinion they quickly learned was anything but true, especially with the conditions they found in and around Port Hudson. Nevertheless, some of them still proved to be courageous, even heroic in perilous situations. Others, mostly conscripts, were sometimes discovered to be deserters, malingerers or cowards who pretended to be ill or wounded, and ran to the rear at the first sounds of battle. Some simply refused to fight because their enlistments were about to expire. A few of them broke down emotionally under the horrors surrounding them, and were hospitalized or sent to the rear. But most of them, in fact the vast majority of these men, were the sort of men that make wars possible in the first place. As a rule, they willingly accepted their duties and responsibilities, crouched down in their holes and trenches, charged when ordered, and grimly agreed to endure whatever was required of them.

This is also an unforgettable story of the leaders who led the common soldiers through this campaign. They were the generals and high-ranking field officers, both Union and Confederate. As to the Confederate officers led by Franklin Gardner, they did a remarkable job organizing and executing the defense of Port Hudson for as long as they did, especially in light of the shortages in food, ammunition, and other supplies. Yet it should be remembered that Gardner and most of the Rebel officers under his command were veterans with at least some prior experience in the hardships of battle. Because of the knowledge and exposure gained from previous campaigns, they were better prepared for the trials of a siege. Finding themselves deprived of outside help, the Southern officers exercised incredible ingenuity in overcoming the difficult predicaments of that brand of warfare. Such ingenuity was particularly true of Franklin Gardner, who, like most other engineers, possessed a clever, problem-solving mind, and was an excellent and resourceful commander in defending against an extended siege.

On the Union side, Nathaniel Banks was unfortunately surrounded by many high-ranking officers who had no military knowledge or experience. In researching this book, I was astonished to learn this. Although it's true that he inherited some of these officers from Benjamin Butler, many of those under his command had accompanied him in his expeditionary force to Louisiana, and were handpicked by Banks. Regrettably, some of those turned out to be as poorly trained as the troops they were supposed to be leading. Others, who were trained, competent, West Point graduates and career military men, were naturally resentful of being commanded by a political appointee such as Banks. To make matters worse, Banks himself had no military background, and never hesitated to promote or appoint a man solely for political expediency, a practice that, time after time, proved disastrous. Even more troublesome, some of Banks's officers neglected their military duties in favor of enriching themselves by seizing and speculating in Southern cotton. All of this, taken together, resulted in a recipe for a poorly led army, and the needless loss of many lives. Thus, for the most part, the book's characterization of Banks as a commander, along with some of his general officers, such as William Dwight, is a harsh one. This is not to suggest that Banks lacked admirable strengths and virtues. He had many. His list of prewar achievements indicated this, and I have tried to give him credit where it was due. But his flaws and miscalculations as a military commander continued to manifest themselves throughout the siege, which will be evident to the reader in the following pages.

These, then, were my reasons and explanations for wanting to write about a long-forgotten and often overlooked occurrence in our great American Civil War. This book is my attempt to present the Port Hudson story using what knowledge and talent I've been blessed with. I'm sure many of the soldiers who fought at Port Hudson also had a story to tell, and I've allowed at least some of them to share it through their letters, diaries and reminiscences. Seen through their eyes, I hope the reader will feel a sense of being present during this time. What remains is the tale of a hard-fought campaign as I understood and interpreted it.

Chapter One

Changes in Commands

On Sunday evening, December 14, 1862, a man wearing the uniform of a United States army officer stepped off the steamer *North Star* and made his way into the Union-occupied city of New Orleans. Onlookers immediately knew that this was a man of some importance. Clearly, they had many reasons for thinking this, not the least of which were the epaulettes of a major general adorning his shoulders. Surrounding this immaculate uniform were a group of bodyguards dressed in their colorful Zouave's uniforms, striking by their distinctive blue jackets, baggy red trousers and matching fezzes. The man under their watch was handsome, dignified, and almost aristocratic, with a full head of thick brown hair, a splendid, broad mustache and round gray eyes. And although he was not impressively tall, standing only five feet eight inches, a newspaperman, noting his erect posture and attractive demeanor, commented how he "stands up square, and looks you square in the face."[1]

His name was Nathaniel Prentiss Banks, and those who knew the forty-seven-year-old general agreed that he had "a genius for being looked at." Even his enemies admired his patrician bearing. Admiral David Dixon Porter, for example, a lifelong military man, and one who had small use for Banks, admitted after the war that he "never saw a more faultless-looking soldier." But looks do not make a soldier and, to his misfortune, looking the part was about all Banks was able to accomplish in his military career. Banks, in fact, had no military training or qualifications, and despite being an articulate spokesman with a resonant voice and a vast knowledge of a number of subjects, he had received very little formal education. He was, however, bright and extremely ambitious, but a person known as a political appointee or commissioned politician, a popular but poor practice employed by both North and South during the American Civil War.[2]

In Banks's case, from the early days of the war, President Lincoln saw a man who could bring a great amount of popular support to his administration, and thus offered him a commission as major general of the army. After all, before the war the popular Banks was Speaker of the House of

Representatives and later governor of the state of Massachusetts. With such credentials, Lincoln knew that Banks's appointment would not only bring recruits to the army, but also give a boost of morale to the war effort. What's more, Banks, like Lincoln, was a moderate Republican, and they were usually in agreement on political issues. Also, both men were self-educated and self-made, lifting themselves up from their humble, working-class beginnings to careers in law and politics. Banks was born in Waltham, Massachusetts, in 1816, and his hopes for the future had looked bleak. He was the oldest of nine children, and like many of the firstborn of those times, he was forced to quit school at the age of fourteen and go to work in a cotton mill that his father supervised to help support the family. There, he was assigned the menial and monotonous job of replacing bobbins (empty reels) when they were full of thread. Later, rising from his lowly origins through a great deal of self-study and determination, he emerged into the political spotlight, and was dubbed with the sobriquet the "Bobbin Boy of Massachusetts," or sometimes "Bobbin Boy Banks."[3]

From the very beginning of "Bobbin Boy's" career as a general, his lack of military experience and knowledge proved to be disappointing. After Banks was thrashed from one end of the Shenandoah Valley to the other by Stonewall Jackson and his small Confederate army, Lincoln, despite the criticism of the appointment, decided to make Banks commander of the Department of the Gulf. And it was clearly an important assignment. By now the Union was closing in on one of its primary war objectives: complete control of the Mississippi River and cutting the Confederacy in two. The planned strategy was for Banks to march his army up from New Orleans, which Admiral David Farragut had taken in April of 1862, and join Ulysses Grant in capturing Vicksburg, a stronghold that both sides referred to as the "Gibraltar of the West." But even though this would be his primary objective, Lincoln also had some other plans in mind, plans that would require the skills of a politician, like Banks, to accomplish. The general, of course, at this time had no perception of Lincoln's intentions or plans for Louisiana, and would only learn of them after he assumed command.[4]

After arriving in New Orleans, Banks officially assumed command of the Department of the Gulf on December 16. Accompanied by his staff, he met General Benjamin Franklin Butler at the Custom House, which, along with the St. Charles Hotel, had served as his headquarters. Although Butler had heard the constant rumors that he was about to be replaced as commander of the department, the sudden appearance of Banks was still a surprise. Banks gave him no explanation, simply presented him with the official order from Washington, signed by Lincoln's general in chief, Henry W. Halleck. Despite being handed the bad news, Butler, a man who possessed an irresistible social charm when he cared to exert it, cordially welcomed Banks and graciously accepted the fact that he was being replaced. Or so it seemed. Butler hated Banks, a feeling which likely came from an envy of the political success of his dignified replacement. Like Banks, Butler was a former politician with no military experience. Although he was formerly a Democrat, who ironically nominated Jefferson Davis for president in the 1860 election, he was also a crafty opportunist who switched parties after Lincoln was elected and was rewarded with an appointment as major general of volunteers. It wasn't long afterwards before Butler moved into the radical wing of the Republican Party, where he remained until after the war, when he became a ringleader in the Andrew Johnson impeachment. Afterwards, as a member of Congress, he once again began changing his party affiliations whenever it happened to be politically expedient.

Major General Nathaniel P. Banks commanded the Union Nineteenth Corps and the Department of the Gulf. Library of Congress.

Unlike Banks, however, the forty-four-year-old Butler had no genius for being looked at. He was a short, dumpy, cross-eyed man with a chubby, mustached face and sagging eyelids and jowls. His head was bald with the exception of some long, stringy hair dangling from the sides and back of it. He was, in sum, a most unsightly man. His looks, however, were not his worst characteristic. Since New Orleans had been captured by the Union and Butler was named its military commander, he had managed to provoke the ire of nearly everyone in the city. It wasn't long before the politician turned general won the nickname "Beast Butler" for his nefarious doings. Even the job of reporting his doings was described by the *Daily Picayune* as a "repulsive one." First, he told the citizens to sign a loyalty oath to the government and renounce their allegiance to the Confederacy. If they failed to do so, all of their property was confiscated and sold as contraband. Sadly, that also included people's silverware, earning him a second moniker: "Spoons." Many of those who opposed him were thrown into prison. Butler sentenced one zealous Southerner who was caught cheering for Jefferson Davis to three months of hard labor. Another citizen, named William Mumford, made the rebellious mistake of tearing down the American flag from the Federal mint, and was tried and convicted of "high crimes and misdemeanors," then hanged in the mint's courtyard. Butler even suspected foreign consuls of aiding the Rebels, and some of them were placed under guard. Newspapers were strictly censored or shut down. Public assemblies were forbidden. Churches were either closed or prohibited from any prayers or sermons dedicated to the Confederate cause. When the ladies of the city expressed their hate for the Union soldiers by glaring at them with contempt, or gathering their skirts and turning away when they passed, Butler issued his infamous order no. 28, otherwise known as the "woman order." That order stated, in part, that if any woman "shall, by word, gesture, or movement, insult or show contempt for any officer or soldier of the United States, she shall be regarded and held liable to be treated as a woman of the town, plying her trade."[5]

Butler's famous "woman order" was met with contempt by officials in the Confederate government as well as his political enemies in the North. Regardless of the general's intent, they interpreted it as an invitation for his soldiers to help themselves to sexually assaulting any woman who offended them. Propaganda aside, most everyone in the South and even people abroad railed against Butler as a barbaric despot. "Thousands," Sarah Morgan of Louisiana wrote in her diary, "would cut the brutal heart from his inhuman breast." Such attacks on the rotund general, did not seem to bother him. Like politicians down through the ages, he was tough-skinned. He also had the politician's inherent gift of gab, and could be most persuasive when arguing his point of view. When provoked by his critics, however, Butler could quickly display an irascible, hot temper. He had a vitriolic, scathing tongue, which provoked hard feelings and bitterness in those who had the misfortune to be lashed with it. New Orleans was a part of his legal empire and, as its king, he adamantly defended his coarse and tactless "woman order." In a letter to one of his friends back in Boston, he explained his reasoning: "The devil had entered into the hearts of the women of this town to stir up strife in every way possible. Every opprobrious epithet, every insulting gesture was made by these bejeweled, becrinolined and laced creatures, calling themselves ladies, towards my soldiers and officers, from the windows of the houses and on the streets."[6]

Aside from the ladies of New Orleans, Butler's most outspoken enemy was clearly Jefferson Davis, who called his behavior "revolting," and ordered him to be hanged if they could ever get their hands on him. After learning of Butler's belligerent order, Davis angrily penned an order of his own, which was contained in the following proclamation: "I ... declare the said Benjamin F. Butler to be a felon, deserving of capital punishment. I do order that he be no longer considered or treated simply as a public enemy of the Confederate States of America, but as an outlaw and common enemy of mankind, and that in the event of his capture the officer in command of the capturing force do cause him to be immediately executed by hanging; and I do further order that no commissioned officer of the United States taken captive shall be released on parole before exchange until the said Butler shall have met with the due punishment for his crimes."[7]

Major General Benjamin F. Butler, Union Military Governor of Louisiana. Library of Congress.

But for all the odious mandates and onerous laws the despotic Butler placed on the grumbling population of New Orleans, none could compare to the graft and corruption he had allowed to flourish under his rule. With the help of his brother, Colonel Andrew Butler, a greedy but jovial man of sizable proportions, the city had been turned into a nest of thieves, swindlers, vultures and speculators, all getting rich, reaping handsome profits from shady business transactions, confiscations and extortions. Planters' cotton, especially, being the most sought after treasure, was routinely seized by the Federals as contraband and sold for booming profits. Because of his lofty position, General Butler knew he must not take an active part in such unethical business dealings. Hence, he chose to remain a silent partner in the widespread thievery, leaving it to his brother, the rotund Andrew, to continue feeding both of their bloated bank accounts.

When complaints of Butler's draconian decrees began to reach Lincoln he felt compelled to replace him. Clearly, there were many reasons. First among them was the matter of reconciliation. The president had hoped to ease Louisiana back into the Union as a loyal state, and Butler had not been helping matters by continuing to infuriate the people of New Orleans. Lincoln was also unhappy that Butler had not been successful in solving the Negro problem. Many of them were homeless, runaway slaves who were destitute and, legally, still not free because New Orleans was under Union control, and the Emancipation Proclamation only applied to those areas still in rebellion. What's more, Butler's conflict with the foreign consuls had grown into a constant and vexing problem for Lincoln's State Department. In sum, Lincoln was satisfied that Butler had to go, and he was hoping for better results with Nathaniel Banks. Although, considering Banks's military record, it's unclear what that hope was based on.[8]

That, then, was the situation facing Banks as he began his tenure as military commander of New Orleans and the Department of the Gulf. Before arriving, Banks had expected his task to be mostly of a military nature with his primary objective being to cooperate with Grant in taking Vicksburg. But now he faced the monumental task of cleaning up the mess Butler had made on the civilian side as well. Within a couple of weeks of his arrival, he sat down and wrote Henry Halleck, unloading his frustration on the man who signed his orders. "The precise nature of the duties devolving upon me in assuming command of this department were not explained to me," he began his complaint. "I find ... on arriving here an immense military government, embracing every form of

President Abraham Lincoln. Library of Congress.

civil administration." He then went on to recount a long list of civil affairs being abused under the military government, the last of which was the business of corruption in "trade" and "commerce," which he described as "most embarrassing." Banks also shared many of these same feelings in a letter to his wife, Mary, and minced no words when it came to describing the corruption: "Everybody connected with the government has been employed in stealing other people's property," he told her, "sugar, silver plates, horses, carriages, everything they could lay their hands on." He would be in New Orleans less than two weeks when he received a note from a man named Smith, which read: "Dear Sir, If you will allow our commercial program to be [carried] out as projected previous to your arrival in this department, giving the same support and facilities as your predecessor, I am authorized on [receiving] your assent to place at your disposal $100,000." Banks, of course, had been a politician his entire life and had doubtless received bribes of this nature before. But this one shocked him with its brazen presumption that he was corruptible. Needless to say, he refused, and told his wife: "It was no temptation. I thank God every night that I have no desire for dishonest gains."[9]

The new commander's arrival was, for the most part, met with wary enthusiasm by the New Orleans populace. No one, they reasoned, could be worse than the "Beast." But the radical wing of the Republican Party was far from pleased that their man Butler was being replaced, and they pressured Lincoln to retain him. However, that was not to be. Butler, along with his wife, boarded a home-bound boat on Christmas Eve, amid the resounding cheers of the people of New Orleans. Before leaving, however, they were subjected to hearing his farewell speech, which was typically self-aggrandizing and aimed at a people he considered to be traitors: "It may not be appropriate, as it is not inopportune in occasion, that there should be addressed to you a few words at parting, by one whose name is to be hereafter indissolubly connected with your city. I shall speak in no bitterness, because I am not conscious of a single personal animosity. Commanding the Army of the Gulf, I found you captured, but not surrendered; conquered, but not orderly; relieved from the presence of an army, but incapable of taking care of yourselves. I restored order, punished crime, opened commerce, brought provisions to your starving people, reformed your currency, and gave you quiet protection, such as you had not enjoyed for years."

Almost immediately after assuming command, Banks began to implement changes aimed at a more lenient regime, and hopefully to promote loyalty to the Union, an important goal of President Lincoln. A series of new orders were issued, which clearly promised a more conciliatory government. Churches, closed by Butler, were finally allowed to reopen. Banks vowed to look into the illegal confiscations. He tried to please the planters by returning runaway slaves to the plantations, provided they must hereafter be paid a small wage. Any other vagrant blacks found within the city were to be employed in the public works or sent to the plantations. Free blacks, however, were allowed to enroll in the militia, and thus to bear arms. This new labor system initiated by Banks had its flaws, but at least it relieved the overcrowding of the Negro refugee camps, put people back to work, and increased the agricultural production. Finally, and critically important, Banks released the foreigners and political prisoners who were wrongly incarcerated by Butler. Most of these measures were welcomed by the military and employees of the department. The citizens, however, although relieved to be rid of Butler, were at best only tolerant of Banks, and remained, for the most part, hostile and defiant. They were, after all, still Rebels, and Banks, in turn, had little sympathy for them.[10]

Banks soon discovered that the civil problems he had inherited were overshadowed by the military ones. After eight months of neglect by Butler, the military, which was apparently an aggravation for him, was in a state of disorder, if not chaos. The new general now had fifty-six regiments in his department for a total of about 42,000 men who were stationed as far away as Pensacola, Florida, although the vast majority of them were located within Louisiana. Thirty-nine of those regiments Banks had brought with him, along with six field batteries. However, of those troops that had accompanied Banks, mostly New England men, twenty-two regiments were nine-month volunteers, counting the days until the following August when they could go home. Most of the troops including those left behind by Butler were poorly trained with hardly any experience. This was especially true of the three Negro regiments which Banks would eventually reorganize. Because of the strong prejudices against black soldiers, he found it necessary to place them under the command of white officers, most of whom were lacking in leadership abilities. Also, many of the officers on Banks's own staff were not only inexperienced, but incompetent. What's more, officers, both commissioned and noncommissioned, who had served under Butler were generally demoralized after witnessing the corruption taking place around them. So, for the new commander, it was clear that there must be a time of reorganizing and training before he could begin his campaign.[11]

Indeed, the only military action taken by Banks at this time was to reoccupy Baton Rouge, Louisiana, a city Butler had taken in the spring of 1862 but abandoned the following August, bedeviled by fears that it could not be successfully defended with the troops he had available. Sending Brigadier General Cuvier Grover with some 10,000 troops to retake the city on December 17 proved to be a wise and successful move for Banks. But the suggestion that that be done actually belonged to Rear Admiral David Farragut, who commanded Union naval operations on the lower Mississippi. In fact, Farragut's gunboats supported Grover's infantry in the operation. Before Banks could commence military action, there were problems which had to be solved. His troops needed more training, and there were civil matters he had to address. These things would require manpower, which he felt was inadequate, since so many of his soldiers had to be detailed to stop the thieves in the illegal cotton market, return idle slaves to their plantations, and skirmish with the menacing Confederate troops threatening New Orleans.[12]

After successfully recapturing Baton Rouge, Banks began reorganizing his command into the Army of the Gulf, which at the time consisted of a single army corps, the XIX Corps. He divided the corps into four divisions. The first he placed under Christopher C. Augur, a major general, Michigan man and veteran of the Mexican War who Banks had tapped for his second in command. Leadership of the second division went to Brigadier General Thomas W. Sherman, a West Point graduate, former Indian fighter, and lifelong soldier from Rhode Island. Notwithstanding his famous last name, Thomas was no relation to the renowned William T. Sherman. William H. Emory, a brigadier, decorated veteran of the Mexican War and Peninsular Campaign, and another West Point man, was awarded the third division. Banks assigned the fourth division to Brigadier General Cuvier Grover, a native of Maine, who, like Banks, had the misfortune of being on the losing end of a tangle with Stonewall Jackson in Virginia. Grover, too, was an 1850 graduate of the Military Academy. In fact, all of Banks's division commanders were graduates of West Point, and each one had prior wartime experience. As will be seen, the fact that Banks was not a West Point man would cause various levels of resentment and distrust among these division commanders in the coming campaign.

Such was the army that Nathaniel Banks planned to lead in the monumental military tasks which had been assigned him: to open the Mississippi River, and cooperate with Grant in taking Vicksburg, both of which would be necessary in achieving the Union's grand strategy of splitting the Confederacy in two. However, what Banks had not planned for—because before arriving in New Orleans he knew nothing about—was a small fortress called Port Hudson standing in the path of his success. It would prove to be an obstinate stumbling block and eventually become his most nagging nemesis.[13]

Saturday, December 27, 1862, a quiet, reserved man with sad eyes and a full beard stepped off a rail car near the banks of the Mississippi River where the spur line of the Clinton and Port Hudson railroad came to an end.

Although he wore the insignia of a major general on the collar of his gray uniform, there was no fanfare or reception such as the one Nathaniel Banks had recently experienced in New Orleans. In fact, this man was alone, without a staff and cadre of guards surrounding him. His name was Franklin Gardner and he was month short of his fortieth birthday. Gardner was born in New York and raised in the North. His father and brother were naturally Union men. But Gardner, who married into the Mouton family in Louisiana, decided early in the war to enter the service of Confederate army against the wishes of his New York family. He was an expert engineer, a West Point graduate of the class of 1843, a veteran of the Mexican War, and an experienced commander of infantry and cavalry in many Civil War battles throughout Mississippi, Tennessee and Kentucky. Now, General Gardner had arrived at Port Hudson with orders to assume command of the garrison there, a post which was under the command of Brigadier General William Nelson Rector Beall, a Kentuckian with sharp, angular features and an exquisitely waxed moustache. Beall was also a graduate of West Point, but had no prior command experience. He was aware that Gardner was scheduled to replace him, but had no idea when he might arrive. After inquiring directions, Gardner, without escort and with no formal announcement, walked to Beall's headquarters and introduced himself. The next day, a Sunday, Gardner made a thorough inspection of the troops, the fortifications and the artillery, and General Beall officially relinquished the command to him.[14]

The assignment of someone as skilled as Gardner to take command of the bastion at Port Hudson was not merely an arbitrary one. It was, in fact, a do-or-die effort by the Confederate government to strengthen what remained of their control of the Mississippi River and, if possible, to retake New Orleans. Everyone from President Jeff Davis to the most ordinary citizen of the South understood the

Major General Franklin Gardner commanded the Confederate garrison at Port Hudson. Library of Congress.

critical seriousness of maintaining control of what they had left, which had by now been reduced to a 110-mile stretch of the famous waterway between Vicksburg and Port Hudson. Within that stretch of the Mississippi lay the intersecting mouth of the Red River, the vital east-west supply line for the Confederacy. Thus, after the fall of New Orleans and the loss of the lower Mississippi, the importance of Port Hudson's defenses had become paramount, second only to those of Vicksburg. The South could certainly not afford another failure such as the one they made by bungling the defense of New Orleans.

New Orleans, after all, was and always will be the all-important gateway to the Mississippi River, and both the Union authorities in Washington and their counterparts in Richmond realized it. Even before acquiring the Louisiana Purchase from France, Thomas Jefferson had felt it was the most important single spot on the Mississippi. "It is New Orleans," he prophetically insisted, "through which the produce of three-fifths of our territory must pass to market, and from its fertility it well ere long yield more than half of our whole produce and contain more than half of our inhabitants." Indeed, Jefferson was right. With a population of 170,000 the Crescent City became the largest in the Confederacy, the center of commerce, finance and its most important port. And what a port it was. Steamboats, packets, and vessels of all forms and sizes piled their goods on the docks and levees there. Coal, timber, sugar, pork, cheese, whiskey, fruits, vegetables, and thousands of other products passed through the bustling city. Visitors to New Orleans came away with the impression they had somehow been transferred to some strange foreign city. One visitor, a man named John Crary, was startled that Sundays were as busy as any other day.

Confederate General William Beall. Library of Congress.

"The whole scene was unique, grotesque and profane," he said as he walked through the crowded streets and markets. "It was neither a gala day nor a carnival, but a heterogeneous composition of all that human tongue, action and motive could inspire for selfish and material gratification." By far, however, the greatest and most gratifying material being bought and sold was King Cotton. By 1860, a banner year, the combined river commerce and ocean trade from the cotton crop came to a staggering $500 million. The tremendous amount that was grown in the antebellum Deep South and exported through New Orleans vaulted the Crescent City over the other major ports, and even bypassed New York City as the busiest port in the United States prior to the Civil War.[15]

Recognizing this, the Confederate government had from the beginning been diligent in guarding the city against an attack from the south, and were smugly confident that Forts Jackson and St. Philip and the many land batteries on the river would make New Orleans invincible against any fleet of wooden warships the Union might bring against them. Of course, they were wrong. Also, President Davis had convinced himself that any attack against the city would come from the north, and that was what he was planning for: "New Orleans," he told the commander there, "will be defended from above." But what no one had properly prepared for was David Farragut's fleet of steam-powered warships sweeping past the forts and into the defenseless city in the cover of darkness, followed by the tramping boots of Butler's 10,000 infantry to occupy it. Surely, the capture of the city in April of 1862 was, to that point in the war, the greatest of the North's spoils, and the South's most grievous loss.[16]

After the fall of New Orleans the citizens initially reacted with panic and anxiety, followed later by weeping, anger and despondency. No one could conceive that the most important city in the South had been taken without so much as a fight. Naturally, the feelings were much the same throughout the South as news of the calamity was rumored then finally printed in the papers. "New Orleans gone," Mary Chesnut wrote in her diary in South Carolina after first hearing rumors, and then reading of the loss, "and with it the Confederacy. Are we not cut in two?" In Corinth, Mississippi, Kate Cumming, who was attending the wounded after the battle of Shiloh, had much the same reaction: "Its loss is a severe one to us, as it commanded the passage of the Mississippi River.... A number of Louisiana troops are here [in Corinth] who are much enraged about it." And close by in Baton Rouge, Sarah Morgan, saddened by the news, wrote: "There is no word in the English language which can express the state in which we all are now."[17]

No one, however, took the news worse than the Confederate president, a stoic, aloof man who was rarely capable of expressing emotions or feelings. But Jefferson Davis was also a Mississippian, and the loss of the lower river and the great port of New Orleans was especially catastrophic for his home state. And for the Confederacy, it was a crowning blow in a series of dramatic losses in the western theater. Shiloh, especially, was painful, being the most recent loss and also occurring in April of 1862, the same month New Orleans fell. Now Grant and Banks were threatening to seize Vicksburg and the last stretch of the Mississippi River under Confederate control. On a personal level, this last stretch of the Mississippi was especially significant for Davis. It was here, on this stretch of the river, lying between Vicksburg and Port Hudson, that his life was invested. He had spent his childhood on his father's small cotton plantation with the romantic name of Rosemont near Woodville, Mississippi, lying just north of Port Hudson. On this same stretch, lying just downriver from Vicksburg, was his own home, a sprawling cotton plantation of eighteen hundred acres of fertile river delta he had named Brierfield. There, he and his wife, Varina, had raised their children, and nearby his brother Joseph owned an even larger cotton plantation, Hurricane, which was one of the largest in the South. Now, with New Orleans gone, his very own piece of the South was under threat.[18]

Confederate President Jefferson Davis. Library of Congress.

Something had gone wrong and someone was to blame for the loss of New Orleans. But Davis was not a man who graciously accepted blame, and he was not about to begin by acknowledging any culpability for the absolute mess in the strategy and command decisions that caused the loss of New Orleans. Nevertheless, he was partly to blame, and privately he could not help but know that he had made a poor choice of appointing his friend, Mansfield Lovell, to command a small inadequate force in defense of that city. Now as he watched the buildup of Union forces in the Mississippi Valley, his concern was growing. Trying to defend every square mile of ground in the Confederate States, he was beginning to see, was an unrealistic goal. His understanding that the defense of Vicksburg, Port Hudson and the river had to become a priority represented the first sign of change in Davis's erroneous belief that the entire Confederacy could be defended with the limited number of troops and resources they had. Grave concerns over defending the river, coupled with a continuing lack of harmony in the chain of command in the Army of Tennessee, prodded Davis to board a train in Richmond on December 10 and head west.[19]

By the time Davis reached Vicksburg and finished his inspection of General John Pemberton's troops and fortifications, he began experiencing a sense of dire urgency that he had yet to feel. For him, the possible loss of Vicksburg would be worse than the loss of Richmond. Determined not to make the same mistake there as he had in New Orleans, Davis began ordering more heavy artillery for the river batteries along with reinforcements from the Army of Tennessee. As to the man in command, John Pemberton, he was a friend of Davis, and the president, who was always loyal to his friends, felt he had picked the right man for the job. Pemberton, though, was Northern born, from Pennsylvania. Like Franklin Gardner, he, too, had married into a Southern family, and opted to serve in the Confederate army, and like Gardner, he was a West Point graduate. Serving in the war with Mexico, he was cited twice for gallantry. Yet Pemberton, because of his Northern birth, continued throughout the war to be suspect in the eyes of most of the South, especially its general officers.[20]

Davis continued his tour of the western theater with a stop in Jackson, Mississippi. There, he addressed the state legislature on the day after Christmas and the day before Gardner arrived at Port Hudson. But the speech was not typical of Davis's flamboyant political discourses, which were normally crammed with metaphors and scholarly rhetoric. Rather, it was the president's best attempt at infusing inspiration and patriotism into his Southern audience. Everyone present was, of course, concerned about the threat to their defenses along the Mississippi River, and Davis devoted a good part of his speech to those concerns. Putting aside his usual optimistic language, he made no attempt at misleading them about the seriousness of the situation. They had to maintain control of the river. Their fight for independence could depend on it. "Will you be slaves, or will you be independent?" he anxiously asked. Instead, he appealed to them to rush all the aid they could muster to the defense of the two river bastions, Vicksburg and Port Hudson. Although much of the speech was spent excoriating the Northern people as nothing more than "a den of thieves," and labeling them "a traditionless and homeless race," he also admonished his listeners to be realistic and not to expect recognition and help from any foreign power, something they had heretofore anticipated. "Put not your trust in princes," Davis told them. "This war is ours," he railed on. "We must fight it out ourselves."[21]

Since he was speaking in Jackson, Mississippi, in front of his own people, Davis's delivery was remarkably passionate and sincere, lasting the better part of an hour. He was not especially known as a man who was famous for inspiration, and it may have been his most successful attempt at voicing his concern over the present danger while, at the same time, remaining confident and optimistic that the South was actually winning the war. "In all respects," the president cajoled his audience, "moral as well as physical, we are better prepared than we were a year ago." He implored them as a resourceful and determined people to make whatever sacrifices were necessary to lend the needed aid to the defense of the Mississippi River. Acknowledging all they had given up to this point, Davis enticed them to give more, and expressed his praise with the thought that the women were more attractive and the men more manly when wearing homespun. Beyond that, he had faith that a godly and moral people such as his fellow Mississippians could invoke the Almighty to assist them in this effort, and he said so: "I cannot avoid remarking with how much pleasure I have noticed the superior morality of our troops and the contrast which in this respect they present to the invader. On their valor and the assistance of God I confidently rely."[22]

Chapter Two

A Natural Stronghold

One hundred and ten miles south of Vicksburg, the mighty Mississippi River makes a sharp bend to the east, then just as abruptly rolls in its bed off to the south again, continuing its course for another twenty-five miles to Baton Rouge, and finally meandering on another hundred miles, give or take, through the city of New Orleans and into the Gulf of Mexico. Upriver, at the point where the river pirouettes to the east and suddenly back south again, its path bends into the shape of an elbow. Here, at the crook of the elbow, stood the small town of Port Hudson. Perched high on a bluff that varied in height from sixty to eighty feet above the river, it overlooked a broad swath of alluvium that had accreted on the opposite shore. The bluff itself fronted the river and extended about two miles around the bend of the Mississippi, rising from the water in an almost perpendicular wall of yellow clay. It was a striking landscape, appearing impregnable to those who saw it. Lying just beyond the bluff, Port Hudson was the quintessential little river town, claiming a couple hundred inhabitants. There were about fifty houses, and the streets were lined with at least a dozen stores, along with rows of warehouses, hotels, saloons, and even a Methodist church. There was also a twenty-two-mile rail line running from Port Hudson to the town of Clinton with a short five-mile spur running northward to Jackson, Louisiana. That rail line, despite its short length, was once an important commercial artery. Although it was technically dissolved in early 1861, it continued serving the Confederate military during the war by transporting supplies (especially salt from St. Mary Parish), artillery and other tools of war. In the surrounding countryside, Louisiana plantations and small farms sent bales of cotton and barrels of sugar by wagon or rail to be loaded on the steamboats that plied the river. Enjoying a peaceful and prosperous existence, no one there realized their serene little town would soon be hopelessly immersed in one of the bloodiest fights of the Civil War.

Indeed, war has a way of seeking its venues in nature's most formidable strongholds, and nature had clearly strengthened Port Hudson. The neighboring landscape lying north and west of town was a labyrinth of hollows,

Chapter Two. A Natural Stronghold

Looking up the Mississippi River towards the Port Hudson site. Port Hudson State Historic Site Photograph Collection.

ravines, creeks, and swampy marshes, all lying within a broken terrain of ridges and knobby hills. Much of it was covered in a dense forest of willows, cottonwoods and thick canebrakes. Elsewhere, where the river was allowed to escape its banks during seasonal floods, the land was covered in black mudflats, stagnant chocolate milk–colored swamps, and a variety of towering trees and smaller saplings. Rising out of the swampy waters were moss-choked cypress and gum trees, and the land abounded with numerous species of mammals, reptiles, fish and birds. East of town and farther from the river, a plateau rose, dominated by flourishing fields of cotton, corn and sugarcane. Several roads fanned out across those fields, leading to Jackson, Clinton, Bayou Sara, and Baton Rouge, Louisiana. Also, extending northeast across the fields was the dilapidated railroad line connecting the river town to Clinton, but terminating there. Below the town of Port Hudson, an enormous canyon-like ravine, sculptured by the liberated river, ran through the bluff, then meandered northwardly and back towards the town. This terrain, coupled with the dramatic bend in the river, was a venue begging to be fortified, and it did not take long for the Rebel brass to realize its potential as a defensive bastion.[1]

As soon as Franklin Gardner arrived at Port Hudson, he put his engineering mind to work, making changes that would correct the flaws he found in the fortifications after his initial inspection. First, he repositioned the artillery to achieve a more concentrated field of fire, and directed the artillerymen to build strong earthen parapets to protect their guns. He ordered construction of a network of roads to move troops and equipment swiftly from one parapet to another. He was constantly trying to increase his arsenal, commissary supplies, medical provisions and tools. Gangs of slaves were gathered from nearby plantations and put to work building redoubts and improving the fortifications. No one was idle. Gardner had nearly everyone, slaves and soldiers, digging the entrenchments that encircled the garrison and stretched a distance of four and a half miles. "A good portion of time was spent shoveling dirt," remembered an exhausted Alabama private.[2]

The bastion at Port Hudson had clearly taken on significant importance for the Confederate government, as evidenced by the reinforcements that continued to pour in during the winter months. It wasn't long before the number of troops increased from five or six thousand to about eleven thousand, with more on the way. Of course with the influx of so many men a housing problem soon arose. Even during Louisiana's brief winter season, troops needed some refuge from the weather. With a shortage of tents, shelter became a necessity to protect them from the frequent rains and cold north winds, or "northers," as the men called them. "We began as soon as practicable to build houses for winter quarters," recalled J.P. Cannon of the Twenty-seventh Alabama Regiment. Arming themselves with axes and saws, the men cut and split logs, and according to Cannon, "Erected very respectable houses, which we covered with boards, 'chinking' the cracks with long hanging moss which grew in abundance on the trees." Generally, the cabin's dimensions measured about eighteen by twenty feet with a crude clay fireplace at each end.[3]

For the most part, the troops were pleased with their new commander. Although Gardner was what one private called "a very strict disciplinarian" who maintained a strict duty schedule, including Sundays, they respected his engineering abilities, his energy, and making whatever command changes that were necessary to improve their chances for survival. Besides, there was much to do; the grueling labor on the earthworks, the guard duty, drilling, and hauling supplies. No one had time to kill, and the fact that there was little free time actually worked to improve the morale of the men as well as the popularity of their commander. Their confidence in Gardner and the good spirits of the men were hard to reconcile with the poor rations, clothing and equipment provided to the typical Confederate

Chapter Two. A Natural Stronghold

Confederate Winter Quarters at Port Hudson, constructed with willow logs and cypress boards, chinked and daubed with mud. They housed about twenty-five men and were approximately eighteen by twenty feet with a fireplace and chimney, but no windows and only one door. Port Hudson State Historic Site Photograph Collection.

soldier. "I have never received anything from the Government yet because the Government has nothing to give me," wrote Robert Patrick, a Louisiana soldier stationed at Port Hudson. "We have to labor under the greatest difficulties in the world," he continued, "and have very little clothing and very scanty fare provided for us." And Patrick's estimate of his government's meager resources was corroborated by the diarist Miss Sarah Morgan when she visited Port Hudson from a nearby plantation to watch the troops on parade: "What a sad sight the 4th La. was, that was then parading! Men that had fought at Shiloh and Baton Rouge were barefooted. Rags was their only uniform, for very few possessed a complete suit, and those few wore all varieties of colors and cuts. Hats could be seen of every style and shape, from the first ever invented, down to the last one purchased evidently some time since. Yet he who had no shoes, looked as happy as he who had, and he who had a cap, had something to toss up, that's all." Concerned also with the living conditions, Sarah continued: "I was watching the hundreds of tents—it looked like a great many—and was wondering how men could live in such places ... poor men! How can they be happy in these tents?" Although, she could not know at this time, in the days ahead she would be repulsed over their living conditions.[4]

Of a more serious nature than the uniforms and shelters were the rations distributed to the troops, something Gardner, despite his best efforts, had not been able to improve. Spoiled beef, inferior corn, and coarse flour continued to be delivered by boat. In camp, there were shortages of nearly everything, especially vegetables and coffee. The only commodity that always seemed to be plentiful was liquor, as evidenced by a significant increase in drinking, during what little free time they had. Perhaps liquor was necessary, most agreed, as a fair substitute for the stagnant swamp water available to drink or, possibly, as a way to fortify themselves for the grueling work they were required to face each day. In any case, the rancid water and the poor diet soon contributed to a great deal of sickness within the garrison. "Owing to bad water and detestable diet, we were soon stricken with a Dysentery which was very distressing," remarked J.P. Cannon in his memoirs. Agreeing with Cannon, Robert Patrick added: "I have been living almost like a dog for the last six weeks, having had nothing to eat but beef and very bad corn bread, and this is so miserably cooked that it was almost impossible to eat it." He also recognized the damaging effects it was having on his health: "My bad health I attribute to bad food we receive, being nothing more than damaged corn meal and very tough beef." However, the "bad food" they were experiencing during that winter was only a harbinger of things to come. Ahead of them they would face grim days when mules and horses would be slaughtered to avoid starvation.[5]

As the number of troops continued to swell in the garrison, Gardner reorganized them into three brigades. The First Brigade was commanded by a thirty-five-year-old Alabama native, General John Gregg, and covered the right wing of the bastion. Occupying the center was the Second Brigade, under the command of General Samuel Bell Maxey, a West Point graduate, former lawyer, and veteran of the Mexican War. William Beall, the general who was in command of the garrison prior to Gardner's arrival, was given responsibility of the left wing with the Third Brigade. Gardner's heavy artillery was put under the skillful leadership of Lieutenant Colonel Marshall Smith, a graduate of the Naval Academy. Spread among the three brigades were seven batteries of light artillery and four batteries of field artillery. Also stationed outside the bastion were a number small units of cavalry, each under a different commander, assigned to watch the enemy's movements and to gather intelligence.[6]

During this time, construction of fortifications and the provisioning of armaments and supplies at Port Hudson did not go unnoticed by the Federal authorities in New Orleans. As might be expected, they made every effort to learn more about those defenses and the number of troops garrisoned there. They were confident that it would not be difficult to send their spies in and out of the camp to gather that information. After all, there was a constant procession of traders, merchants and peddlers bringing in goods and supplies. Also, friends and family of the soldiers were continually visiting, and touring civilians came and went, curiously watching the progress of building a military fortress. Lieutenant Howard Wright recalled an occasion when two ladies, a mother and daughter, stepped off the ferry and announced they were refugees from New Orleans on their way to Jackson, Mississippi, to visit a son and husband who were serving in the Confederate army there. Wright remembered how they described with "rare conversational powers" how they had endured so much woe and suffering before escaping from New Orleans. Claiming to be fatigued from their harrowing experience, they decided to rest at Port Hudson a few days before resuming their travels. They were fashionably dressed, "radiant with smiles." Some of the "gallant young officers" politely offered to make their stay as pleasant and interesting as possible, and escort them through the military facility. Wright readily admitted, "They saw all the works then in progress, as well as the different camps, where, at dress parade, the number of troops could be readily ascertained by the onlooker." Of course the ladies pretended to be "charmingly ignorant" about such things as artillery when they were shown the big guns. "Now do tell me," the younger lady asked one of her escorts, "how far can this thing shoot?" After the officer's explanation of the exact range, she gave a merry little laugh and blushed, "You don't say so; I am a perfect child in such matters." After touring the camp for another day, the ladies departed, leaving some of the officers with broken hearts and enveloped in a "cloud of sadness." It wasn't until sometime later they learned the women were Federal spies sent from New Orleans, prompting Wright to repeat the consoling motto: *Least said soonest mended*.[7]

Under Gardner's supervision, the troops continued to strengthen the fortifications at Port Hudson and everyone continued to wait for the assault they knew was imminent. Rumors, spread mostly by local newspapers, constantly circulated through the camp claiming the Yankee army was on its way. As more Rebel units continued to arrive at Port Hudson the rumors became more plausible. One arriving column passed a huge level field adjacent to the fortifications. The officer leading the column was admiring the bountiful corn crop growing there, and wondered who the owner might be. He asked a civilian on the roadside, who told him, "It is Slaughter's field." Whether he knew it or not, the officer then made a prophetic reply, one which would prove to be an omen of perils to come: "It will be the field of slaughter yet, or I am much mistaken." Indeed, these men were eager for a fight after preparing all winter for one. But except for an occasional shell lobbed from a Federal gunboat, there was no sign of the enemy. In their occasional free time when boredom set in, it was not surprising that many of them began to grow homesick. Those soldiers had not been allowed a furlough, and mail from home was, at best, haphazard and rarely delivered. Robert Patrick, for instance, who was born and raised in south Louisiana, thought often of his home in nearby Clinton. Taking a short Sunday stroll to be alone, think of home, and reflect on his dreary surroundings, he looked back towards the garrison and made a nostalgic entry in his diary: "It looks very lonely and but for the dark line of entrenchments and an occasional company or regiment out drilling, one would suppose that the Confederacy was at peace with all the world."[8]

While Franklin Gardner and his troops were enjoying this time of unaccustomed "peace with the world" and continuing to strengthen the fortifications at Port Hudson, the War Department in Washington was pressuring Banks to join Grant and commence the campaign to open the Mississippi. During the month of February, the dispatches coming from Halleck were growing increasingly curt: "Nothing but absolute necessity will excuse any further delay on your part," he wrote on the second of the month, and then again on the twenty-seventh: "There is much dissatisfaction here at the delay." But Nathaniel Banks was a deliberate man and not one to be moved by pressure. He felt his troops needed more training and equipment before he could move them. In New Orleans, there were still civil matters, such as the illegal cotton trade and the problem of homeless Negroes who had run away from the plantations, to deal with. What's more, there was a small Confederate army commanded by Richard Taylor marauding around in south Louisiana, creating havoc, and forcing him to detail some of his troops to confront them. But most importantly was the Confederate bastion at Port Hudson. By now, Banks knew the troop strength there was about 11,000, and that a frontal assault against a prepared fortification with his present force would not be wise. At the same time, if he were to circumvent Port Hudson in an attempt to join Grant against Vicksburg he would put himself in the precarious position of having the enemy both in front of him and behind him, a risk he could not afford to take. He also tried finding a way to get above Port Hudson through the Atchafalaya Basin, but found the route not only occupied by Taylor's army, but covered with river flood waters, typical during this season, forcing him to abort that endeavor. Thus, the always composed Banks continued to dawdle in New Orleans, trying to come up with another plan to accomplish his part in opening the Mississippi. But, as it turned out, that plan would in fact be concocted by an old navy admiral.[9]

Unlike Banks, Rear Admiral David Glasgow Farragut was not a man given to a lot of deliberate scheming. Rather, he was a crusty old sailor with an impulsive temperament, worthy of his nickname, "Daring Dave." Even though he was a Southerner, born in Tennessee and raised in New Orleans, he was a lifelong navy man, pledged to the government of the United

States. The son of a sailor, who was often at sea, Farragut's father arranged for him to live with Commodore David Porter, whose son David Dixon Porter would later command the mortar boats in the Vicksburg Campaign. After the death of Farragut's mother, the elder Porter informally adopted the future admiral, schooled him in the ways of seafaring life, and introduced him to the perils of battle aboard the frigate *Essex* during the war of 1812 when Farragut was only twelve years old. From that time on, he served as a veteran, piling up fifty years' routine service. When the Civil War broke out, President Lincoln called for the blockade of the South, the so-called Anaconda Plan, and an immense task which involved sealing a thirty-five-hundred-mile coastline. Farragut was given the command of the West Gulf Blockading Squadron, which extended from St. Andrews Bay (present-day Panama City) to the border of Mexico. It was an important sphere of responsibility primarily because it included his foremost duty: to secure the Union's control of the Mississippi River.[10]

Union Admiral David G. Farragut. Library of Congress.

Now, at sixty-two years old, the "old sea dog" had nearly lost all patience with clearing the Rebels off the Mississippi. Moreover, he was raging mad over the recent capture of two Federal ships, the steam ram *Queen of the West* and the ironclad *Indianola*. For the testy Farragut, the only solution to their current problem was a joint army-navy operation against Port Hudson. A diversionary attack by the army, he believed, might result in an opportunity of taking the bastion. However, just as he had done in New Orleans the year before, Farragut would eagerly make the assault alone, but only if he must, telling one of his staff, "I must go, army or no army." And even if that did not succeed in forcing the surrender of Port Hudson, the admiral could still get his ships above it, and cut off the Confederate supply line coming from the Red River. Having accomplished that, Farragut could then move his fleet up the Mississippi, retake his captured ships from the Rebels, and assist Grant in his campaign against Vicksburg. Late in February, when Farragut approached Banks with his plan, the general had misgivings about it, but absent any other choice, he hesitantly agreed. So in early March, Farragut began assembling his fleet of seven ships just south of Port Hudson, intending to run them past the guns of that bastion. At the same time, Banks started gathering his army in Baton Rouge in preparation for the diversionary attack in support of Farragut.[11]

There was, however, a crucial problem in Farragut's plan. Namely, during the months since Farragut had last seen the fortifications at Port Hudson, significant changes had occurred there. It had become a smaller version of Vicksburg. Franklin Gardner's strengthened fortification extending along the two-and-a-half-mile riverfront now included forty-three pieces of artillery, some of which were heavy Columbiad siege guns and rifled cannon, capable of throwing watermelon-size shells over a mile and sinking ships. What's more, reinforcements, including Albert Rust's brigade and three more batteries, had recently arrived, bringing Gardner's troop strength to nearly 15,000, although some of these were not within the actual fortifications, such as cavalry units, which had been detached to other outposts.[12]

Arriving at Baton Rouge on March 11, Farragut began readying his ships for action. His fleet consisted of three big sloops of war: the *Hartford*, *Richmond*, and *Monongahela*. He also had an old side-wheeler, the *Mississippi*, which had served as Matthew Perry's flagship back when he visited Japan in 1853, an event that opened trade with that country. All four of these vessels were wooden ocean-going vessels, and together they were equipped with ninety-five guns. In addition to the large vessels, the admiral had four gunboats and six small vessels armed with mortars. Crews of sailors were kept busy filling shells with powder and loading ammunition. Chains and cables were lowered along the starboard side of the big sloops to afford an armor of protection from the enemy artillery fire and steamers the Confederates were using as floating rams. Cotton bales and chains were placed around the engines and boilers to shield them from the flying projectiles. Wherever possible, guns were moved from the port side to the starboard, where they would be facing the artillery of the Rebel fortress. Finally, buckets of sand were sprinkled around the gun carriages, and wooden boxes containing sawdust were stacked on the decks near the cannons. Thomas Bacon, Reverend of Christ Church in New Orleans who was visiting one of the ships thought the wooden boxes looked like the spittoons used in barrooms. He was no doubt horrified when he learned that the sawdust contained in those boxes and the sand sprinkled around the guns were actually going to be used as absorbents to keep the sailors from slipping down in the slick blood that would soon stand in puddles on the decks.[13]

Admiral David Farragut's flagship, the USS *Hartford*. Port Hudson State Historic Site Photograph Collection.

The next day, March 12, Nathaniel Banks held a grand review of his troops on the parade grounds at Baton Rouge. Farragut, of course, was invited, along with several of his naval officers. Mounted on horseback, Banks and Farragut rode proudly along the lines, inspecting the troops while a regimental band played martial tunes. According to one account, Farragut invited Banks to join him for a drink in his cabin aboard the flagship, *Hartford*. Whether or not the old admiral was attempting to inspire Banks with a pep talk or simply enjoyed pontificating over a captured audience is not known. But he used this occasion to endlessly ramble on about the war. "We have more men and more resources than these traitors and five times as much money," he boasted to Banks. "By God, shall a United

States ship of war hesitate to go in and destroy a dozen of these wretched Mississippi steamers?" Pouring himself another, he blustered ahead: "We must fight this thing out until there is no more than one man left and that man must be a Union man. Here's to his health!" Toasting the Massachusetts politician, he added, "What matters it, General, whether you and I are killed or not? We came here to die." Banks was startled. Although he loved his country and took pride in doing his duty, it was safe to assume that he was appalled at the admiral's morbid suggestion that he, the former Speaker of the House of Representatives and governor of the state of Massachusetts, should be destined to die in this miserable Louisiana swamp.[14]

Following the grand review in Baton Rouge, Banks deployed some troops from a Massachusetts unit to conduct a reconnaissance of the enemy's position. Advancing up the Bayou Sara Road, they skirmished with some Rebel pickets and then returned to camp. They accomplished little, except for stealing some cattle from civilians along the way. Finally, on March 13, a Friday afternoon, Banks sent his army forward. They numbered about 12,000 men. General Cuvier Grover's division was in the van, followed by the divisions of William Emory and Christopher Augur, whose troops didn't get underway until the following morning. Although the distance they needed to march was probably less than ten miles, the weather was unseasonably hot, and the road was enveloped in a shroud of dust. Men began falling out along the roadside, fatigued from carrying the load of too much equipment. Frank Flinn, who identified himself as a "high private," gave an inventory of all the items they carried: "Overcoats, rubber and woolen blankets, dress coats, extra shirts, towels, three days rations, one hundred rounds of ammunition, guns, a canteen of water—just enough goods for proper housekeeping, and too many for an active campaign, especially when you had to tote them on your back."[15]

It came as no surprise that the road behind them was soon littered with discarded blankets, knapsacks and overcoats, all of which contrabands from nearby plantations gladly picked up as they followed the troops. For many of the soldiers, like George Powers of the Thirty-eighth Massachusetts, this was their first combat march, and a few of them were hesitant to part with all their clothing. "Some of the men, not yet having made up their minds to part with their overcoats, cut off the sleeves and skirts to lighten their loads," remembered Powers. Notwithstanding the heat, the troops were in good spirits when they bivouacked on the afternoon of the fourteenth, and Banks was confident they would soon be in a position to launch their diversionary attack. In fact, he said so in a message to Farragut: "We shall be ready this evening." Farragut's plan was to start his fleet forward in the gray of the morning of March 15, but after receiving word that Banks would be ready by that evening, he changed his schedule. At five o'clock the admiral sent a dispatch back to Banks, "stating that he should commence his movement at 8 o'clock." Knowing most of his troops were still strung out on the road several miles from Port Hudson, Banks replied to the admiral not to expect his diversionary attack that evening. After reading the message, Farragut handed it back to an officer with the remark, "He had as well be in New Orleans or Baton Rouge for all the good he is doing us."[16]

All of the troop movements and assembling of naval vessels had not escaped the eyes of the Confederates at Port Hudson. By now, the rumors of an imminent Yankee attack on Port Hudson had become an accepted fact. Small newspapers in Port Hudson, such as the *Courier* and the *Chronicle,* continually reported news of the impending advance. Civilians in Baton Rouge had watched the troop buildup there for weeks. In fact, Gardner had known about the Federal plan to attack since February 24, when he received reliable intelligence reports. Confederate soldiers were actually looking forward to a battle. Robert Patrick, for example, made a diary entry on March 13, after watching five of Farragut's vessels come in sight. "I am not particularly fond of fighting," wrote Patrick, who was a clerk and seldom exposed to action, "but I must say that I would like very much to see an engagement between the boats and the batteries." John Powers, a corporal in the First Alabama Infantry, was convinced of a triumph, and said so: "When old Banks makes an attack on this place he will get a worse whipping than he ever had in Virginia." And from the nearby Linwood Plantation, young Sarah Morgan reacted to the rumors of an attack, writing in her journal late in February: "[At Port Hudson] they are confident that our fifteen thousand can repulse twice the number. Great God!—I say it with all reverence—if we could defeat them! If we could scatter, capture, annihilate them! My heart beats but one prayer—Victory! Victory! I shall grow old repeating it."[17]

Chapter Three

"The Very Earth Trembled"

As soon as the sun went down over the Mississippi River in the evening of March 14, the night grew intensely dark, and the air became stifling, still, silent and heavy with humidity. By ten o'clock each Federal ship was in line and ready to move upstream from Profit Island. Farragut felt he had done all he could to prepare the fleet and compensate for the problems they would face—and there were many. The guns of Port Hudson were located on the east side of the River, perched on high bluffs, allowing the Rebels to fire down on his fleet while his ships would not be able to elevate most of their guns to a position high enough to return the fire. Additionally, since the guns on the starboard side were the only ones that would have any effect, Farragut only had half the firepower of his ninety-five guns. The current of the river was moving downstream at about five knots, which would slow the big sloops to the pace of a leisurely walk. This, coupled with the one-hundred-degree turn to the west the ships would be required to negotiate, would leave each vessel within range of the Confederate cannon for at least an hour during the passage. To offset this, the old admiral had come up with an unusual idea which could offer his large ships some additional power and maneuverability and, at the same time, help protect the smaller gunboats. He wisely ordered three of this four sloops to have a gunboat secured to their port sides. This, of course, could not be accomplished with the fourth sloop *Mississippi,* since she was powered by large paddle wheels on both sides.[1]

Lashed alongside the flagship *Hartford* was the gunboat *Albatross* skippered by Lieutenant Commander John Hart; the *Richmond* was attached to Commander W. H. Macomb's gunboat, *Genesee;* and Lieutenant Commander John Watters's *Kineo* was joined with the *Monongahela.* This, too, was the order of battle for the ships as they advanced, with the side-wheeler *Mississippi* being last in line. Farther down the river, there were five mortar boats protected by the gunboats *Essex* and *Sachem* with orders to hold their fire until the battle was underway. Farragut was painfully aware that any element of surprise was now lost and that Banks would not be making the anticipated diversionary attack. Because of this, he wanted his ships' captains to be sure they understood his instructions, and earlier in the day he called a council of war on board the *Hartford* to reiterate to his commanders what he expected of them. "The object is to run the batteries at the least possible damage to our ships, and thereby secure an efficient force above for the purpose of rendering such assistance as may be required of us by the army at Vicksburg," he told them. "If [you] succeed in getting past the batteries," he continued, "proceed up to the mouth of Red River and keep up the police of the river [Mississippi] between that river [Red River] and Port Hudson, capturing anything [you] can." As a final thought, he advised them, "I expect all to go by who are able, and I think the best protection against the enemy's fire is a well-directed fire from our own guns."[2]

Shortly after ten o'clock the soft glow of two red lanterns appeared off the stern of the *Hartford*, signaling the fleet to get underway. Plying slowly through the dark waters, the steady pulsing of the big steam engines sent an alert to the Rebel artillerymen waiting up on the bluffs. Moments passed, then the glare of a rocket was visible, warning all the defenders of the fleet's approach. Over on the west side of the river, a great bonfire, prepared by Rebel defenders suddenly erupted in flame, followed by others; one after another were lit, until the Yankee fleet discovered itself illuminated in a sort of simulated daylight. Through the ink of night, the light of the roaring fires made the ships clear targets for the guns of Port Hudson. As soon as the first Confederate battery thundered into action shortly after eleven o'clock, the guns from the ships and the mortar boats began to answer. Then, abruptly, hell seemed to break loose. Within the Rebel breastworks of Port Hudson, J.P. Cannon remembered the raucous outbursts of the guns: "The continuous thunder of several hundred guns, the comet-like fuses of large shells as they darted through the darkness, the mortar shells rising high up in the heavens, descending like shooting stars, bursting and scattering fragments in every direction, presented the grandest and most exciting exhibition of fireworks that we had ever witnessed." Agreeing with Cannon's account, Robert Patrick added, "Of all the noises that ever I heard, this beat it.... The very earth trembled." Indeed, for miles around the concussion from the exploding shells caused houses to quiver on their foundations and windows to shatter and fall from their frames. A few miles away at Linwood Plantation, Sarah Morgan, along with her friends and family, were awakened and sprung to their feet. "At half past eleven came the first gun—at least the first I heard," she exclaimed. "Such an incessant roar! All of us prayed aloud ... and at every report the house shaking so, and we thinking of our dear soldiers, the dead and dying, and crying aloud for God's blessing on them. That dreadful roar! I can't think fast enough. They are too quick to be counted.... Gathered in a knot within and without the window, we six

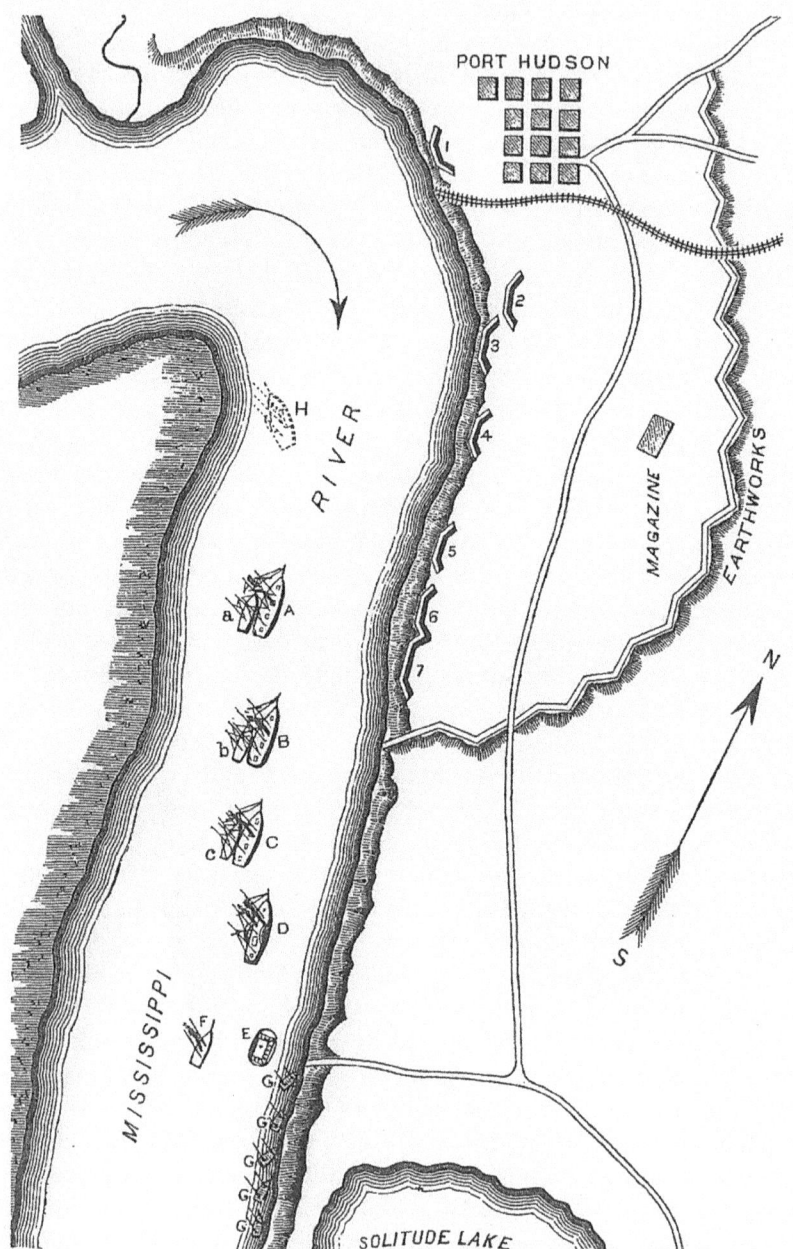

Order of Attack on Batteries at Port Hudson, March 14, 1863.

A. Hartford (flag-ship), Captain James S. Palmer. *a*. Albatross, Lieut.-Com. John E. Hart. B. Richmond, Commander James Alden. *b*. Genesee, Commander W. H. Macomb. C. Monongahela, Captain J. P. McKinstry. *c*. Kineo, Lieut.-Com. John Waters. D. Mississippi, Captain Melancton Smith. E. Essex, Commander C. H. B. Caldwell. F. Sachem, Act. Vol. Lieut. Amos Johnson. G. G. Mortar schooners. H. Spot where Mississippi grounded.

Chapter Three. "The Very Earth Trembled" 37

women up here watched in the faint star light the flashes from the guns, and silently wondered which of our friends were lying stiff and dead. I think we know what it is to wrestle with God in prayer."[3]

The first shot launched that night came from the battery of Lieutenant Colonel Paul Francis De Gournay, a Frenchman with an aristocratic pedigree, whose battalion, the Twelfth Louisiana Heavy Artillery, had fought with Robert E. Lee in the Peninsula Campaign in Virginia. Their service had been so impressive that they were chosen to return to their home state of Louisiana and be a part of the defense of Port Hudson. De Gournay's first shell burst over the *Albatross,* the gunboat that was lashed to the flagship *Hartford.* Following that explosion came the thunder of over a hundred cannons. De Gournay then began rushing about among his batteries and shouting commands. But in the confusion and deafening roar of the cannons his voice could not be heard. From that point on, the cannoneers were left to fight on their own hook, loading and firing as fast as possible.[4]

Out on the river, thick smoke was gathering in the windless night coming from the combination of the bonfires, the artillery, and the steam engines. The smoke shrouded the water and blinded the visibility of the crewmen. Gunners aboard the ships were bewildered in the smokescreen, having no targets to aim at except the muzzle flashes from the Rebel artillery. The flagship, the *Hartford*, leading the fleet, was holding close to the east bank to avoid the mudflats on the opposite shore. She had a visual advantage over the rest of the fleet, being ahead of her own engine's smoke. Although the flagship was hit a few times, injuring and killing men, she managed to slowly crawl forward through the nightmare of exploding shells. Finally reaching the hairpin curve of the river and nearly past the range of the enemy guns, Farragut's pilot, Thomas Carrell, called down to the admiral that the smoke from the guns had become so thick he could no longer see. Then the current swung the flagship around and began sweeping her back into the bluffs and the waiting Rebel artillery. Moments later, the *Hartford*'s hull was scraping bottom with the threat of being grounded. "Back, back!" shouted Farragut to the pilot of the *Albatross*, which was lashed alongside. Quickly, the crew of the gunboat reversed the engines and increased the steam until the two ships finally rocked free and backed off the muddy bottom. Within minutes the *Hartford* and her escorting

Opposite: Map showing the order of attack of the Union ships against the batteries of Port Hudson on March 14, 1863: A/a, USS *Hartford* and USS *Albatross*; B/b, USS *Richmond* and USS *Genesee*; C/c, USS *Monongahela* and USS *Kineo*; D, USS *Mississippi*; E, Ironclad, USS *Essex*; F. Gunboat USS *Sachem*; G, Mortar boats; H, Site where USS *Mississippi* grounded. Loyall Farragut, *The Life of David Glasgow Farragut* (New York: D. Appleton and Co., 1879).

gunboat, the *Albatross,* were past the guns of Port Hudson, and pushing north. Farragut's plan, so far, seemed to be successful.[5]

Following the flagship were the sloop *Richmond* and the most powerful of the Federal gunboats, the *Genesee.* These vessels, being behind the engines and guns of the *Hartford* and *Albatross,* were naturally experiencing a more intense veil of the murky smoke and fumes. The gunners, whose vision was obscured, did their best to return the fire from the Confederate batteries, which had been viciously pounding the ship for nearly an hour. As they approached the bend in the river and the fiercest fire from the enemy guns, A. Boyd Cummings, the executive officer, was trying to direct fire while he stood next to the *Richmond*'s captain, James Alden, when a cannon shot ripped off his left leg below the knee. "Quick boys," cried Cummings. "Pick me up, put a tourniquet on my leg, send my letters to my wife, tell them I fell doing my duty." He was quickly taken below and treated, but died a few days later.[6]

As the *Richmond* began making her turn and closing in on the *Hartford,* a solid cannon shot plunged through her hull and into the engine

Confederate twenty-four-pounder rifled cannon of the Louisiana Heavy Artillery at River Battery 11 (Citadel). Port Hudson State Historic Site Photograph Collection.

room, crashing into a steam pipe and the safety valves. Pandemonium ensued as scalding steam filled the room, burning the crewmen while the pressure to the boiler dropped to a dangerous low. Several men risked their lives rushing into the blazing-hot engine room attempting to restart the furnace. Crippled by the loss of power, the *Richmond* was unable to move against the current, despite the efforts of the *Genesee* to move her upriver and out of danger. Minutes seemed like eternity as the ship came to a standstill, sitting motionless as the Confederate cannoneers poured round after round at their helpless target. Here, two seamen were killed: Charles Catherwood by a shell fragment to his brain, and John Thompson, whose head was "carried off by a shell or cannon shot." Boatswain's Mate John Howard also died after a solid shot ripped off an arm and both legs. Twelve crewmen suffered wounds, varying in severity. During the maelstrom of shot and shell, Confederate observers on the bluff heard one of the crewmen shouting up at them, "For God's sake, don't shoot anymore! We are sinking." But the sloop was not sinking, and the appeal for mercy may have been a ruse or, as a newspaper correspondent for the *Memphis Appeal* put it, "a Yankee artifice." Still struggling to get upriver, the ship began being pushed back by the current, and eventually swung both the *Richmond* and her gunboat around in the opposite direction. Disoriented gunners, confused in the dark and smoke, were not aware they had turned around, and continued to fire on what they thought were enemy guns. Instead, they were shelling one of their own ships, the *Mississippi,* which was firing when the two ships passed each other. Commander W.H. Macomb, commanding the *Genesee,* continued carrying the *Richmond* downstream until they were both out of the enemy's range. Safely dropping anchor about one o'clock in the morning, the *Richmond* had been badly damaged, and Captain Alden admitted, "I was compelled, though most reluctantly, to turn back."[7]

The *Monongahela* and her lashed-on gunboat, *Kineo,* had only begun to run the deadly gauntlet when the *Kineo*'s rudder was disabled by rifle shots coming from the western bank. Approaching the big turn, the *Monongahela* moved from the center of the river closer to the eastern shore when her hull suddenly hit bottom with such a jolting impact that the *Kineo* was ripped from her lashings, and she, too, became grounded. The big sloop struggled but was unable to free herself from the thick mud bottom without the help of her gunboat, which, reversing its engines, soon broke free. For the next half hour while the lines were being reattached to the gunboat, the *Monongahela* was being pummeled with heavy fire from the Rebel batteries. Shortly after midnight, the *Kineo* succeeded in pulling her big companion free. But by this time the Rebel guns had pinpointed their target with lethal accuracy. The floor of the vessel was strewn with the wounded and dead, and the seamen still fighting were unable to keep their footing in the slippery blood covering the deck. Shots striking the sloop were coming at such a rate and velocity that the bridge where the ship's captain, J.B. McKinstry, was standing was shot from beneath him, tumbling him down to the deck with painful injuries. He was taken below and the executive officer assumed command. Continuing upriver, the lines attaching the gunboat once again snapped, and the *Kineo*, without steering, drifted away and back down the river. Then moments later, as the big sloop was again approaching the bend in the river, misfortune struck again. Her engines suddenly shut down, damaged from an overheated crank pin, and the *Monongahela*, like the *Kineo*, began wafting helplessly downriver, back into the shot and shell of the Rebel batteries. By the time she reached safe waters around Profit Island at 3:30 a.m., she was carrying twenty-seven dead or wounded sailors.[8]

Ten-inch Columbiad Cannon of the First Alabama Regiment located at River Battery 5. Port Hudson Sate Historic Site Photograph Collection.

Chapter Three. "The Very Earth Trembled"

Forty-two-pounder Confederate Cannon of the First Alabama Regiment located at River Battery 1. Port Hudson State Historic Site Photograph Collection.

At this point, four of the six vessels attempting to pass through the guns of Port Hudson had failed, with only the *Hartford* and *Albatross* successfully making it north of the Rebel artillery. Only one of the sloops remained in the quest to run the Rebel gauntlet. Farragut, from the beginning, had never felt confident about the chances of the old side-wheeler, *Mississippi*, being able to make the passage. Thus, he placed her last in line. Positioned at the end, the admiral reasoned she would not obstruct the other ships if she was disabled. Beyond that, there was no way that Farragut could foresee the woes and misery the *Mississippi* would endure before the night was over. Blinded by the smoke of the guns and all the preceding ships, she somehow plowed ahead and successfully passed the southernmost of the Rebel batteries. And from that point her tribulations begin.

As the *Mississippi* continued churning upriver, she began passing the crippled *Richmond*, now helpless and being towed back to safety by her gunboat, the *Genesee*. Suddenly, the *Richmond,* whose gunners had become disoriented in the smoke and confusion, opened fire on the big side-wheeler, thinking she was a Confederate vessel. The captain of the *Mississippi*, Melancton Smith, knew that the disabled ship shooting at them must be Federal, and wisely refused to allow his gunners to return fire. Fortunately, little or no damage was reported, and the big sloop continued groping ahead through the smoke and darkness. Although the *Mississippi* steamed past the grounded *Monongahela,* no one on board could see her because of the dense smoke blanketing the water.[9]

Both Captain Melancton Smith and his executive officer, George Dewey, would one day attain the rank of admiral, but on this smoke-filled night of terror neither man was sure of his future. "Both Captain Smith and myself," Dewey wrote later, "felt that our destiny that night was in the hands of the pilot." And as it happened, the pilot did, in fact, succeed in guiding the old sloop through nearly all the batteries and soon she approached the bend in the river. "We had now reached the last and most formidable batteries, and were congratulating ourselves upon having gained the turn," remembered the captain. The pilot then steered the big ship into what he believed to be the bend in the river and shouted for the engines to proceed "full speed ahead." But he was wrong. The pilot's turn was premature, and the *Mississippi's* hull plunged high upon a sand bar, and was desperately grounded. For the next thirty-five minutes the *Mississippi* struggled to free herself. The engine moaned under the strain as Smith ordered the steam increased to the point the boilers could no longer bear the pressure. The unexcitable Smith, now chewing on a cigar, looked at Dewey and calmly remarked, "Well, it doesn't look as if we can get her off." Dewey, who one day would achieve fame at the Battle of Manila Bay in the Spanish-American War, agreed, "No, it does not." The two of them then went about the business of ordering the guns spiked, the engine and machinery destroyed, and the ship abandoned. By now the Rebel gunners had found the range and the ship was exposed to the cross-fire of three Confederate batteries. Dead and wounded sailors began covering the deck, and a shot from the enemy's guns set fire to the forward storeroom. Some, seeking to escape the screaming shells, jumped into the river and drowned in its dark waters. As the lifeboats began carrying the wounded to shore, Dewey became concerned that the oarsmen on the boats would lose courage and not return for the rest of the crew. He leaped into one of the boats to make sure that would not happen. Years later, he thought back on his decision, calling it "the most anxious moment of my career. What if a shot should sink the boat? What if a rifle bullet should get me? All the world would say that I had been guilty of about as craven an act as can be placed at the door of any officer." Throughout his life Dewey recounted those long, frantic moments,

Chapter Three. "The Very Earth Trembled"   43

during the passage of Port Hudson and the rescue operation thereafter, and claimed, "[I] lived five years in an hour."[10]

Under the murderous cannonade from the guns on the bluff, all the lifeboats on the starboard side were destroyed, leaving only three on her port side, which were the ones that Dewey was personally supervising as they abandoned ship. These were soon filled with the wounded and rowed ashore, followed by several more trips to rescue all the crew members. By now fires had spread up and down the deck, and the flames were licking dangerously close to the combustible magazine. The time left to escape was becoming crucial, and Smith and Dewey spent the last few minutes they could spare examining the bodies lying on the deck for any signs of life. Remembering their search, Dewey wrote:

> *We went up and down the decks, examining prostrate figures to make sure no spark of life remained in them, haste impelling us in the grim task on the one hand, and, on the other, the fear that some poor fellow who was still unconscious might know the horror of seeing the flames creep up on him as he lay powerless to move. Meanwhile we kept calling aloud in the darkness that this was the last chance to escape.*

"We found one youngster," Dewey remembered, "little more than a boy, who was so faint he could barely speak. We pulled him out from under the body of a dead man." Rescuing the boy, the only survivor they could find, Smith and Dewey finally abandoned ship. Rather than row to the western shore with the rest of the crew, they made their way downstream to the *Richmond*. Later, in the early morning hours, most of the stranded crew members were rescued from the shore by the ironclad *Essex*.[11]

About three o'clock in the morning the *Mississippi* had been completely abandoned. She then began to slide off the sandbar that had held her for hours, and began drifting down the river along the western shore with her port side facing the enemy. The sight of the hulking vessel, engulfed in flames, elicited a chorus of cheers from Confederate soldiers watching from the bluffs. "It was a grand sight to see her, as she drifted slowly down, lighting up the neighboring shores and the turbid tide of the Mississippi with a lurid glare," wrote the Rebel clerk Robert Patrick in his diary. Another Confederate soldier, J.P. Cannon, recalled how "the burning ship illuminated the country for miles around, and for fear of a general conflagration the rest of the fleet withdrew before her." Indeed, fretful pilots of the mortar boats and other Union support vessels, anxious over their belief in the imminent and inevitable explosion of her magazine, steered out of her path as she approached them. As the heat from the ship's fires reached the guns on her port side, the primers ignited and she began firing at the enemy, although the only crew on board were the dead. Yet she continued moving along and giving battle, even after becoming a ghostly funeral pyre. In Dewey's words,

The Union ironclad USS *Essex*. Port Hudson State Historic Site Photograph Collection.

it was "a dying ship manned by dead men." Just as expected, before daylight in the early morning of March 15, a tremendous explosion occurred on the river, and was heard all the way to the outskirts of New Orleans. Following the shock waves from the deafening blast, nothing was left of the grand old ship, nothing but deathly silence and the remains of charred debris, floating along the muddy surface of the Mississippi River.[12]

It had been a grievous loss for Farragut and his fleet, not only the loss of the *Mississippi*, but the realization that the flagship, *Hartford*, and her escort, *Albatross*, had been the only ships to successfully pass the bastion at Port Hudson. For Farragut the night had been long and distressful. By morning as the firing stopped, Farragut, even though he had no way to communicate with them, was faced with the grim reality that the rest of his fleet would not be coming to join his flagship. They were, in fact, anchored below Port Hudson where sailors were already working repairing the damages to the ships. Doctors were busy attending the wounded, and carpenters grimly laboring to nail the coffins together. According to the account of a reporter for the *New York World*: "The deck of the Richmond presented a melancholy spectacle. Where two men fell there was a great pool of clotted gore, which I saw a seaman tossing overboard with a shovel." During the night the battle had left 99 men killed or missing, most of whom were aboard the *Mississippi;* 138 had been injured with slight to severe wounds, and 48 others were reported to have been taken prisoner by the Confederates, whose losses were slight with only a single man killed and 19 wounded. What's more, not a single Confederate cannon received any damage despite the constant shelling from the Federal fleet.[13]

All night and into the morning hours the Union infantrymen had waited south of Port Hudson for their orders from Banks to begin the diversionary land attack they had anticipated. Of course, no orders came. From their wooded position the troops could not see the naval battle taking place on the river, but they could plainly hear the terrible uproar of the battle. One Massachusetts soldier spoke of the sights and sounds of that night: "The sound of heavy guns was heard in the vicinity of Port Hudson, and the cannonading continued through the night, while the shells from the gunboats could be plainly seen bursting over the fort." By the time reveille sounded at four that morning the firing around the fort had subsided. Although the men knew nothing of the fate of the Union ship, the *Mississippi,* they sensed that something had happened: "The firing at Port Hudson had ceased; but a large mass of flame, which had been supposed to be some portion of the enemy's works, set on fire by the guns from the fleet, began to move slowly down the river, accompanied at intervals by explosions. All eyes were fixed on the mysterious light, and many gloomy forebodings indulged in. Had Farragut been defeated, and the fleet been destroyed by some infernal machine? Suddenly, at daylight, the mass of fire seemed to leap high in the air, followed by a dense column of smoke. The spectators waited in breathless suspense, for a few seconds, for the explosion. Soon it came." It was the *Mississippi.*[14]

In Farragut's mind the entire operation was a catastrophe, and he said so in his official report: "It becomes my duty again to report disaster to my fleet." But the old admiral would remain convinced that if Banks had executed the planned attack from behind Port Hudson at the same time his ships were passing on the river, the fortress would have surrendered. Clearly, his opinion was only conjectural. All the same, Farragut would never forgive Banks. Banks, on the other hand, believed that whatever went wrong was a result of Farragut's rash and impetuous decision to change the timetable of his attack. Moreover, in his official report of the operation, the general ignored the primary objective of forcing the Rebels to abandon Port Hudson, and focused on lesser objectives that were incidentally accomplished, and so concluded, "The complete success of the expedition may be thus justly assumed." Perhaps in Banks's mind the operation was a success, reasoning that even if he had gotten his troops into position for a timely attack, he never intended to actually carry it out against a force he thought to be greater than his own. That would have been suicidal. It was more important, he believed, that Farragut succeeded in getting two of his ships past the batteries, and could then intercept Rebel supplies coming into Port Hudson. Thus, if he chose to conduct a siege, the Rebels would be starved into surrender.[15]

But Banks's optimistic reasoning that the operation was a "complete success" was not shared by his troops. When he congratulated the soldiers for accomplishing the objectives of the operation, they rejected any such notion. Knowing they had accomplished nothing except making a long, grueling march from Baton Rouge, they now found themselves under orders to make a countermarch right back where they had come from. Yet they had seen no action, fired no shots, and did not understand why they were retreating. "The troops were in ill-humor," recalled one soldier, and "the whole movement seemed incomprehensible to them." Many of them had only signed up for a short enlistment, and now they had missed out on whatever glory may have come their way with a victory, or at least a battle. "The impression spreads," according to Corporal James Hosmer of the Fifty-second Massachusetts, "that we have met with great disaster, and are retreating in disgrace. Retreating without firing a shot!" On the march to Port Hudson, they had been eager to engage the enemy, and the popular Banks was cheered as he rode by the columns. Now, as they began the long march back, the troops—most of whom were new recruits with no combat experience—were sullen and demoralized. And as Banks and his staff passed along the long lines of tramping blue coats, they were greeted by a cold, indifferent silence.[16]

Their exodus was dark and gloomy. The column of soldiers, strung out for miles, continued moving south towards Baton Rouge. Their spirits were further dampened by an almost biblical storm of heavy downpours and strong winds, hitting them just as they entered "a dreary Louisiana swamp." Everyone was soaked to the skin. Corporal Hosmer likened it to a "general uncorking among the clouds," and insisted, "I never knew it rain[ed] so hard." The road turned into a quagmire of soupy marshland. Surrounded by snakes and mosquitoes, and without enough to eat or drink, the soldiers had reached what Hosmer referred to as "the bottom of misery." A fatigued Massachusetts private was quick to agree: "We were wet to the skin, and threw off our knapsacks and equipment into the mud. When morning came we were a half-drowned, haggard, bedraggled and hungry set; with an extra supply of wood-ticks." Hungry, disheartened and angry over the retreat, many of them went on a rampage of looting the small farms and plantations in the surrounding countryside. In addition to the provisions and animals they seized, another $300,000 worth of sugar and cotton was also confiscated. No one could stop them. Banks and his officers did not even try. And with all the able-bodied men off with the Confederate armies there was no one left on the farms except women, children, old men and Negroes, who were incapable of putting a stop to the pillaging "I have seen now what a scourge to a country an invading army is," observed a Massachusetts soldier. "All this marauding went on ruthlessly and wastefully. We left the road behind us foul with the odor of decaying carcasses. Cattle were killed, a quarter or so taken out of them, and the remainder left to the buzzards. Pigs were bayoneted, sugar-houses plundered of sugar and molasses, [and] private dwellings entered…. War is horrible, and this feature of plunder is one of its horrors."[17]

Chapter Four

"The Enemy Are Coming"

Nathaniel Banks may not have been a great strategist and, at times, had difficulty seeing the big picture from a military perspective, but he had other qualities which were often lacking in political generals. He paid close attention to detail. He was a superb administrator, and competent with supply and logistics. Notwithstanding his losing record in battle—most of which was against the magnificent Stonewall Jackson—Banks was bold and stout-hearted. He was a skilled problem solver, and understood the immediate one facing him in Louisiana, which was to solve the Port Hudson problem, and move forward to Vicksburg. That, of course, would satisfy Halleck and the War Department in Washington. What's more, he knew he had to do it quickly. But because he believed Gardner to have a greater troop strength than his own, he did not want to risk an attack until he could be reinforced from Vicksburg. Grant had been promising to do just that, but thus far had not sent him any troops. Seeing no alternative, Banks returned to his old plan of trying to find a water route to the Red River through the Atchafalaya River Basin, thus circumventing Port Hudson and then moving north to cooperate with Grant in taking Vicksburg.[1]

By March 25, Banks's army was back in Baton Rouge, preparing to travel through the bowels of Louisiana in a roundabout course to get above Port Hudson in what would become known as the Teche Campaign. The journey would take them through an unforgiving wilderness, known to be a maze of rivers, swampy bayous, lakes and bays. What's more, the route Banks intended to follow would force him to tackle Richard Taylor's small Confederate army, securely dug in behind a strong line of breastworks at Fort Bisland on the Bayou Teche. Taylor's total force defending Fort Bisland only amounted to about 3,000 men, most of whom were conscripts from Louisiana. He also had the captured Union gunboat, *Diana*, armed with a long-range thirty-pound Parrott rifle, which guarded the fort from Grand Lake and the surrounding bayous. It was probable that Banks was at least familiar with his opponent, the Confederate general Richard Taylor, a man who Banks will loathe the memory of in the days ahead.[2]

Chapter Four. "The Enemy Are Coming"

Taylor was a Yale graduate who had fought under Stonewall Jackson in Virginia's Shenandoah Valley. He came from a long line of aristocratic Louisiana planters, but because he bonded well with the common soldier, he was also a popular commander. About the same time Banks was given the command of the Department of the Gulf, Taylor was assigned the command of the District of West Louisiana. Banks, who had always travelled in political circles, certainly knew that Taylor had an impressive pedigree, being the son of a war hero and former president, Zachary Taylor, as well as a brother-in-law of the former United States Secretary of War and current president of the Confederacy, Jefferson Davis.

Confederate General Richard Taylor, son of President Zachary Taylor, commanded the Rebel forces during the Teche Campaign. Library of Congress.

Like his father, "Old Rough and Ready," Richard Taylor was not only a Southern gentleman, but a tough soldier and strict disciplinarian. As such, he was sometimes prone to profanity to chasten his men. Back in Virginia, during the heat of the Battle of Winchester, Taylor, forgetting the presence of the pious Stonewall Jackson, let fly a curse while urging his troops forward. Jackson was not a man who was impressed by his soldiers' family relations such as Taylor's, but was more concerned with their relations with God. Taylor remembered the moment he bellowed the curse: "The sharp tones of a familiar voice produced the desired effect, and the men looked as if they had swallowed ramrods; but I shall never forget the reproachful surprise expressed in Jackson's face. He placed his hand on my shoulder, said in a gentle voice, 'I am afraid you are a wicked fellow' turned, and rode back to the pike."[3]

From Baton Rouge, on March 28, Banks began moving 13,000 troops, first to Donaldsonville, and finally to Brashear City. However, he left General Christopher Augur and forty-five hundred troops in Baton Rouge to guard that place from any possible attack from Port Hudson. From Brashear

City around 8,000 troops from William Emory's division and Godfrey Weitzel's brigade of Augur's division pushed forward to Bayou Teche to attack the Confederate army at Fort Bisland. Meanwhile, Cuvier Grover's 5,000 men were given orders to cross Grand Lake in a fleet of transports and attack the Confederates from the rear to prevent their retreat, and hopefully capture Taylor's entire force. At least that was the tactical plan Banks had in mind.[4]

By April 11, Banks succeeded in having Emory and Weitzel poised to attack the fortifications surrounding Fort Bisland. Their movement up the Bayou Teche, however, was slow and difficult. The earthworks protecting the fort extended 1,000 yards out beyond the Teche, with the ends anchored on both sides by steamy, impenetrable swamps filled with bloodthirsty mosquitoes and venomous snakes. Furrowed fields of row after row of sugar cane which had not been harvested and growing knee-high in front of the breastworks presented still another obstacle for the bluecoats. Over the next several days, Banks's army, with a huge numerical advantage, slowly trudged forward, fighting several battles, and finally maneuvering Taylor's Confederates out of their fortifications with flanking movements and numerous artillery barrages. Grover, however, was delayed by heavy fog, and had difficulty getting his troops across the Teche and behind Taylor's army to block the Rebels' retreat. During this time of delay, Taylor, through what he called, "pleasant intelligence," became aware of Banks's plan to bag his entire command, and quickly ordered his army to move. "There was no time to ask questions," he later wrote. Without delay, his troops began slipping away on the only remaining road that the Federals had not blocked, withdrawing the small Rebel army through Franklin to New Iberia, and finally on to Alexandria. By the time Grover's troops reached Taylor's position, little remained except dead horses killed by the Union cannonade. But there was evidence that they had come close to capturing Taylor's whole force. "The campfires were still smoldering inside of the works," according to one Union soldier, "and the remains of the hasty breakfast of roasted ears of corn gave proof that the rebels had not been long gone." According to one Massachusetts soldier, General Banks offered the following explanation for the foiled plan: "We had the rebels in a bag, and General Grover held the strings, and the whole rebel army was [to be] gobbled up; but the string was rotten, and they slipped through."[5]

Although Richard Taylor had escaped being snatched up in the Union trap, he lost a third of his small force in the process. Most of those, however, were Louisiana conscripts, missing through desertions during the march to Alexandria. Along the way, as the army passed familiar parishes and hometowns, his men simply slipped away from the ranks and vanished into their homes. The most serious Confederate losses, however, were their

Chapter Four. "The Enemy Are Coming" 51

irreplaceable stores. As Banks and the Union army moved up the Bayou Teche, pursuing the retreating Southerners, they seized huge quantities of Rebel supplies, including barges loaded with food, cotton, sugar, guns and ammunition. Cattle, mules and horses, too, were all confiscated. The Confederate saltworks at New Iberia were then captured and destroyed. And once again, the usual looting of private households was rampant, in spite of Banks's orders against such behavior. For Richard Taylor, however, his greatest loss was of a personal nature. Taylor's wife and four children were in Alexandria, but word of the Union army approaching that town caused the family to flee aboard a steamer to Shreveport. No sooner had they arrived there than scarlet fever struck all the children, killing his two sons within a few days. Fortunately, though, the two girls, being older and stronger, recovered. But Taylor, on receiving the news, wrote: "I was sorely stricken by domestic grief." Yet the unexpected news did not absolve him of his responsibilities. "The absorbing character of my duties left no time for the indulgence of private grief."[6]

Like the Confederates, Union losses were heavy. Six hundred men, in fact, had been killed, wounded or captured. Others had become sick, or covered with unbearable skin diseases, a common condition from continually being damp with sweat as they trudged through the humid Louisiana swamps in their thick wool uniforms. "It was a long, weary march that General Dick Taylor led the Army of the Gulf through this country of bayous and plantations," complained a Massachusetts soldier. Unaccustomed as they were to the forced marches, the troops had been tormented with raw, blistered feet. Before the Teche Campaign ended, morale was low, and they began to curse their officers, each other, and the miserable conditions they had been forced to endure. For another soldier from New England the ordeal was difficult to put into words: "The long nights in a Louisiana swamp, the alligators that were killed, the snakes that came out of the water to see us, the mosquitoes that worried us, all of these are better imagined than described."[7]

But for Banks, he interpreted the campaign as an outstanding victory. Writing his wife, Mary, he told her, "Our success has been splendid." Indeed, it was true that Banks had driven Richard Taylor's little army out of their fortifications in south Louisiana. It was also accurate that by taking control of the Atchafalaya Basin, Banks had succeeded in opening a water route from New Orleans to the Red River. But the Mississippi River from Port Hudson to Vicksburg still loomed large, and the conquest and possession of that should have been his first priority. Confederate authorities were pleased that Banks had become distracted and had removed himself from the campaign against Port Hudson to chase Taylor through the Louisiana swamps. That time gave Gardner the opportunity to further strengthen the fortifications at the bastion. On the other hand, Chief of Staff Henry Halleck and the War Department in Washington were clearly not pleased with Banks's excursion. Halleck was actually livid, and claimed to be "exceedingly disappointed" with the general's "eccentric movements" instead of focusing on the Mississippi River, the Union's most important objective. Later, after receiving further reports from Banks on his operations on Bayou Teche, Halleck responded pejoratively, "As this is so contrary to all your instructions, and so opposed to military principles, I can hardly believe it true. I have so often pointed out what I thought ought to be done, and the peril of separate and isolated operations, that it would be useless to repeat them here."[8]

After Banks reached Alexandria on May 7, he stopped the army for several days, pondering what he should do next. Then on May 14, he ordered his troops from Alexandria down the Red River to the town of Simmesport. From there, he could either move up the Mississippi River and join Grant at Vicksburg, or turn his attention back to attacking Port Hudson. Such a nagging dilemma of indecision caused Banks to leave his army and return to New Orleans to consult with Farragut. By this time, however, Banks was aware, through several tardy dispatches from Grant, that he would not be receiving the promised 20,000 troops to aid him in taking Port Hudson. Instead, Grant would like Banks to come north and aid him in the Vicksburg Campaign. All the while, Banks continued to be pressured by the irate Halleck, hounding him to find a way to cooperate with Grant. From a tactical standpoint, moving his army north to tie in with Grant, and leaving Port Hudson in his rear was dangerous, and did not appeal to Banks. On the other hand, if he attacked Port Hudson that would, at least, keep any of the Rebel garrison there from leaving to reinforce Pemberton at Vicksburg; thus he would be lending aid to Grant in a left-handed sort of way. That reasoning finally put an end to Banks's vacillation. He would now move against Port Hudson.

Meanwhile, during the time Banks was spending in pursuit of Taylor's Rebels through the Teche country, Gardner was continuing to strengthen the fortifications and build up the food supply at Port Hudson. But during this time he was instructed to send reinforcements to Pemberton in Vicksburg, who was becoming so hard-pressed by Grant that he began urging Jefferson Davis to order the evacuation of Port Hudson and send Gardner's entire force to his aid. So by the end of April, less than 12,000 Confederates were left under Gardner's command. Moreover, the exodus of even more of his men bound for Vicksburg would continue. As expected, a few days later, on May 4, Pemberton ordered Gardner to join him in Vicksburg with 5,000 men. That, of course, would leave only Beall's brigade and the heavy artillery with the impossible task of defending Port Hudson. Faced

Chapter Four. "The Enemy Are Coming"

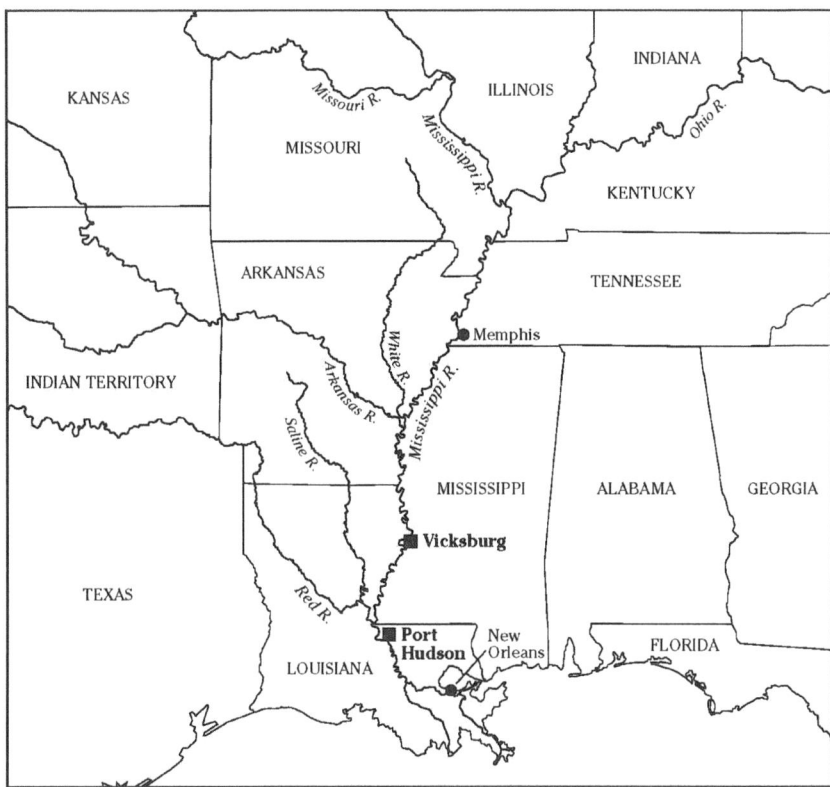

Overview map of Mississippi Valley (created by the author).

with the order, Gardner had no choice but to comply. He immediately sent three brigades ahead, and a few days later he followed with Samuel Maxey's brigade. But he did not get far. He had only reached the town of Clinton before receiving another wire from Pemberton, telling him to return to Port Hudson with 2,000 men, "and hold it to the last." Pemberton's reversal in orders was a result of a telegram that he received on May 7 from President Jefferson Davis in Richmond, ordering him "to hold both Vicksburg and Port Hudson."[9]

So it seemed clear that Confederate president Jefferson Davis was the sole reason that Port Hudson still remained fortified. Pemberton, in fact, was not the only one who wanted to see the garrison evacuated, and thus free Gardner's troops to come to his aid in Vicksburg. Joseph Johnston, who was the departmental commander of the entire military area, also shared the opinion that Port Hudson should be evacuated, but believed that Gardner's troops should be sent to him in Jackson. This was clearly a time of anxiety for the Confederacy and resulted in conflicting orders. Everyone wanted reinforcements, and there were none to give. On May 19, Johnston wrote Gardner explaining that Pemberton had been compelled to fall back within the confines of the city of Vicksburg. In Johnston's words, "He is now invested [surrounded]," and continued on, "so that your position is no longer valuable." Johnston, who had continued to maintain that he intended to go to Pemberton's rescue in Vicksburg, then ordered Gardner: "Evacuate Port Hudson forthwith, and move with your troops toward Jackson, to join other troops which I am uniting."[10]

For the soldierly Franklin Gardner, orders were orders, and he would certainly obey Johnston's orders, assuming that he was given enough time. Most civilians had already been evacuated, and commerce had ceased. But as he began the intricate task of moving his troops and artillery out of Port Hudson, Gardner became aware that Banks's army was closing in on him, making an evacuation impossible. On May 19, the same day that Johnston ordered Gardner to evacuate, Banks had already begun ferrying his troops across the Mississippi River to Bayou Sara, just north of Port Hudson. At the same time Christopher Augur was moving his division north from Baton Rouge, and Thomas Sherman's division, which had been defending New Orleans, was about to be transported upriver by boat. Soon Banks's army would be reunited, increasing his strength to about 28,000 men, and giving him a four-to-one advantage over Gardner and his Port Hudson garrison, which by this time had been reduced to about 7,000 defenders as a result of all the troops that had been transferred to Vicksburg, and those defenders were about to be hopelessly encircled. Furthermore, the Federal fleet was now in control of the Mississippi River, both north and south of Port Hudson. Thus, with these advantages, Banks now stood a much better chance of seizing Port Hudson than he had in the past.[11]

Lieutenant General John C. Pemberton commanded the Confederate stronghold at Vicksburg, Mississippi. Library of Congress.

During the early days

of May while Gardner was transferring troops from Port Hudson to Vicksburg, Admiral Farragut left his flagship, *Hartford,* with the Federal fleet at Vicksburg under David Porter, and journeyed south by way of the Atchafalaya River to resume command of his fleet. In that role, Farragut planned on aiding Banks in the campaign against Port Hudson. Thus, the Union naval forces actually began operations against Gardner and his garrison before Banks and his army. On the morning of May 8, Farragut brought his mortar boats up the river to a point on the left bank about four and a half miles below Port Hudson. There, after finding their range, they commenced firing on Port Hudson, a bombardment that took place primarily during the night and would not stop until the eighteenth of June. The day after Farragut's mortar boats commenced raining their shells down on the Confederate river batteries, Colonel Paul De Gournay brought four rifled cannons downriver to Troth's landing, where they could attack the mortar boats and hopefully drive them away. De Gournay and his men worked all night digging earthen redoubts from which they could position their big guns. By dawn the next morning they were blasting away at the Union mortar boats. Neither side was particularly effective in inflicting damage, although the Southern gunners did manage to land a couple of shells into the hull and rigging of the sloop *Richmond,* but the damage was minimal.[12]

The mortar schooners continued their bombardments on the Confederate river batteries throughout the month of May. Remarkably, there were but few casualties among the artillerymen. However, when they did occur, they were usually fatal. The first incident happened on May 9, when a thirteen-inch shell slammed into a Rebel's neck with such force that it propelled him head first through the gun's wooden platform he was standing on, leaving nothing but his feet protruding above it. Over a week later on May 17, a mortar shell fell to the ground and buried itself beneath four of De Gournay's men who happened to be sitting around that spot. The shell exploded, catapulting the men into the air, killing three of them and wounding the fourth. Soon after these men were buried another mortar round ploughed into the graveyard throwing coffins into the air and exhuming some bodies in the process. Two more soldiers were struck with shell fragments, and lost their legs. These casualties, according to one witness, were the extent of the losses caused from the Union mortar boats during the siege. Indeed, such few losses were incredible, considering the frequency of the falling shells that excavated huge fifteen-foot caverns as they exploded throughout the Rebel breastworks.[13]

Although the relentless bombardment by the Federal fleet did not cause many losses within the Rebel ranks, it had other consequences which were probably unintended, but which created a good deal of misery for the defenders. As in any siege where the confined are subjected to constant shelling, it deprived them of much-needed sleep at night and, still worse, left them with psychological scars. With projectiles coming from every direction, men's nerves became exhausted with fear. A Louisiana officer described some of the collateral effects of the cannonades: "Trunks of trees were pierced through and through or shivered into splinters, their limbs lopped off and the leaves scattered over the ground; houses were ventilated in the most unexpected fashion, balls going in and out … the earth was plowed up and roads were raked, wagons were smashed, and beeves, horses and mules were butchered while grazing in the fields or woods. The riot of destruction raged throughout the whole place, and had there been any weak-nerved people there they might have searched in vain for an abiding place." There was, however, at least one incident when the shelling produced a favorable outcome for the Rebel soldiers. During one of the May bombardments, an errant missile from the Federal fleet fell in the river and exploded with such force that some eighty fish floated to the surface, stunned by the concussion. Right away, some hungry and enterprising Rebels launched a couple of skiffs, and collected a huge catch. Considering that fish "were then selling among the soldiers at from five to fifty dollars apiece, according to their size, this proved to be a valuable haul."[14]

On May 20, with Augur's division steadily approaching Port Hudson, a series of cavalry skirmishes began to break out in the vicinity of a two-story building known as Plains Store, which stood near a crossing of two roads. The next day, around noon, Gardner ordered Colonel William R. Miles to send four hundred of his infantry and a battery of artillery out to reconnoiter Augur's position, and assist Colonel Frank Powers and his cavalrymen. Near the store, in a tangled thicket, Miles's Confederates ran into the leading elements of Augur's division, engaging them in a number of quick firefights. These small skirmishes did not rise to the level of even a small battle until Major James Coleman ordered two companies of Louisiana boys to charge a battery of Yankee artillery. They stormed out of an apple orchard shouting and yelling, and for a time had possession of the enemy's guns. But the bluecoats staged a counterattack which set off an hour-long struggle for possession of the cannons. Because the horses that pulled the gun carriages had been killed in the engagement, Coleman's men had no way of pulling the cannons away as Augur's men advanced. The outnumbered Rebels, unable to claim the guns, were finally forced to fall back in the face of the fierce Yankee counterattack. Nothing was accomplished by either side in that first clash of infantry near Port Hudson except the shedding of first blood: the death of twelve of Miles's men, fifteen of Augur's, and the wounding of over a hundred other men, mostly Federals. Beyond that, Plains Store, which the battle was named after, as well as the pristine woods surrounding it, were savagely battered in a storm of canister and grape shot.[15]

Chapter Four. "The Enemy Are Coming"   57

While the Federal troops continued to mass around Port Hudson, it was beginning to appear as if Franklin Gardner and his little garrison were in a hopeless situation. That, however, was hardly the case. Although the number of Confederate troops now at Port Hudson had been reduced to a third of the force needed to defend the four-and-a-half-mile length of breastworks, their position was superb. The works were complete, formidable, and had strong interior lines that would allow troop movement from one threatened position to another. Moreover, any Federal assault would be faced with crossing a hostile landscape that was laced with tangled undergrowth and treacherous ravines. Gardner also was able to bring in provisions on flats or barges from the opposite side of the river, even in the presence of the Union fleet. Up until they were completely surrounded, he succeeded in bringing in three hundred head of beef, four hundred head of sheep, 4,000 bushels of corn, and large quantities of sugar and salt. One drawback, however, was the lack of proper warehouses for the storage and protection of the food and other supplies. That aside, the Rebel general certainly had reasons to be confident. Thus while the battle at Plains Store was underway he quietly listened to the distant sounds of the guns during a final inspection of the works. After being reassured that the cannoneers manning the artillery on the river were ready to fight, Gardner pointed towards the sound of the fire, and vowed to them, "The enemy are coming, but mark you, many a one will get to hell before he does to Port Hudson."[16]

By the morning of May 23, the investment of Port Hudson was complete. Like its counterpart, Vicksburg, it was now under siege. The Federal lines stretched from left to right, beginning with Thomas Sherman's division whose left was anchored on the east bank of the Mississippi River and extended northwardly over the road to Baton Rouge until it met Christopher Augur's division that held the section of line covering the Plains Store Road. Following the Union line as it began bending back towards the river, Cuvier Grover's division was stretched across the Jackson Road. Completing the encirclement, Godfrey Weitzel's division and the brigades of William Dwight and Halbert Paine held the Union right and blocked the Telegraph Road leading to Bayou Sara. Behind the lines, protecting the intersections of the roads, and defending against the Rebel cavalry, Benjamin Grierson and his cavalrymen were positioned. These horsemen may well have been the most experienced troops under Banks's command. After all, Grierson and his veteran horsemen had only recently returned from their daring and famous six-hundred-mile rampage through the state of Mississippi, where they created havoc on Pemberton's supply and communication lines.[17]

In preparing to defend against the Federal assault, Gardner had divided the Port Hudson garrison into three sections, commanded by his most trusted senior officers. William Beall, a brigadier and his second in command, was assigned to hold down the center with twenty-three hundred men and three batteries of artillery. Colonel Isaiah Steedman, who was also the regimental commander of the First Alabama, had the responsibility for the left wing, which numbered about twenty-one hundred infantrymen, assigned to him from other units in the garrison. Because Steedman's section of the line fell within the swampy terrain around Big Sandy Creek and Little Sandy Creek, Gardner had not expected an assault from the north and consequently had not fortified it as well as the other parts of the line. But with Union soldiers now advancing on that sector, he became aware that his left flank was vulnerable. Thus, the first task facing Steedman's men was to dig rifle pits and trenches into the high ground opposite the creeks. And this they did, beginning on May 25, a Monday night. Lastly, Gardner placed his right wing under the command of Colonel William R. Miles, who may have had the toughest job, since he was ordered to hold the entire right wing with a little less than a thousand infantrymen and two hundred cannoneers. In addition to these forces, Gardner had three hundred heavy artillerymen posted throughout the line and along the river commanded by Colonel Marshall Smith, Gardner's chief of artillery. There were also approximately twelve hundred cavalrymen commanded by Colonel John Logan, who were not within the perimeter of the bastion, but were an important part of the defense of Port Hudson, since they were constantly tormenting Banks from the rear.[18]

Tuesday evening, May 26, Banks called a council of war of his commanders to issue orders for a general assault the next morning. The meeting took place at the nearby Riley Plantation, where Banks, brimming with confidence, prepared to lay out his plan for the attack. And given his huge numeric advantage over the Rebels that self-assurance was understandable. Gathered inside the house were a group of West Point–educated generals who, in some degree or another, were all proud, self-important and highly opinionated men. As career soldiers, they were smugly resentful that a civilian such as Banks was leading them in military matters. Sherman, Augur, Grover, Weitzel, and a number of the other senior officers, including Banks's chief of staff, General George Andrews, were present. Also, there was the ubiquitous watchdog, Richard Irwin, Bank's adjutant, who was described by a Michigan colonel as "a red-headed regular army officer who … has been sent here by the West Point authorities in Washington to act as a *quasi*-keeper for the civilian Major General. He is represented to have been a favorite, long employed in the War Department, where, in addition to his contempt for volunteers, he got great ideas of his own importance."[19]

As soon as Banks announced his plans for an immediate assault, General Augur spoke up and voiced his disagreement, claiming it would be

Chapter Four. "The Enemy Are Coming"

foolish to send the troops over such a tangled and unfamiliar terrain as the one surrounding Port Hudson without a proper reconnaissance. Augur also argued that the place should be heavily bombarded with artillery before any attack could be contemplated. Another strenuous objector was Sherman, who agreed with Augur, and favored a defensive fight or a siege to starve the Confederates into surrender. But Banks ignored both their protests. In fact, according to Adjutant Irwin, he had already made up his mind before the meeting, and quickly responded to their opposition with the order: "Port Hudson must be taken tomorrow." He then reminded them—and correctly so—that half his army was composed of nine-month volunteers whose enlistments would expire within a few weeks, rendering a long siege impossible. Furthermore it was now imperative, according to Banks, to quickly finish taking Port Hudson and move to Grant's aid against Vicksburg. Then, as Thomas Sherman continued to argue that the attack would result in too much bloodshed from their troops, Banks, ever the politician, reddened in anger and curtly replied, "The people of the North demand blood, sir."[20]

Chapter Five

A Miserable Loss

When the first gray streaks of the May 27 dawn were just beginning to peek through the willows and canebrakes along the Mississippi River, Federal cannons suddenly roared to life, breaking the morning stillness and sending the Confederate artillerymen running to their own big guns. The cannonade was furious with ninety pieces of artillery belching fire up and down the six-mile-long Yankee line. Out on the river, the Federal navy soon joined in the raucous shelling, lobbing their melon-sized projectiles into the garrison, something they had already been engaged in for the past several days in preparation of the assault. After the morning artillery bombardment, Banks's plan, as he perceived it, was to launch a coordinated and simultaneous attack by all divisions, beginning with Weitzel's division on the right wing. Unfortunately, Banks, the author of the plan, was the only one who even remotely understood it. His order was clouded with ambivalent and confusing directions. More importantly, his division and brigade commanders did not have a clear grasp as to what their role in the assault was supposed to be. Nebulous language contained in the document, such as "Take instant advantage of any favorable opportunity, and … if possible, force the enemy's works at the earliest moment" and "Take advantage of the attacks on other parts of the line," left the various commanders scratching their heads. The only conclusion they were able to draw from this was that they had the discretion to attack or not to attack. Yet what was just as puzzling was that a man such as Banks, a former wordsmith, had composed such a poorly worded document filled with competing instructions. As a politician, Nathaniel Banks had excellent communication skills, and was known as someone who could inform and persuade huge crowds with facts, figures and details. So, whether Banks's vague instructions were evidence of his lack of military training or an indication of overconfidence in his commanders that they would independently exercise prudent initiatives was unclear. But for whatever reason, Banks had failed to communicate to his commanders his plan for attack, which apparently amounted to nothing more than a simultaneous sequence of movements of nearly

30,000 men who, for the most part, had little battle experience in charging through a swamp-ridden, densely wooded country they knew nothing about. Thus, it didn't take long for his plan—what little there was to it—to fall apart.¹

Brigadier General Godfrey Weitzel, a twenty-eight-year-old engineer from Cincinnati, Ohio, and son of a German immigrant, waited patiently in the dark woods, preparing to move his division forward in columns of brigades. He was, as one officer remembers, "a very different man from most of the regular army subalterns who have been suddenly made brigadiers and major-generals. He actually went with his men in the assault." Initially, Weitzel advanced with fourteen regiments, mostly men from the Northeast with little or no experience. It was shortly after five o'clock when these regiments stepped off through the woods under a canopy of magnolia trees and began pushing their way forward through a series of deep ravines. Lieutenant Colonel Willoughby Babcock was in command of the two leading regiments of skirmishers, the Twelfth Connecticut and the Seventy-fifth New York. In a letter home, Babcock described the difficult ground they had to cross: "Our way led through the woods, over the most broken ground I ever saw, obstructed by deep gulches, running every way, trees and brush, and in some places by rude abatis made by the enemy." By six o'clock, the leading columns arrived at a more open space where they stopped, reformed, and tried to catch their breath. "While we were resting here a sharp firing of infantry commenced on the right and front of us," remembered Lieutenant William Root, a New Yorker, "and we started in that direction." The source of the firing, Weitzel's men would soon discover, was from the Confederate skirmish line, numbering about five hundred men and commanded by Colonel M.B. Locke of the First Alabama

Union General Godfrey Weitzel. Library of Congress.

Regiment in Steedman's section of the line, who had advanced his troops beyond their fortifications. They crossed Sandy Creek, and were waiting in every gully, hollow and ravine, preparing to meet the Yankee advance. Locke's Alabamans were supported by a large cannon behind them. As the Union lines came closer Lieutenant Root recalled the effects of the big Rebel gun and the skirmishers' fire. "This gun cut off a tree larger than my body and grape and canister as well as rifle balls were flying on all sides cutting down our brave soldiers."[2]

Although the outnumbered Rebel skirmishers contested every inch of ground in a furious hour-long fight, they were grudgingly forced out of one position, then another, by the surging blue lines. Finally, they were driven back over the creek and into their main works. After entering the safety of their fortifications, Colonel Steedman, commanding the Confederate left wing from Commissary Hill, ordered the four-gun battery there to open fire on Weitzel's men. "The fight has opened," John Kennedy of the First Alabama Regiment wrote in his diary. "We are laying in our rifle-pits, awaiting the hated foe. The artillery is deafening; it is one continual roar." Weitzel's troops continued through the brutally raking-fire from the artillery and muskets, stepping over the fallen bodies, until they reached a ridge about two hundred yards from the Rebel lines. By this time, the regiments were beginning to break apart into squads, which mingled together like an unorganized mob. From that point, which was closer to the enemy lines, Federal sharpshooters managed to creep forward and pick off many of the artillerymen atop the hill until they eventually silenced the Rebels' big guns.[3]

Rebel riflemen watched from their breastworks, as the Federals reorganized and prepared to resume their assault. There was little time to construct the cover from which they would fight, but Steedman later recalled how "the regiment had rolled logs and piled rails, making a sort of breastwork." After Colonel Locke was wounded by a ricocheting bullet, the First Alabama Regiment was led by Major Samuel L. Knox. They appeared "cool and determined," according to one of their infantrymen, who prophetically added: "The Yanks are laying under the hill, but if they come in sight they will catch it, sure as two and two makes four." And, indeed, they did *catch it* as Weitzel ordered them forward in wave after wave, only to see them mowed down by the lacerating musket fire pouring from the hot barrels of the Alabama infantrymen. Steedman, in his after-action report, could only describe the results of the Yankee charges as "repulsed with great slaughter." Recounting the determined stand of Steedman's line, Lieutenant Howard Wright wrote: "Column after column and regiment after regiment was hurled against them, shells and shrapnel burst around them, and the minie balls maintained a ceaseless whizzing, but, like the British squares at Waterloo, they stood like the rock-bound coast against which the mighty waves of the ocean dash furiously but in vain." Still, Weitzel's boys would not give up. "Every man seemed to be fighting on his own hook," recalled a New York lieutenant. "It was more like Indian fighting than a charge." Off to the left of Weitzel's troops, Halbert Paine's Third Brigade under Oliver Gooding appeared in their support, extending the blue line, and striking the Confederate line at a weak point known as the "Bull Pen." Paine, a curly-headed lawyer and abolitionist from Ohio, was the only brigadier under Banks's command who did not attend West Point. At first, Paine's Second Brigade of New Hampshire and Wis-

Union General Halbert Paine lost a leg leading the charge of June 14. National Archives.

consin men under Colonel Hawkes Fearing, which had moved in behind Gooding's brigade, seemed to be making progress as a few of his men reached the Rebel breastworks. But Steedman, again seeing the threat, sent three regiments of Arkansas men rushing forward to stop their advance. Although heavily outnumbered the Arkansans managed to hold the line and kill the colonels of the Eighth New Hampshire and Thirty-Eighth Massachusetts Regiments in the process. Without support, Paine's attack was another piecemeal effort that failed.[4]

Weitzel's advance had now come to a grinding halt with his men either hugging the ground for cover or retreating to the rear. About midmorning, General Cuvier Grover, trying to provide some support for Weitzel, sent two regiments double-timing to unite with Paine's left, and attacked a hill jutting out on the far right of Steedman's line which was held by Colonel Ben Johnson's Fifteenth Arkansas Regiment. After Grover's first two regiments clawed their way through the tangled woods and reached the hill, they launched a charge and came within thirty yards of the breastworks, only to be turned back in the face of the galling enemy fire. But Grover, another West Point man and native of Maine, had no intention of giving up, and ordered three more regiments forward, with the intent of flanking the quarter-mile-long lunette held by the Fifteenth Arkansas. For the rest of the morning a wild battle ensued as wave after wave of Grover's bluecoats stormed that part of the Confederate line which would, for obvious reasons, come to be known as Fort Desperate, and was the scene of the hardest and bloodiest fighting that day. In every attack, the outnumbered Rebels allowed them to advance within a close distance of the breastworks before rising up and delivering a furious point-blank blast of musketry and canister from their artillery. The results were disastrous. Still, a number of the troops from Maine somehow managed to reach the top of the parapet and plant their flag, an act which brought the gray defenders out of their ditches, impaling the New Englanders with bayonets and driving them back to seek cover in the ravines.[5]

When the advances of Weitzel and Grover had both stalled, the other Union commanders on the right were becoming desperate for some way to

Ruins of Confederate stronghold Fort Desperate, defended by the Fifteenth Arkansas Regiment. Port Hudson State Historic Site Photograph Collection.

Chapter Five. A Miserable Loss

break the Rebel line. General William Dwight, believed he had a scheme to create a diversion and possibly break that line in the process. Under his authority were the First and Third Regiments of the Louisiana Native Guards, composed entirely of black soldiers, and commanded by Colonel John Nelson. They were at that time stationed along the Telegraph Road which ran along the Mississippi River between Port Hudson and Bayou Sara. The First Regiment consisted of free blacks from New Orleans, some of whom were educated and prosperous, and thus were capable of serving as line officers for the regiment. The Third Regiment was made up of former slaves, led by white officers. The Native Guards, like all black soldiers who had participated in the war, experienced the widespread prejudice among whites that they wouldn't fight. Banks, as well as his predecessor, Benjamin Butler, had small use for the black soldiers, although Banks, a man influenced by political currents, later swallowed some of his prejudice, and was credited with the organization of the Corps de'Afrique. Earlier, however, when Butler first formed the Native Guards into a militia in New Orleans, a Union officer overheard him remarking on their capabilities: "Colored troops will probably be kept near and used to garrison unhealthy positions; they will be called on for fatigue duty such as making roads, building bridges and draining marshes; they will be seldom put into battle, and will afford small chance of distinction." Thus despite their desire to prove themselves in combat, they were usually consigned to menial jobs such as teamsters, cooks, laborers, and guards. But on that day, their greatest misfortune was being assigned to the command of Brigadier General William Dwight, who saw this as a challenge "to test the negro question."[6]

William Dwight was a short, pig-faced, balding specimen of a man from Springfield, Massachusetts. Even the uniform of the thirty-one-year-old brigadier did little to improve his looks. "Ah, there he is," commented an officer who had heard him described but was seeing him in a crowd for the first time. "I need not be told which he is ... what a countenance." Aside from his unsightly features, Dwight was not a man who had won the least bit of respect or approval of his troops or his superiors. To be sure, most regarded him with contempt. Thus, it was difficult to understand how such a man had risen through the ranks to become a general officer. One reason, perhaps, was the hero status he achieved in the Peninsula Campaign back in Virginia. There, Dwight, as a lieutenant colonel, was wounded, left for dead, captured and finally exchanged. He was rewarded with a promotion to brigadier general and sent to Louisiana. Another reason, supposedly, was his claim to a military education from West Point, declaring that he had resigned shortly before graduation in 1853. Actually—though he was careful never to mention it—Dwight had been expelled from West Point for failing grades, drunkenness, and "shameless association with obscene women."[7]

On the day of the assault, Dwight was drunk before breakfast, a condition he found himself in on a daily basis, but rarely that early. But even in his inebriated condition, Dwight knew this would be the first time in the war that black troops would be used in major combat. The night before the assault he wrote his mother, telling her, "I have had the negro regiments longest in the service assigned to me. I am going to storm a detached work with them. The Negro will have the fate of his race on his conduct. You may look for hard fighting, or for a complete run away. I shall compromise nothing in making the attack.... I regard it as an experiment." Dwight had not conducted a reconnaissance of the ground, and had no idea about the terrain the men would be expected to cross. But when asked by Colonel Nelson to describe the ground they would have to negotiate in making the attack, Dwight told him; "You will have the easiest way into Port Hudson." That, of course, was a lie and Dwight knew it. Because of the tangled and difficult terrain, it was perhaps the best protected approach to any of the Rebel fortifications. The Native Guards would have to make their advance against a high bluff about four hundred yards long near the river. That position was occupied by the Thirty-ninth Mississippi Regiment, commanded by a doughty colonel named William Shelby. The Mississippians were supported by two batteries of six cannon as well as the heavy artillery of the water batteries on the river.[8]

As soon as Dwight gave the nod, the two regiments of the Native Guards, composed of about a thousand black troops, crossed Sandy Creek and advanced at the double-quick through a patch of willow trees to the edge of a clearing. Although they began receiving fire about four hundred yards from the Confederate line, it wasn't until they got within two hundred yards of the fortifications that the canister from the artillery and the balls from the Mississippians' rifles begin ripping huge holes in the oncoming

Union General William Dwight. Library of Congress.

Chapter Five. A Miserable Loss

columns. Choosing not to accompany the Native Guards, and letting them fend for themselves, Colonel Nelson remained on the other side of the creek, and beyond that point, even farther in the rear, was General Dwight who safely listened to the fire grow heavier. Charging up front and leading Company E of the First Regiment was Captain Andre Cailloux, a free black from New Orleans, who was an ex-slave, but a prominent man in that city. He took pride in his African lineage, and delighted in referring to himself as "the blackest man in America." He was urging his men forward, shouting orders in French and English, when he was wounded in the elbow by a rifle ball. Ignoring the wound he continued on with his arm dangling at his side until he was killed by a cannon shot. Men were falling everywhere. Sergeant Anselmas Planciancois, who was in charge of the colors, told Colonel Nelson before the attack, "Colonel, I will bring back these colors in honor or report to God the reason why." Yet early in the attack, during the first wave, he was hit in the head by a shell that splattered his brains over the flag he had pledged to bring back. It was only a short time after the charge began that the ground was littered with dead and wounded, and after two more charges many of the blacks were demoralized and frightened and began to fall back in confusion. A Rebel defender reported: "The Negroes fled every way in perfect confusion, without firing a gun." They were soon splashing wildly across the creek and scrambling for cover. But there the runaway was halted and they were reformed. Colonel Nelson, seeing the futility in continuing the attack, sent an officer "far to the rear" to find Dwight, explain their horrendous losses, and obtain his permission to withdraw. The officer finally located the general, finding him lounging against a shade tree. Nelson's messenger, panting with excitement, then explained that the black regiments had lost half their men. Dwight, still fortifying himself with liquor, appeared indifferent to the plight of his black soldiers, and casually responded, "Tell Colonel Nelson I shall consider he has done nothing unless he carries the enemy's works.... Charge again."[9]

Knowing another charge would be suicide, Nelson disobeyed Dwight's orders, although he employed a little chicanery in doing so. Satisfied that Dwight would never get close to the front lines and only monitored the charge by listening to the noise, he ordered the black soldiers to take cover in the trees and continue firing, deceiving the inebriated general into believing the attack was still in progress. Later, after Dwight had become what one officer described as "uncommonly drunk," Nelson was handed a final order from the general: "Keep your Negroes charging.... When there is only one man left, let him come to me and report." Thus throughout the rest of day the Native Guards continued to fire at the enemy from a safe distance, and Dwight continued to believe he was making history by *testing the Negro question*.[10]

The Native Guard's losses were severe with a total of 308 men killed, wounded or missing, most of whom were from the First Regiment, while the defending Mississippians did not lose a man. Assessments of the black soldiers' conduct varied, ranging from courageous to cowardly. There is no argument that the attack of the Native Guards failed to succeed. Yet it was only one of many that failed on that day. By some accounts, they did all they could in an impossible situation, whereas others were less favorable. After giving a critical account of their performance during the charge, Howard Wright, a Southern officer, added: "This was the last we saw of Negro troops at Port Hudson." However, in Banks's after-action report, he gave them an unexpected high commendation, considering that up until then he had expressed little faith in the ability of the colored soldiers "It gives me pleasure to report that they answered every expectation," Banks wrote. "In many respects their conduct was heroic." Later, on June 11, 1863, the *New York Times* published excerpts from Banks's report, and opined the following compliment:

> *The official testimony settles the question that the Negro race can fight with great prowess. Those black soldiers had never before been in any severe engagement. They were comparatively raw troops, and were yet subjected to the most awful ordeal that even veterans ever have to experience—the charging upon fortifications through the crash of belching batteries. The men, white or black, who will not flinch from that, will flinch from nothing. It is no longer possible to doubt the bravery and steadiness of the colored race, when rightly led.*

As expected, the people of the North were encouraged over the blacks' performance at Port Hudson, which they saw featured in other newspaper editorials such as the *Washington Daily National Intelligencer*. The charge of the Native Guards during the battle was certainly significant and newsworthy in view of the fact that it was the first major engagement between white and black troops in the Civil War. As it often happens, however, at least some of those articles tended to present exciting, if not exaggerated, accounts of their spirit and bravery. One such example was an illustration in *Harper's Weekly* depicting the Negro troops storming a Rebel parapet in a close and desperate struggle, although evidence from primary accounts confirmed that none of the Native Guards approached closer than two hundred yards of the Rebel lines. There were also accounts of black soldiers in hand-to-hand combat with the Mississippians, who took them as prisoners and were subsequently tortured by Shelby's men. Those accounts were clearly fabricated and rebutted by soldiers on both sides. Nevertheless, the engagement of the Negro troops at Port Hudson changed both the military and public opinion regarding their willingness to fight in this war.[11]

Around noon, after the failed charges on the Union right by Weitzel, Grover and Dwight, a brief stillness settled over the battlefield. Licking

Chapter Five. A Miserable Loss

Artist illustration of the Louisiana Native Guards on May 27, 1863, making the first assault by black troops in U.S. history. *Harper's Weekly*.

their wounds over the morning beating, Weitzel and Grover decided to wait for Generals Augur and Sherman to open their offensives on the center and left before resuming their attacks, or at least wait for new orders from Banks. Banks, meanwhile, could not understand why the attack seemed to have died, and from his nearby headquarters had still heard no sounds of firing from the center and left. Frustrated and "greatly disturbed by the silence on the left," Banks mounted his horse and galloped off to find General Sherman. Arriving at his position, he saw the men of his division sitting around idly and waiting for orders. Entering the general's tent, he found Sherman enjoying a luncheon with his staff. Banks maddened at the sight, and according to Richard Irwin, "Hot words passed, the precise nature of which has not been recorded." What was recorded, however, were Banks's words to Weitzel when he notified him that "Sherman has failed utterly and criminally to bring his men into the field." The red-faced Banks then hurried back to his headquarters, and ordered General George Andrews, his chief-of-staff, to ride to Sherman's headquarters and assume command of his division.[12]

By the time Andrews arrived at Sherman's position, which was about 1:30 p.m., he found the recently reprimanded general sitting in the saddle with his division deployed for battle. Because of the high esteem in which Andrews held Sherman, he did not deliver Banks's order that he was there to relieve him of his command. Instead, he spoke briefly to Sherman, and remained to "witness the operation." Andrews, after some thoughtful reasoning, felt justified in his decision to decline assuming command. While it was true that Sherman had already voiced his objection against making the attack, and did not think it had a chance to succeed, it was also true that he was not a man who would knowingly disobey orders because he disagreed with them. It was possible that Banks's unclear orders of the night before may have left Sherman confused over what was expected of him. Moreover, Andrews, a military man who graduated first in his 1851 class at West Point, knew that Sherman was a good general, and agreed with Richard Irwin's description and assessment of the situation: "Sherman was an officer of the old army, of wide experience, favorably known and highly esteemed throughout the service for his intelligence, his character, and his courage. Neither in his previous history nor in his conduct in the present exigency was there anything to his personal discredit as a man or as a soldier."[13]

Union General Thomas W. Sherman lost his right leg leading the assault of May 27. Library of Congress.

Shortly after two o'clock in the afternoon, Sherman ordered his division forward to attack the Confederate center. Sherman and his staff rode between the brigades of General Franklin Nickerson and General Neal Dow. Out in front of these troops were three hundred Negroes, known as Pioneers, who carried no weapons, but instead were burdened with long, heavy poles or planks that were intended to be used to span the wide ditch laying in front of the Rebel breastworks. Following these men were a group of volunteer soldiers known in the ranks of Banks's army as the "Forlorn Hope," a most appropriate name considering the miserable task that lay before them. Their job was to carry the planks that would be used to span the poles, and thus provide a bridge for the combat soldiers to get across the ditch and into the Rebel's breastworks. But before they could reach that point, all of the Union men had to cross an open field owned by a man with the ironically fitting name of Slaughter, the same field a Confederate officer had earlier predicted would become "the field of slaughter." Unlike the dark, broken, woodsy terrain where the morning fight took place, the unobstructed ground on the cornfield exposed the attackers to a murderous fire. Slaughter's Field, as it would hereafter be known, stretched out for about five hundred yards, and was cluttered with felled trees that were intended to hinder their crossing, along with several rail fences, and finally the fifteen-foot-wide moat they would be forced to negotiate. All the while, as they were scrambling over this ground, the bluecoats would be subjected to the pounding artillery of the Confederate batteries. Assuming they succeeded in getting near the moat, they would then face a close-range fire from the brigade of General William Beall, whose command had just been timely reinforced with some Louisiana troops from Colonel William Miles, positioned on Beall's right.[14]

"The enemy advanced in beautiful formation led by a general officer and his staff, who rode together in advance of the colors. A strong breeze was blowing, which made their splendid silken flags stand out like boards," remembered John Kendall, a Confederate officer from Louisiana, who was watching Sherman's troops as they emerged from the woods and began crossing the field that bristled in the stubble of young cornstalks. As soon as the bluecoats appeared within the sights of the Rebel artillerymen, the air was filled with flaming projectiles that either exploded over their heads or plowed up the dry ground around them. Although the Yankee batteries answered with their own guns and disabled a number of Beall's guns, the Rebel cannoneers were clearly taking a much heavier toll on the unprotected blue columns. Kendall recalled how Captain George Abbay, commanding a battery of the First Mississippi Artillery, encouraged his gunners while blowing billows of smoke from his squatty little pipe. "Now boys," he yelled from under a badly crushed gray cap, "I want you to stick to the pieces and give the Yankees hell." "The order was obeyed with a vengeance. At the right moment the guns were run up into position and delivered their charges of canister directly into the advancing lines. At the same moment the infantry opened with volleys. It was frightful to witness the destruction of the advancing Union lines which ensued." During this attack, there was only a minimal loss among the Confederate infantrymen. However, there were some severe losses among the Rebel batteries, particularly on Commissary Hill, where guns had been placed to guard the approaches to the grist mill. Against that point, there was a concentrated fire from two Union batteries equipped with heavy Parrott guns that succeeded in wrecking some of the lighter Rebel batteries as well as killing and wounding a number of the cannoneers. Indeed, the life of an artilleryman was far from a charmed one, but rather one that was constantly fraught with danger and death.[15]

A typical experience of an artilleryman was taking place this same day, as a detachment of Battery K of the First Alabama Heavy Artillery went through the complex routine of firing shot and shell into the advancing lines of Union infantry. The Alabamans were manning a twenty-four-pound brass rifle located near the Jackson Road. That gun, like many of the heavy ones at Port Hudson, had been moved to its position from the river batteries when the siege began, and replaced with a Quaker gun. The brass gun supposedly remained there on the Jackson Road until the surrender. Before the siege was over, it suffered multiple direct hits by enemy artillery, and was dismounted from its carriage on several occasions. But during the attack of May 27, the gun itself escaped damage, but nearly all the cannoneers serving it, including the commander, Lieutenant Frank, were either killed or wounded. Daniel P. Smith, a member of Battery K, described the afternoon's carnage, as his fellow soldiers, one after another, fell beside their gun while fighting. "While ramming a charge home, Private Henry Smith was mortally wounded by a sharp-shooter; Corporal Fergerson promptly stepped to his place, and was instantly [and] fatally shot. In the meantime, Private Hayes had been stricken down. Private Sears was busy attending the wounded and Lieutenant Frank and Sergeant Ellis fired the gun themselves several rounds, the former pointing and the latter loading. While doing this Lieutenant Frank fell, pierced by a minie ball." Later that night Lieutenant Frank and Corporal Fergerson died of their wounds. The rammer, Henry Smith, lingered until July 10, when he, too, died. Hayes, whose wound was not serious, recovered.[16]

As Sherman and his troops drew within two hundred yards of the enemy breastworks, long rolls of musket fire thundered from the Rebel lines, sending volleys of grapeshot buzzing, like angry bees, into the blue lines. At the same time, Confederate cannoneers loaded their guns with double charges of canister, unleashing the deadly metal missiles into the faces of the oncoming Union soldiers. Unable to stand the withering fire, the black pioneers threw down their poles and hugged the ground for cover. Seeing it was futile to continue, the "Forlorn Hope" followed their lead, and began casting away the planks and boards they carried. Dashing off in every direction, they dove or scrambled behind whatever cover they could find. General Sherman, close to the front, was one of the first to fall as shell fragments struck and killed his horse along with several of his staff. Springing to his feet, he tried to continue on foot, but another shell slammed into his leg, shattering it below the knee. "O, my God, my Country," he cried, while some of the New Hampshire troops dragged him safely out of the line of fire. With Sherman wounded and removed from the battle, command should have devolved to General Neal Dow, a fifty-nine-year-old, smug and self-righteous prohibitionist from Maine. But before he could assume that role, he, too, was shot, first in the arm and then the leg, and carried away to the rear. Franklin Nickerson would have been the heir to the command following Dow's departure, but was never informed of it. Consequently, there was not a commander on the field to control the direction of the battle. This, of course, resulted in bedlam, and men began fighting in whatever fashion they thought was best. Most of them instinctively hid behind fallen

Chapter Five. A Miserable Loss 73

trees, stumps and logs, and fired blindly at the Rebel parapet. Casualties continued to mount throughout the afternoon, especially in one of Nickerson's regiments of New Yorkers, dressed in their colorful Zouave uniforms of baggy red trousers and caps. A Confederate officer observed: "The gay colors of their uniforms contrasted brilliantly with the green and somber shades of the trees and field, making a fine mark for our fire." Although several disconcerted charges were made, the attackers were mowed down and driven back with heavy losses, including the death of two regimental commanders, Colonels David Cowles and Abel Smith. Soon, the constant flaming of the artillery fire became so furious that it ignited the trees and brush around Slaughter's Field, leaving many of the wounded Yankees helpless and in jeopardy of being burned alive. Finally, following a second failed charge by Nickerson's brigade, Sherman's attack began to break apart, and men fled in panic for the rear, or cowered in terror under the cover of a nearby ravine.[17]

Still seething over his confrontation with Sherman, Banks was apparently not paying attention when he failed to hear the rumble of that general's guns, and was thus late in ordering General Christopher Augur to send his troops into the fray. Augur, another West Pointer, who possessed an outrageous set of wiry mutton-chop whiskers, was Banks's second in command, but felt obligated to wait for Banks to give a direct order to attack, which he received too late to achieve a coordinated attack with Sherman. To his credit, he had his division ready to move all morning, but unlike the chivalrous Sherman, he had no intention of personally leading them. "Now boys," Augur instructed his men, who were mostly from Maine, Massachusetts and New York, "charge, and reserve your fire till you get into the fort; give them cold steel, and as you charge, cheer! Give them New England." Private Henry Johns of the Forty-ninth Massachusetts remembered listening to the words of encouragement from an excited Lieutenant Colonel James O'Brien, commanding the two hundred volunteers of Augur's division that composed the "Forlorn Hope," as they started their advance: "Come on boys; we'll wash in the Mississippi to-night." Leaving the cover of the timber, Edward Chapin's First Brigade Augur's division deployed in line of battle, and followed O'Brien's troops, both groups crossing an open field from which they could see the Rebel breastworks in the distance. Albert Plummer, a trooper in the Forty-eighth Massachusetts remembered the moments before his regiment began their advance, and the "zip of the rebel bullets was getting unpleasantly frequent. General Augur, who stood very near, seeing the men dodge their heads at the disagreeable sound said, 'No use boys to dodge them after you hear them,' a fact we soon learned by experience." Private Johns's account was typical of others engaged in this charge: "Full two-thirds of a mile distant we saw the parapet lined with rebels, and great volumes and little jets of smoke, as muskets and cannon bade us defiance." Soon Johns and his comrades began to encounter the obstructions of trees chopped down by the Rebels, which slowed their progress. "It was impossible to keep in line," remembered Johns. "As best we could we pressed on; shells shrieked past or busted in our midst, tearing ground and human bodies alike; grape and canister mowed down the branches, tore the leaves, or lodged in trees and living men. Solid shot sinking into the stumps with a thumping sound or thinning our ranks, minie balls *zipping* past us or *into* us, made our progress slow."[18]

Up ahead, the two hundred men making up the "Forlorn Hope" were doing their best to stay in advance of Augur's men but, like their counterparts in Sherman's division, they simply could not keep pace under the strain of the heavy weight they carried while at the same time withstanding the blazing artillery from the Rebel lines. Henry Johns thought "they looked more like loaded mules than men, and watched them as they struggled to keep up. I could see one after another drop, and round me voices moaned out, 'O, God! O, God!' And bleeding men dragged themselves to the safe side of the felled trees." Exhausted, they began dropping their loads, lying behind the fallen trees, and leaving the infantrymen to devise their own way to bridge the ditch. Elsewhere, scores of men were tumbling to the ground, including the highly conspicuous brigade commander, Edward Chapin, a flamboyant New Yorker, who was wearing a white panama hat with his dress coat when he suddenly fell with a bullet crashing through his nose and into his brain. "My God! They have killed me," he cried while throwing his hands in the air. By the

Union General Christopher Augur. Library of Congress.

time the remnants of the brigade approached the proximity of the Rebel breastworks, the firing was so heavy that the survivors were hugging the ground for cover. O'Brien, who claimed they would "wash in the Mississippi tonight," was among them. After being pinned down for an hour, he jumped to his feet, waved his sword, and yelled, "Charge boys! Charge." He was immediately killed, along with the few men who were bold enough to follow him. By now, Banks, in desperation, was considering sending in Augur's reserve brigade, but before he could do so, he received word that Sherman's attack had also failed. His adjutant, Richard Irwin, recalled the moment when they heard the disappointing news: "At last it was clear to the most persistent that the day was miserably lost." It was also clear, at least to the participants of the charge, that uncoordinated, piecemeal attacks against a strongly fortified position would inevitably end in failure. Indeed, and the soldiers in Augur's division understood the price they had paid as they came streaming back from the assault: "As we came back from the front," wrote a Massachusetts infantryman, "we had our first sight of the dreadful effects of a battle and burial of the dead in one line, about twenty dead bodies lying at the side of the road, and the long trench all ready to receive them. Poor fellows, with no coffin and no shroud but the blue uniform in which they had shed their blood for the flag they loved."[19]

Chapter Six

"Death Was Always with Us"

All night long the stretcher bearers picked their way through the woods and fields, following the light of bobbing lanterns, and removing the Union wounded to the field hospitals in the rear. It did not take long before these crude hospitals were overflowing. With no shelter to put the wounded, orderlies were compelled to lie the suffering men under the trees. Because the surgeons in the field hospitals were unable to cope with the growing numbers of casualties, many of them had their wounds quickly bandaged and then carried away to hospital ships out on the river. James Hosmer, who was serving as a nurse aboard the *Iberville* recalled that night in his diary:

> *Early after dark, word comes from the front of the repulse and terrible loss of the storming party; and the surgeons are warned of the approach of a large number of wounded. We hear of the fall of generals and colonels, and rank and file without number; and close upon the heels of the intelligence follow the ambulances, loaded as never before with hastily dressed wounded from the field hospitals in front.... As I enter the cabin door [of the saloon on the hospital ship], the long, handsome saloon from end to end is filled with the victims of the battle just fought. From the rich, bronze chandeliers, light falls upon a ghastly sight,—all the ghastlier from contrast with the elegance about. I can hardly step among the prostrate and gory company. And so they lie all through the long perspective, the great mirror at the farther end repeating it all anew; the stains upon their wrappings, about heads and limbs and bodies, red as the figures of the rich carpet upon which they lie.*

Only the critical that had a chance of being saved received immediate attention, and a Massachusetts soldier remembered the grisly sights of surgeons operating on the wounded in one of the field hospitals. "Seeing the doctors with sleeves rolled up, splashed with blood, here a pile of booted legs, there a pile of arms, was more trying than the horrors of the battlefield." Also enduring a fitful and sleepless night were those who were not seriously wounded, waiting for treatment, and listening to the cries of the dying. "The whole night was rendered dismal to the last degree by the groans of their suffering comrades mingled everywhere," remembered

Chapter Six. "Death Was Always with Us" 77

Richard Irwin, "the wounded with the well, the dying with the dead." Many of the men assisting the surgeons witnessed sights which before that night would have been unbearable, as Corporal Hosmer explained: "I held the leg of a young adjutant while Dr. L____ cut a bullet out of the bones of the knee, in which it had become deeply embedded. It was a painful and critical operation. A few days before, I should have fainted at the sight; but, in such scenes, the sensibilities become blunted."[1]

That same night the division commanders reported to Banks's headquarters and quantified their losses in the twelve-hour fight. It was there that the severity of their defeat became painfully apparent. The butcher's bill came to 1,995 men. Of that number, 293 had been killed, including at least 15 of the officers. The wounded and missing numbered 1,702, and 92 of those were officers. As an added woe, it should be assumed that among the missing (157) most of those were either dead or wounded. After hearing the casualty count, it didn't take long before the commanders began their finger-pointing, blaming others and making excuses. Chief among those was Banks himself, who besides blaming Sherman for not bringing his men on the field in time also claimed the Rebel works to be "impregnable," and went so far as to exaggerate that point to Farragut: "It was the strongest position there is in the United States." To Halleck he complained, "The force placed at my disposal is inadequate to the duty imposed on me." A more plausible justification for the loss came from Augur, who pointed out, "It is far easier to talk of taking a strongly-fortified place than to do it." But perhaps the most straightforward and honest reason for their failure to take the fort came from a lowly artillery officer, who in the aftermath of the battle offered a simple yet fair explanation to his fellow officers: "Well, gentlemen, my opinion is that we would have succeeded better if it had not been for a damned rebellious spirit inside that fort."[2]

The next morning, at daylight, Banks sent Gardner a note requesting a "suspension of hostilities" to remove the Union dead and wounded still on the battlefield. The Rebel general, "as a matter of humanity," of course consented, provided that during the process of retrieving these men, Banks would agree not to move his skirmishers any closer to the Southerners' breastworks than eight hundred yards. Gardner also wanted the Federal fleet to move out of shelling range. Banks would not agree, and a series of messages ensued between the two generals until they finally agreed to an armistice that would last until seven o'clock that evening. During the hours of truce, mass graves in the form of long trenches were opened by the Union burial parties. Into these ditches, scores of bodies were thrown, eulogized only by the shovelfuls of dirt thrown upon them. For the morose Union soldiers, the confidence they had felt prior to the attack was now gone. Gone, too, was their faith in Banks. Adjutant Irwin agreed, acknowledging, "Their reliance on the department commander never quite returned." But across the way, the Confederate soldiers—despite their desperate situation, inferior weapons, scarcity of food, and ragged clothing—were, for the most part, in good spirits. Their losses for the day came to about three hundred in all categories, only a small fraction of what the Union lost. What's more, they felt a sense of satisfying pride because only through their gritty determination they had turned back an enemy force much larger than their own and achieved a great victory. Thus, while the Yankee burial parties worked through the day, gaunt, raw-boned Southerners proudly rose from their breastworks and stared out over the wooded fields and marshlands with a resigned gratification on the work they had done. Before long, while the white flags were still flying, some of the Rebels actually climbed from their holes and ventured beyond their fortifications to mingle with the bluecoats, hoping to trade some tobacco for coffee. However, shortly after the truce ended, about eight o'clock, the bluecoats made another vicious surprise attack against Steedman's line which, like those of the day before, was driven back.[3]

The disappointing and bloody outcome of May 27 forced Banks to come to grips with the proposition of having to conduct a siege, something he had not wanted to do. It was an ancient method of warfare that required the enemy to be surrounded. Without the means to be reinforced or resupplied, such a slow-grinding operation would, over time, compel them to surrender. For Banks, however, time was his problem. Sieges could last for months, requiring patience, and Banks could not afford to be a patient man. Grant, he understood, was now immersed in one at Vicksburg, and Banks would prefer to avoid conducting the same kind of warfare at Port Hudson. However, if he could not take the place by storming it, he was faced with no other choice but to resort to a siege. Actually, if he were honest with himself, he would admit that he was already engaged in one because the essential ingredients for conducting such a military tactic were all now in place. Port Hudson was and had been since May 23 completely encircled, and foreclosed from any hope of receiving help or provisions. Besides, there were, Banks believed, some diabolical methods he could employ to hurry this siege to a victorious conclusion. In the meantime, as this grinding style of warfare continued to weaken the Rebel's resolve, he would begin planning a second and better coordinated assault.

Settling into the siege, Banks relocated his headquarters to the Young Plantation, situated "in a grove of stately oaks" behind the center of the Union lines. Although Banks could have commandeered the entire home for his own private living quarters, he continued to allow the Young family to reside there, except, that is, for one room where his telegraph operator worked. Instead, Banks and his staff were housed on the grounds in "fine

Chapter Six. "Death Was Always with Us" 79

wall tents ... elegantly pitched in the form of a parallelogram, the Major General's tent being at the end nearest to the house," wrote Colonel Edward Bacon of the Sixth Michigan Volunteers. Bacon noticed, however, that even though the general declined the comfort of the big house, choosing to live in a tent like a common soldier, he did not hesitate to enjoy the services and amenities provided by the Youngs' slaves. "I see some fine looking quadroon and mulatto girls are busy in cooking, at the house, the various dishes of food which genteel Negro waiters are carrying to a table which they have covered with a fine linen table-cloth," observed Bacon. As he continued to watch what was obviously going to be a fine dinner for Banks and his staff, he also viewed "two well-dressed, middle-aged slaves, who look as if they had always held positions of trust in great families, carry past me, on silver trays, decanters of liquors and finely-cut glasses."[4]

From his new and well-nurtured headquarters, Banks wasted no time sending out orders in preparation for a siege. First, he ordered the siege train brought up to Port Hudson. It consisted of forty pieces of heavy artillery, such as Dahlgren guns and sea-coast howitzers mounted on carriages. These would be added to his already powerful arsenal of sixty pieces of artillery, giving him some one hundred big guns to pound the Rebel position. And, added to that, he still had the support of the powerful naval guns of Farragut's fleet that continued to throw shells into Port Hudson, day and night. Knowing he would need more entrenching tools to dig rifle pits and saps (zigzag trenches to approach the enemy lines), he ordered an abundance of shovels, wheelbarrows, picks and axes, along with cotton bales to afford the men protection from which they could work behind. Banks also called for the eight regiments of troops he had left in the Atchafalaya area after the Teche Campaign as well as all the Negro troops stationed in New Orleans to report to Port Hudson. From Baton Rouge, he sent for all the available able-bodied Negroes to report for work at Port Hudson, digging the breastworks, ditches and rifle pits. With the addition of men and weapons, and the expectation that the siege might take time, Banks did not neglect to order extra ammunition and provisions.[5]

With the arrival of new troops coupled with the loss of so many officers on May 27, changes in commands and assignments of units to new positions had become necessary. Although the disposition of Banks's forces remained nearly the same, with Weitzel on the extreme right, followed by Grover, Paine and Augur, William Dwight had been given the wounded Sherman's old division on the extreme left. Apparently, Banks had a higher opinion of Dwight than the rest of the Nineteenth Corps. Grover was now in command of the entire right wing while Augur had the left wing, which was composed of both his division and Dwight's. On the brigade level, Colonel Charles Paine was appointed to command the brigade of the flamboyant Edward Chapin, who had been killed in action. Colonel Thomas Clark, a man of questionable character, somehow managed to inherit the command of Neal Dow, who was recovering from the wound he received in Augur's attack of the twenty-seventh. Clark, however, had only feigned his wound, during that same attack. According to an officer in Clark's regiment, there was a rumor that the colonel had been killed. "Is Colonel Clark really killed," he asked a soldier at the hospital. "Not exactly killed," came the reply. "He was knocked down by the wind of a cannon ball in the beginning of the fight." The officer then persisted: "Then he is not wounded severely?" "No," replied the soldier, "he was all right." Yet the cowardly Clark was cited for valor and awarded command of Dow's brigade in Dwight's division. Although the sanctimonious Dow, who was now recovering from his wounds at a nearby plantation, was clearly unpopular with his troops, Clark had always and would continue to prove himself to be just as detestable, and probably more so than his disliked predecessor, Dow.[6]

Across the way, behind the Confederate lines, Gardner was not idle. He continued strengthening his defenses in preparation for another attack. In addition to constructing new works to fight behind, they labored, digging and filling sandbags to shore up their existing breastworks. Because of the incessant bombardment from the Union artillery, Rebel soldiers, like gophers, honeycombed the ground with a network of burrows and caves, and then roofed them with logs, tin and planks to create what they called "bombproofs" or "gopher holes." Such filthy diggings were their only refuges from the daily pounding of the Yankee guns and the hot Louisiana sun. Rarely did the Confederate artillery respond, and for good reasons. They only had about fifty cannon, and many of those were small, obsolete pieces that had been damaged or disabled by the Union artillery barrages. Occasionally, when the Rebel cannoneers did answer with fire, they risked giving away their position and thus invited a real possibility of being destroyed by enemy projectiles. But Gardner's primary reason for ordering the artillery to withhold their fire was the lack of ammunition, which had to be conserved for another attack. One exception, however, was made by the Confederate chief of artillery, Colonel Marshall Smith. He ordered a huge Columbiad mounted on a railroad car. This allowed the Rebels to move the gun up and down the tracks of the Clinton Railroad so as to prevent the Union artillery from pinpointing its position and destroying it. Yankee soldiers soon began detesting the big gun the Rebels had named "The Lady Davis," but which they preferred to call "The Demoralizer." After it was fired by the heavy artillerymen of De Gournay's command, the projectile began catapulting through the air, making an eerie, shrieking sound before plunging down on them. It was a noise they had come to hate and fear. William Tiemann, a captain in a New York Regiment, described it as "an awful unearthly shriek," and recounted how he and his fellow soldiers underwent the cannonades: "Shot, shell and bars were constantly whizzing and shrieking through the air. The firing was usually most severe at night and, lying on our backs, we would watch the bombs from our mortars as they flew through the air like revolving stars, or the shells from the fort as they shot towards our lines, the streaks of light from the fuses of the latter indicating when they were coming in our direction.... They made a horrible sound." The raucous scream of the shells may have been due to the unorthodox ammunition that the Rebels rammed down the muzzle of the big gun, which were usually bars of railroad iron or sometimes just a homemade, hodgepodge of scrap metal and iron bound together in cloth bags.[7]

The routine of the siege was a miserable life for soldiers on both sides.

Columbiad cannon of DeGournay's Louisiana Heavy Artillery, known to the Southerners as "Lady Davis," but as the "Old Demoralizer" to the Union soldiers. Port Hudson State Historic Site Photograph Collection.

Living in trenches and holes, men were covered in filth and grime with no way to wash themselves or their ragged uniforms except from the soaking rain of the almost daily thunderstorms. "We have quit living like men and are living like hogs," an Alabama soldier told his diary on May 28. Food, especially for the hungry Confederates, was a constant problem, and the only water to drink was the dirty swamp water, which caused as much death as the gunfire. Swarms of bloodthirsty mosquitoes and a variety of other insects brought on malaria and other sickness, and drove the soldiers wild. Howard Wright of the Twentieth Louisiana Regiment grumbled that the "continued exposure to the sun, rain and night dews brought on much sickness. Our stock of medicines proved to be even shorter than our stock of provisions." Added to all this was the ever-present stench of half-buried bodies emanating in front of the Rebel's breastworks. In their free time, bored men would break the monotony by playing checkers or dealing greasy cards. Others wrote letters or reread old ones. "Time hangs heavy," wrote William Root of the Seventy-fifth New York Volunteers, "nothing to do but lay around and hear the continual crack of rifles and the occasional louder report of cannon." The Louisiana heat made sleeping almost impossible. John Kendall, a Rebel officer, remembered: "The months of May and June in Port Hudson were the hottest days that I ever experienced. Exhausted by long hours on duty, the men would frequently fall asleep at their posts, and after the fierce rays of the sun had beat down on them for an hour or so they would wake up delirious. Some fell asleep in the sun and never awoke again."[8]

One affliction that tormented the men of both armies was lice. There were body lice, which roamed over every inch of their physique, and crab lice, not so common, confining themselves to the hair. Both species of the irritating vermin made no distinction as to what color uniform a man wore, or what rank he happened to be. Everyone was fair game for the pests. Without a doubt, anyone who saw service in the filthy ditches around Port Hudson was crawling with them. When soldiers first became aware that their clothes and bodies had been invaded by lice, they were understandably ashamed to admit that they harbored such unhygienic creatures on their persons. This was especially true of the more genteel Union soldiers from New England. Soon, however, they began accepting that shameful condition as an inevitable curse, and even amused themselves with stories about the ubiquitous parasites. "We had an enemy, a *gray-back* too [likening the lice to the gray-clad Rebels] within the pits," wrote a Union officer from New York. The crawling enemy was "more persistent and difficult to contend with than his namesake in the fort, the small insect which did much to make life almost unbearable, and a constant *skirmish* was necessary to keep us even partly free from these pests, the sand in the pits being almost alive with them."[9]

Chapter Six. "Death Was Always with Us"   83

All of these troubles preyed on the minds of the soldiers, but nothing was as traumatic as the constant cloud of death that hovered over them day and night. As always, in any siege, death could find them in a number of ways, but none was as treacherous as the sniper's bullet. At Port Hudson, the ever-watchful snipers did more than their fair share of killing. Men dared not move outside their breastworks, or even stand up straight inside their trenches for fear of a ball striking them dead. John DeForest, a captain in a Connecticut Regiment explained to his wife in a letter that "danger is perpetually present," and "the nerves never have a chance to recuperate." "Every morning," he wrote her, "I was awakened by the popping of rifles and the whistling of balls; hardly a day passed that I did not hear the loud exclamations of the wounded, or see corpses borne to the rear." In his recollections, a Confederate officer, across the way, agreed: "There was no safety anywhere else, except close up behind the breastworks ... sharpshooters constantly fired at any moving thing which appeared above the works.... At times it was literally impossible to lift a hand above the shelters without getting a ball through it." And a Louisiana soldier concurred: "With their numerous line of skirmishers pushed up close to our position, the exchange of shot became dangerous work. Anywhere along our fortifications it was almost certain death to look over at the foe. A felt hat, raised slowly on a stick so as to feign the appearance of one of our men raising to fire, would be speedily perforated with balls." Men soon learned that wearing the wrong clothing could get them killed. A white shirt or a wide brimmed hat might draw the fire of a sharpshooter. "Death was always with us," insisted another Louisiana man, "sometimes in the most singular forms. I remember that one of our men was killed while playing checkers." No one knew it until the man took too long to make his next move and his impatient partner suddenly realized he was dead, killed by a sniper's rifle ball.[10]

George Hepworth, a studious Massachusetts officer whose memoirs were published during the war in 1864, took copious notes on the everyday activities of the siege, and was intrigued with the techniques of the snipers. He would travel along the lines and note the little events "which history will think too trivial to mention." After spending some time with the New York Zouaves, he described the tactics of the snipers in their regiment. "Their sharpshooters went out every night, carrying twenty-four hours' rations; and hiding behind some providential hillock, would watch eagerly till some unfortunate head was lifted above the parapet, when *whiz* would go a bullet. Fortunate was the aforementioned head, if it could open its eyes to the world again." The closer the sniper could get to the enemy lines, the more deadly he became. Most of them would try and crawl within about eighty yards of the parapets. "All day" noted Hepworth, "the constant crack of the rifle announced that someone unfortunate had put himself in a dangerous

Typical Confederate entrenchments, known as "rat holes" or "gopher holes." Port Hudson State Historic Site Photograph Collection.

place." As to the enemy snipers, he admitted, "The rebels, too, were good shots [and] there was one man who was a source of great annoyance to us: and many a poor fellow will testify to his existence by showing a very peculiar and ugly wound." According to Hepworth, that Rebel was armed with a "double-barreled shot-gun of English make, with a bore large enough to admit a ball weighing an ounce and a half." Such a load of ammunition would have been twice the size of that used in a standard Enfield rifle. The Rebel gunner was especially dangerous to the Union snipers. Covering himself with the long moss that grew plentiful around Port Hudson, he would climb some forty feet up the big cypress trees where "he could get a fine view of many of the sharpshooters." From his concealed position, he could easily kill the Yankee sharpshooters as well as those troops in the advanced batteries. He could even hit a target three-quarters of a mile away. But because he used a shotgun instead of a rifle, he probably did not kill anyone at that distance. However, as Hepworth was quick to point out, "he made some very disagreeable wounds."[11]

Throughout the siege of Port Hudson, Confederate Colonel John Logan and his twelve hundred horsemen continued to torment the rear of Banks's army. The thirty-year-old Logan, a Mississippi druggist before the war, was operating out of the nearby town of Clinton, and did his best to relieve the pressure on Gardner and his besieged troops. Like a nest of gnawing rats, Logan's men would suddenly appear out of nowhere, behind the Union lines, launch hit-and-run attacks on their troops, wagon trains, and supply depots, then quickly disappear back into the swamps. Irish-born Colonel Frank Powers, who had begun the war as a captain with a Texas outfit called the "Jefferson" dragoons, and Major Thomas Stockdale, two other Rebel cavalry commanders, were also a constant source of aggravation for Banks, surprising Union troops guarding the supply depots, taking them prisoner, and then making off with wagons loaded with supplies, guns and ammunition. But with the siege now underway, Banks was now able to turn his attention to ridding himself and his army, once and for all, of the bedeviling Rebel cavalry that had been hounding his lines. For this, he was depending on Colonel Benjamin H. Grierson, who was given command of all the Union cavalry at Port Hudson. Grierson, during the war years, had become a skilled cavalry leader, in spite of the fact that not only did he lack any military education, but his pre-war background as an Illinois music teacher and bandmaster was hardly suitable for such a position. Nevertheless, before joining Banks's command, Grierson had proven he had a natural aptitude as a cavalry commander as evidenced by his daring six-hundred-mile raid through the interior of Mississippi, creating chaos and destroying railroads, bridges and Confederate warehouses. Up until the time Grierson made his famous raid, the prevalent opinion among Union soldiers was that their cavalry was sluggish and inferior to the Rebel horsemen. According to one Union officer, "The rebels have done more to win respect for themselves by their cavalry raids than by all their infantry movements." Men like Jeb Stuart and Bedford Forrest were brilliant, quick and daring, even to recklessness. Indeed, it was assumed that the Southerners were inherently superior horsemen because of their agrarian and frontier backgrounds. Ralph Waldo Emerson, the sage American essayist and student of life, once observed that the young Southerner "has conversed so much with rifles, horses and dogs that he has become himself a rifle, a horse, and a dog." Yet by 1863 the Union cavalrymen had become quite adept at fighting from the saddle, as confirmed by men such as Grierson. An admirer of this new breed of Union cavalrymen exclaimed: "Our boys will ride at break-neck speed, feet out of the stirrups, swinging their swords in great and little circles, over ditches and through the woods, and into the midst of the enemy; and that is as good riding as you need for cavalry service. Our cavalry horses too, are vastly superior to those of the enemy generally. Northern horses will weigh, on an average, nine hundred pounds; while those of the Southerners, generally a cross between a Creole pony and what is called an American horse, will not average more than eight hundred pounds. In a charge that hundred pounds is worth everything."[12]

On the morning of June 3, before Grierson had finished his breakfast, a young Negro boy appeared, telling him that Logan and his cavalry were on the Clinton Road moving towards Port Hudson. Grierson immediately ordered his cavalry, about thirteen hundred strong, to set out for Clinton. But before they could reach the town Thomas Stockdale and his battalion of 250 mounted Mississippi infantry—who the young boy had apparently mistaken for Logan's entire brigade—became aware of the approaching Union cavalry. Stockdale then surprised the Yankee column with an ambush before it could reach Clinton, and, at the same time, he sent a courier there to warn Logan of the approach of the bluecoat horsemen. The messenger found Logan and Frank Powers engrossed in a poker game, but within a matter of minutes after hearing the warning they had abandoned the table and had their men saddled and riding hard to the aid of Stockdale. At the same time, Stockdale and the outnumbered Mississippians were being pushed back to Pretty Creek, but continued fighting off Grierson's cavalry long enough for Logan and the rest of his command to arrive. As the gray riders approached, Logan directed Colonel Powers to detour around the rear of Grierson's line and strike his left flank while he attacked the Union

General Benjamin H. Grierson commanded the Union Cavalry at Port Hudson. Library of Congress.

Chapter Six. "Death Was Always with Us"

front. The plan worked, throwing the bluecoats into utter chaos and forcing a retreat. Leaving his dead and wounded behind, Grierson was finally able to reform his stampeded column, and then notified Banks that he needed reinforcements to break the stubborn Rebel cavalry.[13]

Grierson waited several days for Banks to respond to his request. As soon as he got word of Grierson's defeat, Banks was more determined than ever to supply his cavalry with whatever muscle it needed to finally drive the troublesome Confederate cavalry out of Clinton and away from the rear of his army. On the morning of June 5, help for Grierson's cavalry arrived in the person of General Halbert Paine, the same former abolitionist lawyer who had supported Weitzel's attack on May 27. The Ohioan joined Grierson with 4,000 infantry and a formidable battery of artillery. Together they moved towards Clinton. The next day, Rebel scouts observed the movement and reported that long blue columns were quickly approaching the town. John Logan, who had asked his superior, General Joseph Johnston, repeatedly for reinforcements to relieve Port Hudson, knew that his position would soon be untenable, and had advised Johnston: "I am at this place [Clinton] with a small command of cavalry and mounted infantry, 1,200 men, doing all I can to aid General Gardner by dashing upon the enemy's lines, destroying his wagon trains & drawing the enemy's troops from Port Hudson." After learning that Grierson was approaching Clinton with infantry reinforcements, he wrote again: "I have met his cavalry and whipped it, but, of course, will have to retire before a heavy column of infantry and artillery." In their haste to leave, Logan and his men were compelled to leave behind some valuable property, all of which they feared would be doomed for loss. Those fears were realized as soon as Grierson arrived, and found the Rebels gone. His first order of destruction was the railroad and telegraph connecting Port Hudson and Clinton, which he immediately had cut and burned. After that was accomplished, Union soldiers and cavalrymen went about the business of wrecking, ruining or confiscating nearly everything of value in the town of Clinton, including "the railroad depot, machine shops, a locomotive, woolen and cartridge manufactories and a large quantity of ammunition." Thus, his mission was partially successful. Although Grierson and Paine had failed to defeat or bag Logan's cavalry, they had succeeded in depriving the Rebels of some important war supplies and, for the time being at least, in driving them north, out of Clinton and away from Port Hudson.[14]

On June 10, the Federals opened a furious bombardment against Port Hudson. From the early morning until well after sundown, the land batteries and the gunboats out on the river continued to roar. The cannonade, Banks hoped, would cause the Southerners to respond with their own artillery, enabling the Union gunners to pinpoint the location of their batteries and destroy them. But Gardner did not have the ammunition to trade cannon shots with the Federals. His shells were limited and would have to be saved for the next full assault, which he believed to be imminent. When the Rebel guns remained silent, Banks decided to force the issue and make them unmask their batteries by launching a reconnaissance expedition early the next morning .In the words of Richard Irwin, Banks's adjutant, there were several purposes in making this sortie, including "harassing the enemy, of inducing him to bring forward and expose his artillery, acquiring a knowledge before the enemy's front, and of favoring the operations of pioneers who may be sent forward to remove obstructions if necessary."[15]

On the morning of June 11, well before daylight, regiments from two Union brigades stepped off into the darkness and into what would prove to be an expedition of horror. In the predawn blackness, men tried to negotiate their way through the brambles and thickets. Following the figure in front of them, they fell or slipped down the steep banks of the ravines and sloughs, stumbling and clawing their way forward. No one knew exactly where they were, where they were going, or what they were expected to do except to attack the enemy's breastworks. It wasn't long before the Confederate defenders became aware of their presence and opened fire. The darkness was then lit up with flashing gunfire from the Rebel lines and continued for about an hour. It only subsided about three o'clock in the morning when a violent thunderstorm struck. As soon as the storm slackened, the firing resumed, and the Union troops, drenched from the torrents of lashing rain, found themselves struggling and floundering to keep their feet in the slick black mud. Two regiments of Maine men, the twelfth and twenty-second in Godfrey Weitzel's brigade, managed to slip through a gorge and draw close to the Confederate lines. The gorge then deepened into a ravine that was beneath a high bluff, upon which the Rebels had erected a crude slaughter pen for cattle. The discarded remains from the butchered cows had been thrown down into the ravine. Trudging into this mess, the Maine bluecoats suddenly found themselves, wading not only in the mud, but through the rotting and decomposing entrails of the Rebel cattle. Overwhelmed by the decay, they panicked and began scrambling away in every direction, trying to free themselves from the putrid refuse and mire. Some, losing all sense of direction, fled and wandered aimlessly into the Confederate lines, where they were quickly captured. The next day, Weitzel, in his report of the action, admitted defeat and added that when they were ordered to fall back there were "two companies in the ravine, and [I] cannot ascertain their whereabouts as yet." Although there was never an accurate report of the number of casualties incurred, it was estimated to be well over two hundred men. Those who survived the expedition agreed it was not only poorly planned, but suicidal. Lieutenant William Root was a little more euphemistic in his assessment: "It was a strange movement and I cannot understand its object nor learn of any beneficial result."[16]

That movement was another mistake made by the impatient Banks, provoked by his fear that the siege would take too long. In the days that followed, Banks was made aware of several matters which were convincing him that there was trouble in the Rebel ranks, and persuading him that it was time for another attack on Port Hudson. Night after night, hungry, barefoot Rebels continued slipping out of their own breastworks, crossing the Union lines, and giving themselves up. The deserters told the Union officers that they were on half rations because of a dwindling food supply, and morale was low. They also told them that as a result of the desertions and battle casualties the Rebel troop strength had been reduced to about 4,000 men, and that there were shortages of other provisions, especially ammunition and medical supplies. What's more, Banks was faced with some of his own woes, problems which could only be solved by ordering an attack, one that would be successful in taking Port Hudson. Specifically, he hoped that taking the offensive would improve the morale of his own troops which had worsened during the monotonous siege. Many had lost faith in their commanders because of the failed attack on May 27. Moreover, the enlistments of the troops who had only volunteered for nine months was about to expire. The fierce but unsuccessful bombardment on June 10, along with the failed troop maneuver the next morning, had only added to his concerns. Banks was thus satisfied that the time was right for another full-scale second assault. This one, he believed, would be the final one, the one that would succeed in the capture of Port Hudson.[17]

Friday evening, June 12, Banks finalized his plan of attack, and late the next morning, about 11:00 a.m., he ordered every cannon and mortar in the Union arsenal as well as the gunboats out on the river to open fire on Port Hudson. The cannonade was furious, with shells exploding and kicking up dirt throughout the Confederate fortifications at a rate of one per second. So fierce was the bombardment that the gray defenders could do nothing but dive into their "caves and gopher holes," and pray for the blazing barrage to end. But it continued in an apocalyptic thunder for a terrifying hour that seemed to go on forever. Although the Confederates—who were accustomed to taking cover at the sound of a cannon—only lost a few men, they had three of their heavy cannons blown from their carriages and destroyed during the attack. The most severe of the losses that day was Colonel De Gournay's thirty-pound Parrott cannon, which was hit several times and reduced to a pile of twisted metal. However, what was more important, at least to Banks, was that he had demonstrated the awesome firepower of the Federal artillery which could be unleashed whenever he chose to order it.[18]

When the hour ended the Union's big guns grumbled to a halt, and

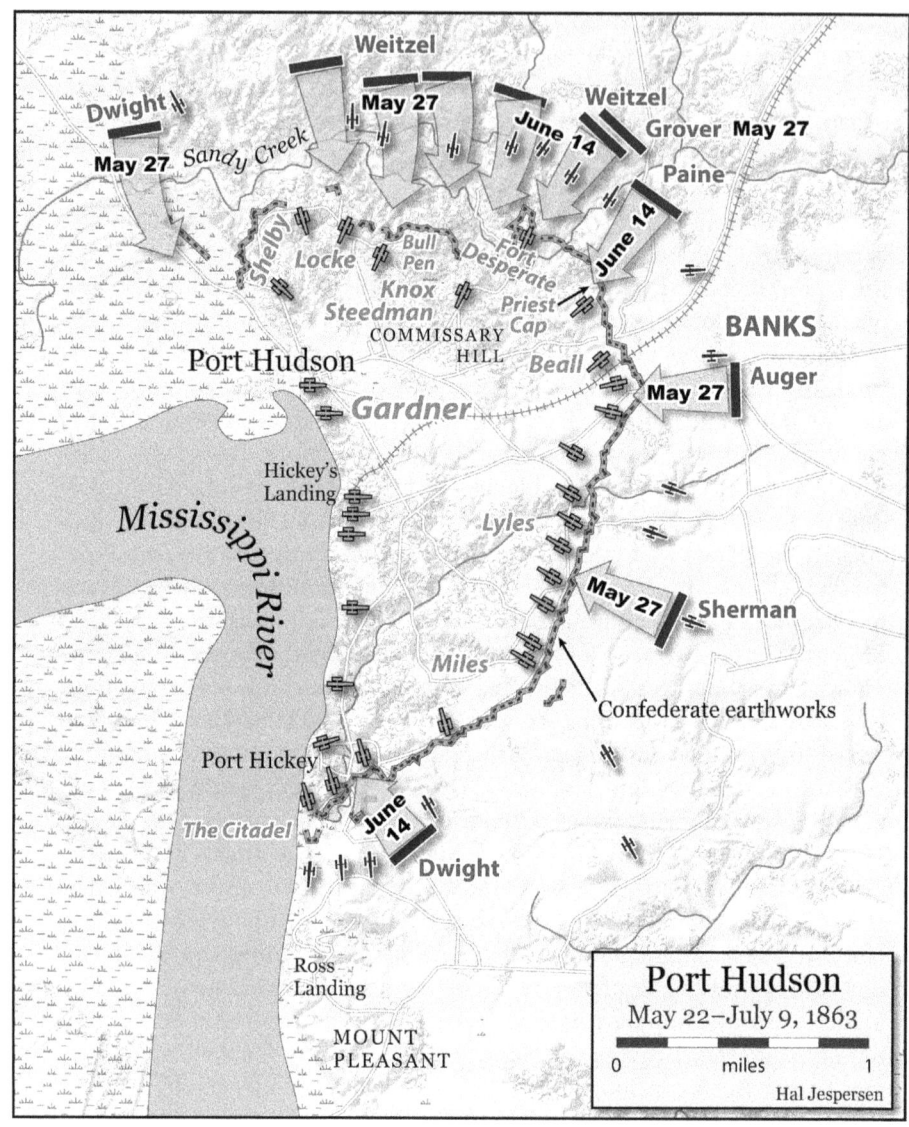

Map showing positions of Union and Confederate forces at Port Hudson on May 27 and June 14. Map by Hal Jespersen, www.cwmaps.com.

Richard Irwin recalled, "The cannonade ended as suddenly as it began, and profound silence followed close on the intolerable din." Watching the Rebel breastworks, a Union colonel realized that very few of the defenders had been killed, and remarked, "Appearances indicate that the rebels are only shelled into their holes … for along the parapet, both ways from the redoubt,

Chapter Six. "Death Was Always with Us"

up come the graybacks out of their holes, like so many prairie dogs." Right away, at one o'clock that afternoon, while the memory of the spectacular barrage was fresh on Gardner's mind, Banks sent over a courier under a flag of truce, asking for the surrender of the garrison. The message made it clear to Gardner that he knew the hardships under which his men were existing, and reminded him that he possessed artillery "seldom equaled ... which no ordinary fortress can successfully resist and an infantry force of greatly superior numbers." As a final caveat, Banks, in a subtle implication of a possible massacre if he refused to surrender, admonished Gardner that "the protection of life" might well be beyond the control of his commanders after the Union forces had overrun the garrison. Having made his case, Banks solicitously came to the point: "I desire to avoid unnecessary slaughter, and I therefore demand the immediate surrender of the garrison, subject to such conditions only as are imposed by the usages of civilized warfare."[19]

In the house that served as his headquarters, Gardner, was seated with Sergeant Crawford Jackson and some of his staff beside an open window when Banks's message was given to him. Opening it, he began reading, and his facial expression suddenly changed from a stony and solemn one to a beaming, wide grin. "Ah Gentlemen," he exclaimed, while he began laughing and tugging on his beard, "What do you think? Why Banks has notified me that to avoid unnecessary slaughter he demands the immediate surrender of my forces!" Gardner then ordered two of his staff to mount their horses and ride to the field officers, with the warning "to have their men ready ... in order to repel the enemy." Later in the afternoon, Gardner dictated his answer to Banks: "Your note of this date has just been handed to me, and in reply I have to state that my duty requires me to defend this position, and, therefore I decline to surrender." The reply was delivered about an hour before sunset, and according to Sergeant Jackson: "From that time until the next morning the mortar boats kept up an incessant bombardment."[20]

Behind the Union lines, there was much speculation about the effects of the bombardment, and the probability that it might force a surrender. Some thought that had the cannonade been extended several hours it may have caused the garrison to surrender. Others believed that no artillery barrage against prepared earthworks could ever be successful, and cited the siege of Sebastopol during the far away Crimean War as an example. Two of the Union generals, Cuvier Grover and Godfrey Weitzel, who would become heavily involved in the coming attack, had been anxiously waiting to hear how Gardner would answer Banks's demand for an immediate surrender. After what seemed a long wait, a Rebel messenger came through their lines under a flag of truce and delivered Gardner's reply. Grover, who apparently knew Gardner from the old army, was told of the contents of the message and turned to Weitzel, who was standing nearby. Grover shook his

House that served as General Franklin Gardner's headquarters during the siege of Port Hudson. Port Hudson State Historic Site Photograph Collection.

head and, according to a bystander, said, "No surrender yet," then he added, "Old Gardner was always as obstinate as a mule." Accepting their fate with a stoic resignation, Weitzel replied, "Well, we know what is to come next."[21]

Later that same evening, Banks notified the division commanders to gather at his headquarters to receive their final orders for the morning attack. Shortly before midnight, with everyone seemingly understanding their roles, Banks ended the meeting. He felt optimistic. After all, his command had been strengthened since the first attack. And, since that time the constant digging during the siege had moved his lines closer to the Rebel position, tightening the ring around the garrison down to a distance of some three miles. The plan was set and Banks believed it was a good one. The artillery near Christopher Augur's position on the Federal center was to open up at 3 a.m. on the morning of June 14. After thirty minutes of the cannonade, William Dwight would make a probing attack with two regiments of his command against a fortification known as the Citadel lying on the south end of the Confederate works where their line neared the river. When the Union cannons ceased firing, that would be the signal for Christopher Augur's division to feign an attack on the enemy's center as a diversion, and convert it to an actual attack if the opportunity should arise. The main attack, however, was to be made at this same time by Cuvier Grover, who now commanded the entire Union right wing. Since this would be the primary thrust, Banks had reinforced Grover with two New York regiments from Augur's command. Grover's troops would strike near the northeastern salient of the Rebel line at a position the soldiers called the Priest Cap, probably named because of its shape. That attack was to be made in two columns and preceded by skirmishers, then pioneers armed only with their tools, followed by the volunteers of the "Forlorn Hope" to bridge the ditch, and finally the infantrymen, who would march in "lines of battle, as far as the nature of the ground would permit." Grover had tapped Halbert E. Paine and his division to spearhead the attack against the eastern face of the Priest Cap. Godfrey Weitzel's division, on their right, would be in close support and strike the northern face of that fortification. Banks was so confident of success that his cavalry was ordered not only to picket and protect the Union rear, but to block the road leading out of Port Hudson towards Bayou Sara, the route he believed the Southerners would attempt to escape from the garrison when their lines broke.[22]

Union General Cuvier Grover. Library of Congress.

Chapter Seven

"This Day of Blood"

In the early morning hours of June 14, a Sunday, an impenetrable fog blanketed the woods and fields surrounding Port Hudson. So dense was the fog that when the planned cannonade opened at three o'clock the sounds of the big guns were muffled in the pea soup and could not be heard at a distance of one hundred yards. As Halbert Paine's men lined up in the mist-shrouded darkness, a morose spirit lingered among most of them. Corporal Hosmer recalled the officers giving final instructions: "No talking in the ranks; no flinching. Let everyone see that his canteen is full, and that he has hard bread enough for the day. That is all you will carry beside gun and equipment." They could not forget the failed assault of May 27, and their confidence in Banks and his generals was, at best, unenthusiastic. Moreover, many of them whispered in soft undertones that an attack on Sunday, the Lord's Day, was blasphemous and it would likely incur God's terrible wrath upon them with another bloody defeat. "By some ill-advised calculation, Sunday was fixed upon for the assault," complained a Connecticut captain, "Sunday assaults are seldom successful." Thirty-seven-year-old Paine, a devout man himself, agreed with his troops, wishing they had not been ordered to fight on a Sunday. Nevertheless, orders were orders, and Paine, who insisted on personally leading his troops into battle, quietly passed in front of them, regiment by regiment, giving last-minute instructions and words of encouragement.[1]

Across the way, in the Rebel lines, Gardner's men were ready for an attack. The bombardment of the day before, followed by Banks's demand for their surrender, was correctly interpreted as a harbinger of an impending assault. Any hope which Banks may have held that this would be a surprise attack had by this time vanished. What's more, despite their many hardships, desertions and hungry bellies, most of the ragged Rebels were in surprisingly good spirits and confident of victory. Even Colonel Steedman, who commanded the Confederate left wing, and worried constantly about discipline and morale, agreed: "Our men seem to be vigilant, and in as good moral condition as the mud and slop and surrounding circumstances will admit." Looking back on it, the men realized that they had little trouble holding their position against the May 27 attack, and since that time they had been working to the point of exhaustion, strengthening their fortifications to the extent that they were confident of once again turning back a Yankee attack of any proportion that might attempt to overwhelm them. Although their own supply of ammunition had been dwindling, they still had a sufficient amount. Additional ammunition and more weapons had become available in the days after the May attack when Rebels crept out of their works and scavenged the bodies of dead Yankees for cartridges and guns. In point of fact, on the morning of this June attack, many of the Confederates were awaiting the Union assault armed with two guns. Each of the weapons had a particular purpose, explained Lieutenant Daniel Smith of the First Alabama Regiment: "a musket loaded with buck and ball for use at close quarters, and a rifle for sharp shooting." The Rebel soldiers had also been cleverly efficient in picking up spent Yankee minie balls in front of their works. These served not only as lead for their Enfield rifles, but also as canister load for their artillery. After the May attack, Smith recalled gathering the plentiful leaden missiles: "[They] were so thick on the surface of the ground within our lines, that it was but the work of a few minutes to pick up enough to charge a 12-pounder gun."[2]

The Southerners' dogged morale remained strong because of their faith that they would be rescued from their entrapment. There was still the hope that Joe Johnston would soon send troops from his army in Jackson to attack Banks and lift the siege. Gardner had already sent many couriers to Johnston asking for assistance, but because the dispatches were not answered and none of the messengers ever returned it was assumed they had been killed or captured. But Gardner kept trying. Just a few days before the Sunday attack, he penned another coded message to Johnston: "I have repulsed the enemy in several attacks but am still closely invested. I am getting short of provisions and ammunition of all kinds and should be speedily reinforced." This time, however, Gardner meticulously picked the courier he believed would succeed in such a dangerous mission. Captain Robert Pruyn was the general's choice. Pruyn, according to a fellow Louisianan, was "a man of rare courage and unlimited resources." After receiving his orders, Pruyn discarded his uniform and dressed in civilian clothes, an attire that he believed would assist him in passing through the Union lines, but also one that would get him shot as a spy should he be discovered. Ignoring that risk, on the night of June 11, he quietly waded into the dark Mississippi River, intent on first drifting downstream to Prophet's Island, which was near his home. On a small raft, crafted out of canteens, he floated all night, stealing his way through the Federal fleet, and finally went ashore the next morning. After a brief rest at his home, he continued on horseback up the Woodville Road and on to Johnston's headquarters in Jackson, Mississippi. Days passed before Pruyn was able to deliver Gardner's dispatch to Johnston, who seemed pleased at receiving it. The general explained to Pruyn that he had tried to get a message to Gardner of "utmost importance" on several occasions, but none of the couriers could succeed in getting through the Federal lines. Of course, the adventurous and dauntless Captain Pruyn immediately volunteered to return to Gardner with Johnston's coded message, and then boldly set out to repeat the perilous journey.[3]

Lieutenant General Joseph E. Johnston commanded the Confederate Department of the West. National Archives.

Back at Port Hudson, about four in the morning, Halbert Paine directed the first wave of his 3,000-man assault to move forward. Leading the division out of the woods and onto a rolling plain was the skirmish line made up of men from Wisconsin and New Hampshire. Behind them were several companies of grenadiers, carrying both rifles and hand grenades. Next came Colonel Oliver Gooding's Third Brigade with the point regiment being made up of sweating Massachusetts men carrying cotton bags, which they planned to use in filling the ditch fronting the Rebel parapet. They were followed by Colonel Hawkes Fearing and the Second Brigade, and lastly Colonel Samuel Ferris's First Brigade. Interspersed in the procession were the pioneers and engineers, lugging tools and building materials to bridge the ditch. Ormand Nims's battery of artillery remained in the rear waiting for Paine's division to break the enemy's line and then move into their works.[4]

The guns behind the gray lines were silent until Paine's division reached the crest of a ridge, at a point within a hundred yards of the left side of the Priest Cap. Then rifle shots began to whistle around the leading formations, freezing the skirmishers in their tracks. The ground over which they had to advance was a rolling field, and offered little protection in terms of trees and ravines. Paine, who had moved to the front of the formation, noticed his men were hesitating, and rushed ahead of the column of sharpshooters. In a deep booming voice he ordered the men to charge. No sooner had the bluecoats lunged forward than a wicked, lacerating fire poured out of the Rebel works. Those guns were in the hands of the First Mississippi and the Forty-ninth Alabama regiments, and although their vision was limited in the misty and dim light of the morning, the volleys still found their mark. Paine's men were cut down by the score. It was no surprise that one of the casualties in the first blast of musketry was "the gallant Paine," as Richard Irwin referred to him. Crumbling to the ground in agony, Paine's thigh bone was crushed and shattered by a well-aimed rifle ball. In the hail of bullets, all attempts by his men to come to his aid were unsuccessful, and two stretcher bearers were both killed in the effort. Finally, a wounded soldier lying near him succeeded in tossing Paine a canteen, an act which probably saved the commander's life.[5]

With the wounded Paine lying helpless and unable to direct the troops, the attack lost its momentum. The storming party, pioneers and bridge crews discarded their tools and pontoon materials. Throwing down the sandbags they had carried to fill the ditch, they crouched behind them as cover from the heavy fire. Even so, some of the New Hampshire and Wisconsin skirmishers, along with a number of Connecticut and Massachusetts boys, somehow managed to momentarily get across the ditch and claw their way over the parapet. One Rebel defender recalled the moment: "The smoke was so thick that nothing could be seen more than twenty steps in advance, and before our troops were aware of it the enemy were pouring into the ditches and scaling our breastworks on the left." Here, curses filled the air, and the battle turned into a brawl with men trying to kill each other with rifle butts, bayonets, and even their bare hands. There were not many Mississippians defending the point where the parapet was breached, but they were quickly reinforced with troops from the First Alabama who rushed to their aid and turned back the bluecoats. "Again and again they rallied," remembered one Southerner, "but each time repulsed.... In several instances their skirmishers succeeded in gaining our ditches and hurling their grenades over the parapets." But their fuses were cut too long, giving the Rebels time to pick them up and hurl them right back where they had come from, exploding among the grenadiers who had thrown them. Those bluecoats still fighting within the Priest Cap were killed, wounded or taken prisoner, and those still trying to drag themselves over the parapet were clubbed and gunshot until they tumbled back into the muddy ditch. Looking beyond the ditch, a Rebel defender recalled, "The ground in front of our works was blue with their uniforms, and the weeds and bushes still further forward, were strewn with them."[6]

The rear of Paine's division then fell back behind the cover of the hill, but those who had been in advance were forced to hug the ground around the ridge while incessant Rebel gunfire ripped over and around them. Perhaps they could have mustered another charge and, perhaps, that one would have been successful. But without Paine's leadership and enthusiasm it could not and would not happen. Moreover, these were New Englanders whose enlistments were about to expire. Precious thoughts of home were on their minds and they could see no reason to risk their lives for honor and glory on some faraway, horrifying battlefield. On top of that, they could not forget their friends and fellow soldiers who had been killed or maimed in the battle of May 27. Thus, at least for these men, the decision not to fight was elementary. Their battle was over, and it was only five o'clock in the morning. Yet rather than risk being shot by leaving the field and exposing themselves, they chose to remain lying with the wounded and dead all day on the blood-stained ground in front of the Priest Cap, unprotected from the burning rays of the Louisiana sun. Yet, during this time, many of these men did their best to help those around them, sharing the water in their canteens. "In this unfortunate situation," recalled Banks's adjutant, "the sufferings of the wounded became so unbearable, and appealed so powerfully to the sympathy of their comrades, that many lives were risked and some lost in the attempt to alleviate the thirst, at least, of these unfortunates." Indeed, there were many men who had fallen in the assault. Looking over the carnage, George Powers of the Thirty-eighth Massachusetts lamented: "More than one-third of the Thirty-eighth, and one-quarter of the Fifty-third, lay wounded and dying on the hills and in the ravines ... and that voice which had inspired the whole movement was no longer heard. Whatever chance of success there may have been at the outset, the fall of General Paine destroyed it."[7]

According to the instructions of Banks's plan, Godfrey Weitzel's division was supposed to be supporting Paine's with a simultaneous attack on the right side or north face of the Priest Cap. But because of some of the same problems that caused the defeat on May 27—a lack of leadership, poor planning, and discipline problems with the short-term enlistees—there was, once again, a failure to make a coordinated mass attack. Furthermore, in the predawn blackness that covered the Port Hudson woods, entire brigades and regiments of Weitzel's command found themselves lost, or guided in the wrong direction by bewildered staff officers, who had not received proper instructions. As a result, it was seven o'clock that morning before they were finally ready to move forward with their attack. And even then, they still had to approach the parapet through a series of deep gorges, creek beds, and finally a large ravine with steep banks that led to an open space below the ridge of a hill where the Rebel breastworks were frowning

Chapter Seven. "This Day of Blood"

Ruins of Confederate fortification known as the Priest Cap. Port Hudson State Historic Site Photograph Collection.

down on them. Emerging from the ravine and starting up the hill, Weitzel's men came under heavy fire. Even so, they pressed forward "with a rush and a cheer." But the rush came to an abrupt halt at the crest of the hill. Most of them had, by now, already been shot down, driven back, or left cowering down among the dead and wounded, afraid to move. The few who managed to reach the breastworks were dropped by gunfire while attempting to climb through a ditch and over a parapet. That ditch had now gained a reputation of infamy as a place that would long be remembered by those who survived it. As in Paine's attack, the ditch was soon full of the dead and dying. "That awful ditch," remembered one of the attackers, "yawning like a grave." Indeed, "a grave" was an excellent description in view of the fact that "charge after charge had been made and repulsed; the ditch was an obstacle which could not be overcome." The One Hundred and Fourteenth New York Regiment led a gallant charge in Weitzel's last attempt to get across the infamous ditch and take the Rebel entrenchments. "With desperation amounting to madness, our boys jumped to their feet and made another impetuous rush towards the entrenchments," remarked Harris Beecher, the regimental surgeon. "They ran and shouted, until they had once more reached the ditch. Into it they leaped, and made a desperate but ineffectual effort to scale the works. The charge was the last throb of expiring courage."

A plea for reinforcements was sent back to Cuvier Grover, commanding the Federal right wing. Although he sent two more brigades into the fray around 10:00 a.m., there were no high-ranking general officers to lead them. Colonel Joseph Morgan, who was the officer Grover had ordered to take them forward, was said to be drunk and cowering behind a log during the battle. Before the reinforcements could reach the hillside, they ran into a sea of humanity made up of a mob of skulkers, retreating soldiers, and hospital orderlies who were trying to move the wounded from the field. Finally, they made their way up the hill and to a narrow ridge where they met the same tormenting fire as had Weitzel's earlier assault. Here, one of the brigade commanders, Colonel Richard Holcomb, was among the first to fall when a Rebel bullet struck his head and blew out his brains. It soon became apparent to those actually doing the fighting that the assault had failed, and the orders that were relayed from the rear by absentee commanders were ignored by regimental officers who refused to renew the charge. One strenuous objector was Colonel Simon Jerrard, who had taken charge of Grover's First Brigade after Holcomb was killed. Jerrard flatly refused, saying, "If General Banks wants to go in there, let him go in and be damned. I won't slaughter my men that way."[8]

Grover's Third Brigade had been ordered to support Colonel Holcomb's First Brigade, and before Holcomb's death some of their regiments had become inextricably mixed with Holcomb's command. In fact, the Thirteenth Connecticut Regiment of the Third Brigade had not only followed Holcomb's First Brigade into battle, but had overtaken them and were being led by that colonel before he had fallen. Captain Homer Sprague, a company commander in the Thirteenth Connecticut, tried to describe the ground over which they had to cross: "It is impossible to convey in words any adequate idea of the difficulties, natural and artificial, presented by the ground between us and the enemy. There were forty or fifty rods of standing timber, and many precipitous, crooked ravines, filled with a tangled mass of felled trees, vines and brambles; and the level ground was scarcely less obstructed; all being in clear view and point-blank range of the enemy's works, from which arose incessant puffs of smoke, as their men fired from safe cover." Charging over this ground, Sprague remembered how they were "instantly exposed to the hottest fire." Men seemed to be falling everywhere when a young private named Blake rushed up to Sprague in wild-eyed excitement and said, "Captain, Colonel Holcomb is killed!" Sprague discounted the private's report as just another rumor, and replied, "Get back to your place, sir. It's no such thing!" But Private Blake was adamant, and blurted out, "But Captain, he certainly is killed! See, here are his brains all scattered over my coat." For Sprague, a quick glance confirmed the private's account. By now, most of the troops around them had almost vanished, and they were thrown into confusion. Sprague pushed his troops forward until, by chance, they reached a ravine in which they could find shelter from the terrible shot and shell from the Rebel guns. "Into this ravine we poured pell-mell," Sprague thankfully confessed. But insofar as Sprague was concerned there was no hope for victory, and he admitted it: "Colonel Holcomb having fallen, and almost the whole of the advancing column being thrown into confusion by the well-nigh insuperable obstacles, and most of the storming party greatly retarded by logs, bushes, briers, and gullies, and the leader of the movement killed, the assault failed." Sharing the same ravine for cover was the One Hundred Fifty-ninth New York Regiment, which had been ordered in as a reserve and met the same fate as Sprague and the Connecticut men. After being forced to seek the cover of the ravine, Captain William Tiemann recalled the experience: "Here we lay, our eyes saddened by the sight of our dead and our ears tortured with the groans of our wounded … under a blazing sun without shelter we lay exposed to a constant fire until 9 p.m. when all the forces were drawn off, with the exception of the regiments left as pickets."[9]

In the Union center, General Christopher Augur was under orders to simulate an attack in order to draw the Confederates' attention away from the right and left where the actual attacks were supposed to occur. Assuming the feigned attack was successful, it would cause the Rebels to divert troops to the center, thus weakening their defense against the attacks of Grover and Dwight. As ordered, before dawn Augur sent a regiment of skirmishers forward, inching their way as close as possible to the Confederate works. A couple of hours later another infantry regiment moved in behind them and Augur's artillery opened with a roar. The riflemen and the artillery created a raucous commotion. But that was all. The mock attack drew some fire from the Confederate breastworks, but the military objective of a diversion failed. Losses on both sides were light. And for the Union troops that was a fortuitous blessing, considering that many of them had filled their canteens with whiskey before advancing. The only real danger Augur's bluecoats experienced that day was the erratic fire pouring into the backs of the Forty-ninth Massachusetts, the leading regiment. Those bullets were blasted from the rifles of an inebriated regiment of Union soldiers that had moved up behind them. "The miserable fellows thought, in their drunken valor, that they were the nearest regiment to the foe," complained Henry Johns, a Massachusetts private. "So imminent was the danger from their guns, that it became a questionable matter, which was the safer side of the logs."[10]

Another soldier who had famously fortified himself with an extra ration of whiskey was the odious William Dwight, the general commanding the Union left. In the ranks, questions continued to arise as to how a man as inept in military matters as Dwight was not only tolerated by Banks, but after the wounding of Thomas Sherman was given command of an entire wing of the army. The answer remained a mystery, but rumor suggested that Banks owed a great deal of money to Dwight's rich Bostonian father, and was perhaps trying to redeem his debt. Dwight's orders from Banks were to first send two regiments against the fortification known as the Citadel, which was situated on a bluff near the river on the extreme right of the Confederate line. However, Dwight, shortly before the attack, decided to embellish those orders to include the capture of the Confederate commander, Franklin Gardner, whose headquarters were supposedly in a house located within the Citadel. After learning of this in his Special Order No. 32, the officers who were to be engaged in such a foolish scheme believed that a plan so quixotic must have come to Dwight in one of his a drunken reveries, and they assumed that he would forget all about it after he sobered up.[11]

But Dwight did not forget about it, perhaps because he was never completely sober. In fact, prior to the attack, he called a meeting of the officers involved to come to his headquarters. Lieutenant Colonel Edward Bacon, commanding the Sixth Michigan Regiment, was among them. Bacon, who was often cynical in his opinions of his superiors, was especially loathing of Dwight. But in Bacon's defense, the contempt and disrespect for Dwight was shared by most of the Nineteenth Corps. As soon as Bacon arrived, one of Dwight's staff officers offered him a drink. Knowing, though, he was about to have an interview with the general, Bacon declined the offer. The officer then responded that it made no difference, remarking, "The General was tight himself." Once in Dwight's presence, the boozy general produced a map of the Rebel works, and pointed towards two Rebel deserters, who were also present at the meeting and had volunteered to act as guides for Bacon and fifty of his men. "With this party," remembered Bacon, "I was to have fifty picked men, who were to be disguised so as to look as much like Rebels as possible. I was to pass in through the citadel, and proceed immediately to General Gardner's quarters and take him prisoner." Of course, no one, including the deserters, seemed to know the location of Gardner's headquarters. Bacon then questioned Dwight as to how he was to find the Rebel general's headquarters. "You must make a prisoner of the first man you meet," answered the red-faced Dwight, "holding your revolver to his head, extort the information from him." Then, after listening to some absurd tactic about signaling him with rockets after accomplishing the mission, Dwight glared at him with a grave look and sputtered, "Your men must be desperate men—men that will fight!" "There was something in the tone of his last words so comical," recalled Bacon, "that I could hardly keep from laughing in his face." After Dwight's rambling instructions, Bacon and the other officers were honored with an invitation to dine with the general and his staff. It was a lavish feast of chicken, mutton and beef, complemented by fine wine and brandy, and all served by "two gentlemanly waiters, the most valuable servants that could be found." There was only little discussion of Dwight's proposed project and the upcoming attack. "The General," remembered Bacon, "was too far gone to say much while we were at dinner." However, after they returned to camp, one of the officers who was unfortunate enough to be included in the risky mission remarked to Bacon, "We are all turned over to Dwight to be disposed of."[12]

In the early morning hours of the Sunday attack, Bacon and his regiment, the Sixth Michigan, waited patiently in the darkness, listening to the sounds of the assaults taking place all around them. The plan had called for him to move his troops forward at four o'clock that morning, but he had not received the orders to do so. As the hours continued to creep by, Bacon questioned himself: "Can it be that I have been here until the morning is almost ready to dawn? ...and yet no order for us." It was almost broad daylight when the sound of a horse's hoofs alerted Bacon of an orderly approaching his camp and bearing a message from Dwight, which instructed him, "March your regiment immediately, and join the column under Colonel Clark." Dwight, then, had apparently given responsibility for executing his bizarre plan to Thomas Clark, a favorite of the general, who had promoted Clark to command of the First Brigade of the division. The promotion was puzzling to Bacon, since Clark was currently facing several charges of acts unbecoming of an officer, including "drunk and unfit for duty and cowardice and neglect of duty." Bacon then protested to the orderly: "I am informed that this regiment is not in Clark's brigade." The courier then explained that Clark was given command of more troops than his own brigade, and that he was quite certain that Bacon's regiment was ordered to join Clark's brigade.[13]

Soon after the orderly left, Colonel Clark suddenly appeared on horseback and ordered Bacon to send two captains, John Cordon and Henry Stark, along with a detail of 250 men to capture the Rebel general Gardner in the Citadel, as instructed by General Dwight. He then told Bacon to take the rest of the Sixth Michigan, and join his main column to storm the Confederate works near the river. The cowardly Clark, "in the most amiable tone of voice," invited Bacon to accompany him when he led the column in the attack. Watching the gallant colonel ride slowly away, Bacon noticed that he went "down a winding by-road, through thickets, toward the river, every step taking him farther from his column, which must have been waiting some time for him to lead it." After Thomas Clark rode away, the 250 men detailed to capture Gardner marched forward. Bacon studied them as they trudged past and lamented, "I see in the faces of officers and men that all understand well what kind of a horrid scrape they have got into. I hear among them the words, 'Pile up our bones, to make a reputation for somebody.'"[14]

From that point, nothing seemed to go right for Dwight's division. The attack was so poorly planned, timed and executed that it hardly resembled an attack at all. From atop the high bluff of the Citadel, Rebel cannoneers clearly saw the advancing regiments approaching in the morning sunlight, and opened up on them with every artillery gun in their arsenal. After crossing a muddy ravine, they needed to cross a low open area and then climb a steep ridge to enter the Citadel. "When we came out from the shelter of the woods," recalled Albert Plummer of the Forty-eighth Massachusetts, "the fire of the enemy was terrible, but the column moved forward firmly; the rebel line of breastworks was clearly defined before us, with the Citadel frowning in the front." As the firing began to increase, the Massachusetts men quickened their forward pace, moving from quick time to a mad rush. Plummer continued recounting their awful experience: "The air hissed with bullets and shell, the groans of the wounded mingled with the cheers and yells of the charging troops, the shouts of fellows, losing their presence of mind, would try to dodge the flying missiles as they passed to bury themselves with a sickening *thud* in some other doomed comrade's body; it seemed as if pandemonium was let loose, and when we overtook and passed over the prostrate bodies of the red clothed fascine bearers, who had started in advance of the main column and who, unable to face the leaden storm, had dropped their burdens and taken shelter behind them, they were greeted with cries of derision, which quickly change to cries of dismay when we came into the vortex and saw the ground swept as it were by a whirlwind, and every man sought shelter in ravines, behind stumps, logs and any object which could afford shelter."[15]

While hugging the ground Bacon and the Sixth Michigan Regiment could plainly hear the victorious Rebels from William Miles's command taunting them, "How do you like it" and "Why don't you come on." While the debacle continued, there were no orders being given, as no one seemed to know the whereabouts of General Dwight. Colonel Clark was also missing, although Bacon, while on the way to join the main column, claimed to have seen him skulking in the bushes, supposedly suffering from an attack of dysentery, and feeling "very poorly." As to the raiding party led by Captains Cordon and Stark, it goes without saying that it failed to capture Gardner, and, in fact, they were unable to come anywhere near the Citadel.

Chapter Seven. "This Day of Blood" 105

Destroyed cannon of a Mississippi battery located on the left flank of the Citadel. Port Hudson State Historic Site Photograph Collection.

Also, it seemed that prior to the attack Dwight, through another delusion of grandeur, had ordered a saber-flashing cavalry charge into the Citadel by Colonel Benjamin Grierson and his horsemen, in the hope of adding luster to his victory. That, of course, never materialized since Grierson considered the order preposterous and ignored it.[16]

Except for a few cracking sounds of sporadic shooting, by 11 a.m. the assault had come to a grinding halt, signaling yet another bloody repulse for Banks and his Nineteenth Corps. Nothing had been gained except advancing their lines a few yards closer to the Rebel works. In addition, a small hill or eminence overlooking the Citadel had been taken, which Dwight's division, by chance and not design, successfully occupied. Although the combat was mercifully over, the suffering was only beginning. Throughout the blazing-hot afternoon, the wounded men who could not move or be moved continued lying in the baking sun, suffering from thirst, fatigue and a loss of blood. Lieutenant George Carpenter, one of the Green Mountain Vermont boys, remembered that scene: "All that hot June Sabbath day the men lay there in plain sight—the dead, the wounded, the unhurt, together, but no help could reach them, for the enemy's gunners were unusually active, and woe to the man who showed signs of life on the field, and the pitying comrade who ventured forth on a mission of relief. The least movement drew the fire of a score of sharpshooters. Many who lay wounded before the works were killed during the day; and several brave men who set out to carry relief to their fallen mates were ruthlessly shot." Among the wounded was General Halbert Paine, still lying in a cotton field, "his wound alive with maggots," but afraid to move a muscle. Somehow, he managed to survive until nightfall when the stretcher bearers were able to reach him and carry him to safety. Though he would lose his leg, Paine was more fortunate than many of the wounded whose lives were drained from them while lying on the battlefield. Behind the Federal lines, men engaged in sullen conversations about the outcome of the fight. "We know nothing certainly," admitted Corporal Hosmer of the Fifty-second Massachusetts early that afternoon, but then added, "There are rumors, thick as the rifle-balls, of this general killed, that regiment destroyed." Soon, however, the awful reality of the defeat became certain. "We hear of poor wounded men lying without shelter, whom the ambulance men cannot yet reach on account of the enemy fire.... We begin to know that the attack has failed," lamented Hosmer.[17]

Not only had it failed but, like the May 27 attack, the toll in casualties was shocking. After the losses are counted they numbered 1,805, and although only 216 were listed as killed it should be noted that of the 1,401 wounded many of those would die later. Also, there were 188 men reported missing, and most of those were surely dead. When the sun finally set in the west, a New England soldier expressed his relief to see the day disappear into history, and entered in his journal: "The sun goes down on this day of blood." And a surgeon in a New York Regiment added these words: "Thus ended the battle of the 14th of June. It had been such a decided defeat, and had been productive of such frightful carnage, that it cast over the whole army a spirit of gloom and despondency. Not a joyous laugh was heard, not a smile was seen, [and] not a particle of advantage had been gained over the enemy. In fact, the poor sufferers were tormented with the shouts of the victors, which the breeze wafted over from the rebel works." Indeed, across the way, behind the Rebel lines, there was a feeling of jubilation and thankful prayers. Bugles blared and drums beat while weary men broke out in songs, such as "The Bonnie Blue Flag," "Dixie," and even some of their favorite hymns. There was also a relief that their losses were trifling as compared with those of the Federals, totaling only forty-seven, with twenty-two deaths and twenty-five wounded. Yet even in victory they, too, were grateful that this day was finally over.[18]

Chapter Eight

Unspeakably Dreadful Days

Nathaniel Banks may not have been a man possessed with a great deal of military ability, but no one should have doubted his bullish tenacity. Before the sun set on June 14, Banks admitted to Farragut, "The attack did not succeed," but insisted that it came close to a triumph, claiming, "The merest accident separates success from failure. I am still confident of the final result." In other words, Banks was not about to give up. As a politician, he knew any suggestion of a defeat at this point would be tantamount to self-destruction at the polls when the war ended and he resumed his public career, something he could not allow to happen. Thus Banks continued to maintain a confident façade, but privately he was becoming frustrated and impatient with the loss of more and more men and the failure to take Port Hudson. "I swear terribly," he confessed in a letter to his wife, Mary, "I wake up at night and swear. We have great trials—so many poor men." But the day after the battle, June 15, Banks was again brimming with his usual confidence and feisty poise, circulating a report to the troops and congratulating them on "the steady advance made upon the enemy's works." With bullish optimism, he added: "One more advance and they are ours!" He then called on the corps for a thousand men to volunteer to join a storming column and "to vindicate the flag of the Union and the memory of its defenders who have fallen." As an extra incentive, Banks promised accolades and rewards to anyone who volunteered for this perilous adventure, including medals and promotions.[1]

While Banks waited for the morose troops to mull over the offer to join another version of the "Forlorn Hope," he turned his attention to the wounded Union soldiers who were lying within Port Hudson as prisoners of war. Under a flag of truce, he sent a courier to the Confederate general, Gardner, offering drugs and other medical supplies for the treatment of not only the wounded bluecoats but for the Rebels as well: "I have the honor," Banks wrote, "to request your permission to send a small quantity of medical and hospital supplies within your works, for the comfort of my wounded in your hands and such of your own as you may desire to use them for." Gardner, of course, wasted no time in accepting what appeared to be a most generous and humane offer, but reminded Banks that there were dead and wounded men still lying on the battlefield, needing burials or medical attention. However, to Gardner's surprise, Banks refused to allow a cessation of fighting to remove the Federal dead and wounded. Apparently, Banks had decided to follow Grant's example at Vicksburg by refusing to grant a truce which might somehow be construed as an acknowledgment of failure or defeat. As a result of such haughty stubbornness, many of the wounded Union soldiers died unnecessarily.[2]

Another man who hastily rejected the notion of granting a truce to bury the dead was none other than the thoughtless William Dwight. Even though the Confederates extended an offer to send out parties of their own men to carry the dead and wounded bodies closer to the Federal lines and a safe distance away so they could be either treated or buried, Dwight would not agree. When one of Dwight's officers approached him and begged him to accept the Rebel offer, he angrily snapped at the man: "No sir.... They know that they will be stunk out if the bodies rot there, and they cannot get them away on account of our fire. No, sir; I'll stink the rebels out of the citadel with the dead bodies of these damned volunteers, if I cannot make the cowards take it by storm, as I have ordered them to do." Dwight then dismissed the officer with a threat: "Clear out, sir, or I will have you executed ignominiously."[3]

By June 17, the blistering Louisiana sun had been beating down on the bloated, fly-blown corpses for three days. The bodies began decaying and turning black, and the stench became almost unbearable for the soldiers. Even civilians living in surrounding areas near the battlefield began to complain. "The stench became so terrible that we could scarcely breathe, especially at night," recalled a Southern woman years later. Because Banks and Dwight had both refused to grant a truce to bury the bodies, Gardner instructed General William Beall, commanding the center section of the line, to appeal to the Union general Christopher Augur, and ask for a truce to collect and bury the Union dead lying between their respective commands. Augur agreed and a truce was granted, but it was limited to only his part of the line. Working parties of men wearing both blue and gray combed the battlefield for the dead and wounded. "Our men collected and delivered one hundred and sixty-seven corpses," remembered a Rebel soldier and "found one poor fellow able to speak though desperately wounded ... whose face, neck and hands had been completely fly-blown." James Hosmer, a Massachusetts corporal, glumly complained about the ghoulish business of gathering 114 dead bodies, calling it "unspeakably dreadful." He remembered: "The decomposition of the bodies was so advanced, that the flesh slipped from the arms as our men tried to raise them, the heads fell

Chapter Eight. Unspeakably Dreadful Days 109

away from the trunks sometimes, and the worms crawled from the dead upon the hands of the living." Another Massachusetts soldier, Sergeant Solomon Nelson, wished this gruesome duty could have been done sooner, since it was obvious that some of the men had died before help could reach them, and said so in his diary entry of June 17: "Very many had lived a long time, as was evident by the appearance of their surroundings. In some cases they had tied their handkerchiefs above the wounds and made twists with their bayonets, forming what is termed in medical parlance a tourniquet, thus stopping the flow of blood. But the extreme heat was too much for nature. Decay had commenced, and the most sickening sight to be conceived of was here beheld." As to those parts of the line where a truce could not be arranged, the bodies remained conspicuously unburied throughout the siege. Henry Gardner, a New York artilleryman, after walking over the battlefield as late as July 8, told his diary: "I saw the remains of some of the stormers still unburied." And, according to at least one Rebel soldier, on some parts of the battlefield none were buried: "The bodies of the slain could be seen from the breastworks on the day of the surrender, twenty-six days after the fight."[4]

About this same time, unofficial truces also began to occur, here and there, on other parts of the line. These informal interludes of cease-fires were always initiated by the enlisted men in the trenches, who waved white handkerchiefs or rags from their breastworks, then came out in full view of the enemy without the threat of being shot by sharpshooters. Both sides honored the integrity of the truces although, at times, soldiers took the opportunity to verbally abuse one another from a distance. On such occasions when hostilities were suspended, it allowed the men to work on their breastworks in some measure of peace. And, of course, there were times when they even met each other half way between the lines and exchanged tobacco, coffee, newspapers and even a little food, the latter being a commodity the Rebels sorely needed. These close-up exchanges were usually amiable, as if the soldiers were not enemies, but good friends. It seemed strangely inexplicable that during the most horrific of circumstances, men were, by nature, still social creatures. But, after a time, someone would call out to the other side to take cover because they are getting ready to commence firing, and everyone scurried back to their ditches. However, after this had continued for several days, high-ranking officers became aware of these unauthorized détentes, and ordered them stopped.[5]

Wickham Hoffman, a Union officer, gave his version of these strange unofficial truces in a postwar account: *It was curious to observe the sort of entente cordiale which the soldiers on both sides established during the siege. When they were tired of trying to pick each other off through the loop-holes, one of them would tie a white handkerchief to his bayonet, and wave it above the parapet. Pretty soon a handkerchief, or its equivalent—for the rebs did not indulge in useless luxuries—would be seen waving on the other side. This meant truce. In a moment the men would swarm out on both sides, sitting with their legs dangling over the parapet, chaffing each other, and sometimes with pretty rough wit. They were as safe as if a regular flag were out. No man dared to violate this tacit truce. If he had done so, his own comrades would have dealt roughly with him. After a while, on one side or the other, someone would cry out, "Get under cover now Johnnie," or "Look out now, Yank; we are going to fire," and the fire would recommence.*[6]

There were, however, one group of soldiers who did not get to experience the unofficial truces. Those were the thousand men who had volunteered for Banks's special storming force, once again labeled the "Forlorn Hope." At first, volunteers were slow to respond. But by the twenty-eighth of June the ranks of that unit had been filled and divided into two battalions, with command awarded to a Connecticut Colonel named Henry Birge. Not everyone who volunteered for the mission was accepted, such as ninety-one black men from the Louisiana Native Guards, who after the fight on May 27 had been relegated to "fatigue duty," or digging the trenches on the Union right. Those volunteers who were accepted were sent to a camp in a pleasant grove situated in the rear and close to Banks's headquarters. Here they were made to feel they were a part of an elite command where officers trained them in the use of weapons, the terrain which they would encounter, and some different and improved tactics that they would have to employ during the next assault, all of which seemed to improve the morale of the men. Yet they all knew that there was dangerous work ahead of them. In an attempt to inspire them for the mission, Banks visited the camp on June 30, and made a speech which only a polished politician like himself could deliver: "A little more than a month ago you found the enemy in the open country far away from these scenes. Now he is hemmed in and surrounded. What remains is to close upon him and secure him within our grasp. We want the close hug! When you get an enemy's head under your arm, you can pound him at your will." Many of the troops were roused and encouraged by his words. Others, knowing the unshrinking tenacity of the Rebel defenders, were silent and unresponsive. All thought of their futures. Those who had anything to leave made their wills, and everyone took some time to write what may have been their final letter to their families. One young officer, identifying himself only as "Willie," wrote home to his family and attempted to explain his reasons for volunteering. "Something must be done. You will wish to know why I came when our regiment is so short of officers, and I am so easily fixed now. I came on principle. I did not come for the reward or promotion, but because I deemed it my duty to come. Bold men are wanted. If I am not bold, God will make me so." Then he

Chapter Eight. Unspeakably Dreadful Days   111

closed his letter with an acknowledgment of the uncertainty of his life: "If I die, you will think of me as one whose short life was not wholly without a purpose. I hope to come to you with honor—with the medal on my breast."[7]

Banks never bothered to set a date for the assault of his latest version of the "Forlorn Hope" for one important reason. That was, in order for it to be successful, they must be able to get closer to the Rebel breastworks, and that would take an undetermined amount of time. One of the causes for the failure of the past attacks, he believed, were the long distances over open ground the Federal troops had to cover before reaching their objectives. Thus, in solving this problem, several points along the line were identified, and Union troops, along with gangs of slaves taken from neighboring plantations, began digging deep saps, or zigzag trenches, towards the Confederate fortress. Based on the terrain and position of the enemy, the direction and pattern of the saps were carefully designed by Federal engineers and draftsmen. They were planned with the intent of not only providing protection by angling the trenches, but also to connect them with a number of Union batteries.[8]

Night and day, the men doggedly worked on the diggings that were intended to approach four main strongholds along the Confederate line: the Priest Cap, Fort Desperate, the Citadel, and the Slaughters' house. Progress varied at each point, depending on the terrain and the amount of resistance the Rebels offered. In those areas where there was too much opposition from the defenders, the work was mainly done at night. The heat of the June days became almost unbearable. Men on both sides fell from the ranks, suffering with heat stroke, malaria, diarrhea and just plain exhaustion. The work was hard, slow and dangerous. While digging these saps, sweating men toiled all day behind the cover of cotton bales or large sugar casks that had been emptied and filled with dirt or cotton that were known as hogsheads. Those not engaged in the digging were armed, and served as sharpshooters trying to protect the workers from the constant and harassing gunfire from the Confederates, who were not about to idly stand by and watch as the trenches crept closer and closer to their fortress. At all times, both sides were constantly improvising ways to kill or keep from being killed. Union artillerists, for example, were a favorite target for Rebel marksmen and were routinely picked off until the Yanks devised a hinged, flat iron shutter with a small eye hole mounted in front of the guns to protect their gunners, who could then safely operate and fire the artillery.[9]

The men from New England had an especially difficult time adjusting to the fevered Louisiana heat. Private Henry Johns, who was accustomed to the more pleasant summer days of Massachusetts, probably best described their ordeal with the weather: *The "Sunny South" sounds nicely enough ... but here, with that mercury at 95 degrees in the shade for weeks at a time, the poetry all disappears.... You can think of nothing but a "furnace of fire." An hour after sunset or an hour before sunset, and it is seemingly as hot as at noon.... For the whole twenty-four hours your body is moist or dripping with perspiration. If you are cool at night, it is nothing but the dank moisture driving fever to your vitals. Showers have been infrequent and the dust, pulverized by the tread of thousands of men and beasts, is more than ankle deep. The trees and bushes are covered with it, and in the sunlight look like smoldering fires. We dress accordingly. A straw hat, a shirt, a pair of breeches and shoes (sometimes stockings) complete our wardrobe.*[10]

Another New Englander, George Carpenter from Vermont, agreed with Private Johns about the stifling heat, but spoke of other tribulations he wanted to relate to the people back home: *I often wonder whether our friends at home have a realizing sense of the situation of affairs here in camp. I hardly think they do—in fact, I am sure they cannot. Let me tell you. The men of this command have been confined for more than a month to the ditches, in which they live, eat, sleep and fight. In front are embankments of their own building, on top of which are sand-bags and logs, forming loop-holes, through which they watch the enemy, and shoot at the sight of anything that moves.... Along a large part of the line the men are obliged to approach the trenches crawling on their hands and knees. Here too they sleep, if they sleep at all.... If the night be ever so rainy, all they can do is to lie or stand and take it. When the ground gets very slippery, so that they slide too much, they must drive some stakes to brace their feet against. Many of the men have dug holes in the bank large enough to admit their bodies, so that they literally live in caves of the earth. You can readily imagine that the men are of necessity very dirty and ragged, for their clothes soon get terribly filthy, or wear out. So much is their appearance altered that you would recognize but few of the men or officers. Occasionally a few get out and stretch their legs and get washed, and those who are fortunate enough to possess a change of shirt put on a clean one. But as a rule the poor boys are unshaven, their hair is long and frequently uncombed for a week or more; and, if a close inspection were made, it might surprise their wives or mothers to find vermin living on their heads and bodies. Think then of living in such a place week after week, with the burning southern sun pouring down upon you, while a hundred pieces of artillery boom around night and day, not to mention the bursting of rebel shells in your very bedroom, and the reports of ten thousand musket to lull you to sleep. What say you to this?*[11]

And from the diary of Sergeant Solomon Nelson, a Massachusetts soldier added his version of the Port Hudson summer: *Here we sit in the dirt with a blazing July sun pouring its serenest rays upon our heads. By stretching blankets across and holding them in place with our bayonets a little shelter is obtained; the sun strikes us enough to give every man a sunstroke. If one straightens up his head above the line of dirt in front, this is recognized by a*

Chapter Eight. Unspeakably Dreadful Days 113

rebel, who shoots his rifle at it. The only variation from dirt and sweat and impatience has been for somebody to hold his cap upon a stick to draw the fire from some of the southern chivalry. During the day the cook comes to the edge of the woods, and in squads we go on all fours to the right flank and satisfy the cravings of hunger. As we have to work under difficulties, having a wholesome dread of the rebel sharpshooters, the dirt and sweat mingle and plow deep furrows down our bronzed cheeks.[12]

Throughout the stifling June days, the Southerners spent their time improving their own breastworks or repairing the damage constantly done by the enemy's artillery. And all the while, they were doing their best to interrupt the work on the Yankee saps. Hardly a day passed when the Confederates failed to engage in a trench raid or small skirmish to halt or hamper their work. Other times, they rolled hand grenades or lit mortar shells into the Union trenches. During the dark nights, small parties of adventurous Rebels would sally out to torch or shoot flaming arrows into the cotton bales and sugar hogsheads (large casks or barrels) in an attempt to burn down the protective cover of the workers. Yet despite all their efforts, the saps kept moving closer, and by the latter part of June some of them, such as the one approaching the Priest Cap, had been pushed to within thirty yards of the Confederate works. As the saps drew even closer, Union engineers began designing mines that tunneled their way under the Rebels at both the Priest Cap and the Citadel. The idea, of course, was to load the mines with barrels of gunpowder, blow up the Confederate positions, then send in the troops who would be led by the thousand troops of the "Forlorn Hope." But before the two mines at the Priest Cap could be completed, the Rebels became aware of the tunneling, and quickly employed some of their own ingenuity. They dug a countermine, loaded it with explosives, and blew it up, causing one of the Union mines to cave in, and covering the workers with an avalanche of dirt. But despite their predicament, the panic-struck Yankees who were trapped inside were eventually able to dig themselves out without losing a man.[13]

Although life in the trenches was nothing short of misery for both sides, the besieged Southerners by far suffered the most. Short of medicine, ammunition and other supplies, their situation grew more desperate with each passing day. A Louisiana officer, writing after the war, recalled the shortages of medicine and the impact it was having on the defenders: "The continuous exposure to the sun, rain and night dews brought on much sickness, materially reducing our effective strength. Our stock of medicines proved to be even shorter than our stock of provisions with a large and constantly increasing list of chills and fever cases the quinine was exhausted. Ipecac was resorted to in its place, but that also came to an end. Finally there was nothing to be had to check fever except a decoction of indigenous barks, which did not effect any wonderful cures. Still, the sick suffered uncomplainingly, and a great many of them preferred remaining at their posts so as to give aid in repelling another assault, should it be made."[14]

Weeks ago, when they had found themselves officially besieged, they only had a ten-day ration of meat. By mid-June, the scanty rations had to be cut in half. The Federal troops, on the other hand, were enjoying a better quantity and quality of rations, but they, too, had their problems receiving provisions. Those problems, for the most part, were due to the Confederate cavalrymen who were constantly plundering behind Banks's lines, raiding supply depots and capturing supply wagons en route to the Union lines. Specifically, the missions were accomplished by either Colonel John Logan's horsemen operating in and around Clinton, or the Irishman Colonel Frank Powers, who made his headquarters at Freeman's Plantation. Both men had

Confederate Commissary Building, located behind Fort Desperate. Port Hudson State Historic Site Photograph Collection.

Chapter Eight. Unspeakably Dreadful Days   115

successfully continued to torment Banks's supply lines despite the efforts to stop them by Benjamin Grierson's Federal cavalry.[15]

After making a number of successful raids against outlying Federal campsites and supply trains, the notorious Frank Powers began planning another strike. Powers, who was listed as a "laborer" in the 1860 census, had no military background or education, but according to his men was "a daring sort of fellow." For that reason alone, they had chosen him as their colonel. But it was only an honorary title because the Confederate government never officially awarded him a commission to that rank. At dawn, on June 15, the day after the last assault, Powers led his four hundred Tennessee and Louisiana horsemen on a raid against the Fourteenth New York Cavalry Regiment, camped at Newport, only a couple of miles from Port Hudson. Powers was joined by Major Thomas Stockdale's Mississippi battalion numbering about 250 men. But even with the added strength of Stockdale's battalion, Powers was still outnumbered, as the New York regiment boasted a full complement of eight hundred men, mostly foreigners from Sweden who had only recently arrived in America.[16]

Thundering through the Yankee camp in the early morning hours, the Rebel horsemen caught the Swedes completely by surprise. Many of them were still asleep. Those who were awake were preparing their breakfasts. The attackers swept through the camp "like a hurricane, firing into the tents, right and left, and yelling at the same time like demons," according to one of the riders. The Swedes, unaccustomed to such a savage brand of warfare, were hysterical with fear, and threw themselves down on their knees, babbling and begging for quarter in their foreign tongues. Without losing a man, Powers and Stockdale took seven hundred prisoners, captured sixteen hundred pistols, eight hundred sabers, large quantities of ammunition, and all the stores of the quartermaster, including eight wagons and their mules. While the cavalrymen were gathering all the commandeered supplies, arms and wagons, the captured Swedes were marched away under guard, and through an interpreter were told that "any attempt to escape would mean death." Just as the gray riders were preparing to leave, scouts reported that Grierson's cavalry was close by and rapidly approaching. But once again Grierson arrived too late to confront the enemy. All he found were the dead killed in the raid, and the scant remains from another piratical Rebel raid. Once again, Frank Powers and his pugnacious horsemen had struck without warning and disappeared into the forest.[17]

Despite the danger of the Rebel cavalry marauding in his rear, on June 20, a Saturday, Banks ordered a foraging party to the little village of Jackson, Louisiana, just to the northeast of Port Hudson, where two plantations were located. There, the expedition was directed to gather supplies, especially cotton bales, ostensibly to be used in the fortification of the Union lines. Such a mission was of course a large task, requiring a train of 140 wagons, stretching out for two miles along the Jackson-Clinton Road. The train was protected by the Fifty-second Massachusetts infantry and the One Hundred Fourteenth New York Infantry, together with a detachment of Grierson's cavalry and two light cannons. They reached the plantations in Jackson without being attacked, and the soldiers stacked their arms and retired under the shade trees to eat their dinner. Sometime later, as the foragers began looting the houses and barns and loading the wagons, the sounds of rifle fire rang out in the distance. Corporal James Hosmer of the Fifty-second Massachusetts remembered watching two Rebel regiments and a body of horsemen coming towards them: "The Philistines were upon us," he later wrote. Pickets came rushing in from their posts, and the soldiers scrambled for their weapons. What followed was a scene of bedlam and wild confusion. It was a beautiful summer's day as described by Hosmer, with the "infantry skirmishing, cavalry charging with drawn sabres, the snap of rifles from the distant woods, the rush of animals and fugitives to get out of danger." The sounds of battle and the charging Rebels terrified the Negro drivers and their teams of mules. "The mules are in full gallop," Hosmer observed, "some with, some without drivers; over ditches and fences, crash through groves of young pines, over logs and stumps. The Negro drivers yell, and brandish their whips. All is perfect uproar and panic." Halbert Greenleaf, a Massachusetts "imperturbable" colonel leading the expedition, wisely ordered the wagon train to retreat to Port Hudson. The two pieces of Union artillery that were "extremely well served" held off the Rebel horsemen for a while, but the raiders led by Major Thomas Stockdale eventually caught up with them, and in Hosmer's words, "swept like a whirlwind through our long straggling line." Again the artillery turned them back, and the corporal admitted, "If it had not been for them, we might all have been on the way to Richmond." When it was over, and they counted their losses, the foraging journey to Jackson had been costly: sixty wagons and their drivers had been captured, along with two hundred mules and fifty prisoners. It was estimated by Hosmer that eight to ten of Grierson's cavalrymen were killed.[18]

While raids such as these were clearly a problem for Banks and his army, they were not the only measure of annoyance the Yankees faced from the Rebel cavalrymen. Besides the surprise attacks, there was at least one other occasion involving a cloak-and-dagger escapade. Late in June, Colonel John Logan, Powers's counterpart in command, was informed through a local resident, a Mrs. Brown, that Brigadier General Neal Dow, who had been wounded in the attack of May 27, was recovering at a nearby plantation owned by a well-to-do lady named Cage. Logan saw this as an opportunity, not only to capture a Union general who would have important information valuable to the Confederate war effort, but also for a daring act, which would further demoralize the Federal soldiers at Port Hudson. Logan picked a squad of three men from the Seventeenth Arkansas Mounted Infantry. The men chosen were joined by two young Southern sympathizers who lived in the Port Hudson area. Lieutenant John McKowen, a local who was home on furlough from Lee's army in Virginia, was appointed to lead them because of his thorough knowledge of the area.[19]

On the night of June 30, about ten o'clock, the intrepid little band of men approached the Cage home. John Simms, one of the Arkansas soldiers, remembered that moment: "The dogs barking and the moon about half-full…. Rapidly, leaving our horses, we entered the house, and capturing two orderlies who were lying on the gallery, we proceeded into the room where the General was to be, but he was gone!" Mrs. Cage, who was also a Confederate patriot and knew that the raid to capture Dow was to take place on this night, told the men that the general had gone to another house to meet with two of the officers in his regiment. Dow, in his recollection, maintained he had just gone to the Cage home to get some of his things and return to the front, worried that he was about to be discovered. "I feared that … my whereabouts might be learned and a raid made to capture me."[20]

As McKowen and his men mounted their horses to leave the Cage house and track down Dow, something in the moonlight caught their attention: "Just then," recalled Simms, "looking off to the left, inside the lot, in the shade of a tree, sat a man, clad in white, on horseback" He was still within the confines of the spacious yard, which was surrounded by a high board fence. Simms and another Arkansas man named Petty galloped across the yard with their revolvers drawn, and demanded to know if he was General Dow. "Yes sir," replied Dow. "Surrender or I'll kill you," shouted a Rebel horseman. "I was alone, without weapons," recalled Dow, "and there was nothing but to submit to the demand made upon me to surrender."[21]

That same night Dow was taken on the twelve-mile ride to Logan's camp, and the next morning, under guard, commenced the long journey to Richmond. Apparently the general was treated well after his capture, and such was indicated in a letter to his wife: "You will be glad to learn that all the officers seemed disposed to make the situation as endurable as possible. I was treated very courteously, and was made as comfortable as the situation and exigencies would permit." Whether or not the Confederate government extracted any valuable information from Dow was not reported, but is doubtful. Nevertheless, he was considered important enough to exchange for one of Robert E. Lee's sons, "Rooney" Lee, who had been captured by the Union at Brandy Station, Virginia. As for John Logan's hope that Dow's capture might demoralize the Federal troops, he was sadly mistaken. If anything, Dow's loss was received as a welcomed riddance by the men of his regiment, who had grown to despise their general. For them, his self-righteous moralizing and anti-liquor crusade had deprived them of not only their whiskey ration, but newspapers, candy and anything else that might make their days at Port Hudson a little more bearable. Thus, whatever miseries destiny may have had in store for the captured Dow did not concern them.[22]

Although Dow's capture had no adverse effect on the morale of the Federal soldiers, there were other matters that were causing serious problems with their spirit, self-esteem and confidence. Discipline was beginning to break down to the point that there was a mutinous attitude festering in many of the units, mainly among those twenty regiments that were made up of nine-month volunteers whose enlistments had either expired or were about to. These men were nearly all New Englanders and since the campaign began had continuously been on bad terms with the three-year soldiers, who considered them slackers and cowards who had only joined to receive a bounty and lacked the will to fight. Sergeant Solomon Nelson, a nine-month soldier from Massachusetts, recalled one such incident when he was passing by a three-year volunteer resting under the shade of a tree, and the man asked him: "Are you a soldier, or a nine-month man?" However, the nine-month soldiers felt otherwise. That is, they believed their units were overused and had suffered heavy casualties in the attacks of May and June while the three-year men had been used sparingly by the commanders. As a result, they were now refusing to go into battle again, since their enlistments were nearly up. Banks, while explaining to Henry Halleck why it was taking him so long to take Port Hudson, attributed the blame to the short-timers, telling him so in a letter dated June 18: "A large part of my force consists of nine-month men, who openly say they do not consider themselves bound to any perilous service." As for the rest of his troops, he pointed out: "The men enlisted for the war do not like to lead where the rest will not follow." What he neglected to tell Halleck, however, was that most of the troops, regardless of their terms of enlistment, had lost confidence in him and the other generals, and what's more, some of those had also vowed never to follow another one of Banks's orders to charge the Rebel breastworks. In sum, a serious disharmony existed within the ranks of Banks's Army of the Gulf, which by now was on the verge of instigating open mutiny.[23]

Chapter Nine

The Whisky Charge

Much of the discontent within the Union ranks could be attributed to several of the general officers who were either incompetent, unqualified, egocentric, constantly drunk, or in the pathetic case of General William Dwight all of the foregoing. After the failed assault of June 14, Dwight's desire to break the Confederate line and be the hero of the siege of Port Hudson became a nagging obsession. Soon after his failed attack in June, he directed his chief engineer, Joe Bailey, to begin construction of a mighty fortress atop the bluff his troops had taken from the Rebels during the attack. Dwight was somehow convinced that his project, known as Battery No. 24, would enfilade the Rebel right wing and weaken the Citadel to the point where his infantry could overrun the place. Seventeen pieces of heavy ordnance were to be moved from other points on the line into log redoubts high atop the bluff. "By God," Dwight swore to Bailey, "I'll have an artillery fire that will drive every soul out of this part of Port Hudson." Bailey, who was only a captain, had delusions of grandeur, dreamed of being a general, and was a master at pandering to his superiors. Following Dwight's orders, he went right to work, commandeering gangs of Negroes to work around the clock to build the great fortress Dwight envisioned, and hopefully to win his approval, along with a promotion.[1]

In the early morning hours of June 16, Rebel soldiers woke up seeing the spectacle of the massive earth diggings, log foundations, and protective cotton bales, all piled along the bluff only two hundred yards away. Uncertain of the intention of the Yankees in creating this site, they naturally responded with "sharp rifle fire," but it only lasted a little while. As soon as word of the creation of this great parapet was reported to Franklin Gardner, he ordered the firing stopped. As a competent engineer, he knew that a battery placed here would not create much of a problem for the Citadel. But for every cannon moved to this place, there would be one less in other parts of the line, completely removed from the siege. As the guns ceased, the Federal soldiers and Negro workers who had fled for cover from the enemy fire felt safe in getting back to their labor. They could not help but notice that the ragged Rebel soldiers in "slouched hats and dirty grayish clothes" were sitting idly in plain sight atop their breastworks, watching them work. As the cotton bales were stacked thicker and higher, Bailey began mounting the great guns within the redoubts. Still, the Rebels did not resist. In fact, according to a Federal colonel, enemy spectators "even offered to come over and help us." Such behavior, of course, confused Dwight's officer. Dwight, though, was convinced that the enemy simply did not understand what he intended to do, and bragged, "My building this parapet right before the rebels' eyes is one of the greatest stratagems that ever was." Bailey also failed to understand that the Rebels knew exactly what he was doing and could care less. He was overheard remarking to one of the officers: "I think that the rebels have given up in despair, and if they let me get along a little further with my work, I am the man that'll have the credit of takin' Port Hudson."[2]

Somewhere during the process of building the general's impressive battery, Captain Bailey discovered another opportunity to indulge Dwight's massive ego. He suggested building a kind of bunker near the battery, "A thing that will surely keep you safe," he told him. Bailey envisioned the place as a command post from which Dwight could direct the charges, observe all the action, and be built so formidable that "no cannon can ever shoot through it, and you can sit inside and watch everything through the little loop-holes.... I would not have you expose your precious life," said Bailey in his most solicitous voice. He then went on to describe how he

Union battery overlooking the Citadel, known as "Dwight's great cotton bale battery." Port Hudson State Historic Site Photograph Collection.

would construct the general's safe shelter: "I will make three sides of a log house [and] pile up a great haystack of dirt against the outside of the logs." Describing the inside, he explained: "There is a floor, a table, an easy chair, and other seats; also a strong camp chest, for containing nice things to eat and drink." Beaming at the image of his engineer's idea, Dwight praised him: "Bailey, what a genius you are."[3]

Under Bailey's watchful eye, the structure began to rise from the bluff. Everyone, including sick men, were compelled to work day and night on Dwight's safe house as well as continuing their work on the battery. Government wagons roamed the countryside, gathering the finest logs and confiscating cotton bales from the surrounding plantations. Stout men with axes hewed and cut the choice logs to the lengths and sizes specified by Bailey. The most skilled carpenters in Dwight's division were commandeered to conduct their trade in constructing the bunker's timbered walls. There was also a "small army of Africans" laboring in the hot June sun with picks and spades, shoveling dirt and clay for the protective embankments. As soon as one of the gangs of Negroes began to tire, Bailey ordered in another fresh gang. He demanded silence, and threatened to kill any man that made too much noise and drew the fire of the Rebel guns against his structure. With astonishing speed, Dwight's safe house along with the battery were soon completed.[4]

With the sunrise, Rebel soldiers were astonished to see Dwight's new command post looming large on the bluff near the battery. "What is that?" someone hollered over from the Rebel lines. "Is it an Indian mound? Are you going to have a sacrifice on it?" Indeed, the structure was odd. Now complete, it had the appearance of "a large well packed mound, in the shape of half a globe." Despite its bizarre appearance, Dwight was delighted with his new command post, and "with a peculiar majesty," seated himself in the chair of honor which offered him the option to peer through any one of the three holes that faced the Citadel. Staff officers began filing in and out, congratulating the general and his engineer on the structure, while the quartermaster was busy stowing away an abundant supply of Dwight's favorite whiskey into the camp chest. Thus stocked with liquid courage, Dwight, on Friday, June 26, ordered all seventeen of the big guns of his Battery No. 24 to open fire on the Citadel. He was completely satisfied that a savage bombardment from his cannons would soften up the Rebel stronghold, enabling him to march his troops right into the place, and guarantee his aspiration of becoming the hero of the siege of Port Hudson. Unfortunately, though, when Dwight's guns began thundering from the bluff, very little damage was inflicted on the bastion, and the Rebels simply hunkered down in their log and earthen fortifications out of harm's way. What damage was done was just as quickly repaired. Although the Confederates were not able to answer the cannonade with all of their batteries, cannons commanded by Paul DeGourney tore nineteen holes into the Union flag and wounded the Yankee major who was directing the Federal fire. For the soldiers in blue who watched the cannonade, it became clear that the enemy ramparts were every bit as indestructible as Dwight's safe bunker. "The more of our projectiles that sunk into their parapet the stronger did it become," confessed Colonel Edward Bacon of the Sixth Michigan Regiment. "Nobody knew what a failure his battery was to prove." But as his noisy failure turned into a *notorious* one, a dejected Dwight glumly instructed Bailey to return to the tedious work of digging the zigzagging saps, which were apparently the last and only means of attacking the Citadel.[5]

Work on the major saps, such as the approaches to the Citadel and the Priest Cap, were making steady progress by the latter days of June. The mostly straight-line sap at Fort Desperate, however, would eventually have to be abandoned because of the intense sharpshooting from Arkansas riflemen, whose line of fire was not hampered by the zigzagging pattern of the other saps. However, it was no small wonder that even two of these diggings continued to make progress in approaching Port Hudson, considering the never-ending fire from the Confederate sharpshooters and the routine night attacks of small bands of Rebels who continually burned down the protective cotton bales. Much of the credit for digging the saps, according to Corporal James Hosmer, should have been given to the numerous slaves seized from the many surrounding plantations. "Sambo," as he referred to them, "has the courage to stand close to the rebel rifle pits all the time, and the strength to handle this unyielding earth. These big black fellows, with arms like our legs almost, and with muscle piled in great layers about rib and back, have done the main work." And while the slaves relentlessly labored in the ditches, the Federal soldiers did what they could to provide at least some protection for them. "For the most part," Hosmer claimed, "we have had it for our work to keep sharp watch from our cover, and never allow a rebel head to appear above the opposite parapet." Of course, it was understandable that by this time in the siege the Union soldiers could no longer be counted on to handle the hard labor of digging the saps in the sweltering June sun. "What would have become of us," Hosmer asked, "if the work of the siege had fallen to us to do? I do not know." Physically, they were a spent and worn-down lot. "The gloss of military show had all worn off," wrote Hosmer. "The men were brown—attired as they chose to be—shaggy and stained with their bear-like life in ravines and behind logs." Mentally, too, their spirit was broken: "Our life is a monotony of perilous exposure. The regiment remains in its advanced position, constantly under fire, and occasionally losing a member, killed or wounded."[6]

As the Union lines inched closer and closer to the Rebel parapets, the danger grew in commensurate proportions. Simply moving up to the advanced positions of a newly dug sap where the work was being done was hazardous for the soldiers. Private Frank Flinn of the Thirty-eighth Massachusetts Regiment gave a vivid present-tense account of the perilous journey he and his comrades made to relieve the men of his regiment guarding the sap. *We will now go into the ravine and know what sights and sounds it is our business to be familiar with. First we must creep out of the ravine, through the tops of the prostrated trees. Your head now comes in range of riflemen in the trees over there. A few steps more and we come within full range from the parapet; but do not stop to look. Stoop as low as you can, and run. We soon gain the cover of the woods, and are comparatively safe. Down through a little gully and we enter the beginning of the sap. Behind the angle is the station of the ambulance men. They wait there, day and night, with stretchers ready. Three or four a day out of the brigade and working party are carried out. We pass out into the sap. Here is the most dangerous point of all, just at the entrance. You can see how the rebel parapet commanded it. 'Tis just in front, with an old shot-pierced building behind it, and white sand-bags laying on top of the tawny slope. Every day or two, there is a sharp-eyed Mississippian with his rifle pointed through some chink. The trench goes under a large trunk, stretching from bank to bank, and from here we are tolerable safe. Only tolerably. The sap is here about six feet wide, and four feet deep, dug out of the hard soil, the dirt being thrown out on the side toward the enemy, forming a bank rising about five feet from the surface, and therefore about nine feet above the bottom of the trench. Here, now, are our boys, the few that are left, barely twenty.*[7]

While the Union troops and slaves worked on the zigzagging ditches day after day, the Southerners were busy conducting numerous trench raids, skirmishes, and defensive precautions to impede their progress and discourage an assault. On the Confederate right, where Dwight was advancing his ditches, fifty Louisiana men from Miles's Legion, led by a young lieutenant named Bankston, ventured out in the predawn darkness on June 20 and succeeded in driving off a greatly superior advance force of Yankees threatening the Citadel. At the Priest Cap, on the Confederate left, the Union diggings were drawing dangerously close to the position occupied by the First Mississippi Regiment under Colonel Steedman's command. Preparing for an assault, Lieutenant Fred Dabney, an engineer, supervised the construction of a daunting and elaborate defense system in front of the salient angle of their line. There the Mississippians planted a large number of sharpened stakes, known as *chevaux-de-frise*, which were all frowning towards the enemy approaches. Throughout the maze of stakes, wires were stretched about a foot and a half from the ground to trip any charging soldiers. Added to that were artillery shells or torpedoes, attached to fuses, and buried like land mines, set to blow up any intruding Yankees brave enough to attack. Still, the bluecoats continued to advance their ditches, and were protected behind huge cotton bales they used as cover while they worked. On the twenty-fifth of June, Corporal L.H. Skelton volunteered to risk the enemy fire, venture out alone, and set the cotton bales on fire. It was an adventurous undertaking, requiring Skelton to crawl from the breastworks in broad daylight, light the bales, and hold off the Federals with his Enfield rifle until the fire was sufficiently blazing, then somehow manage to return to the Rebel lines. This he did, successfully and without being wounded, which earned him the thanks and praises of General Gardner, who was astonished by the corporal's courage and determination.[8]

Behind the Confederate lines, life was getting worse for the soldiers. For many days the troops had been on half rations, and on June 29, the last small ration of beef was issued to them. It did not take long before hungry men became desperate men, hence the next day the first mule was killed, butchered and served as an experiment in the limits which men would go to satisfy their famished stomachs. "All those who partook of it spoke highly of the dish," claimed John Kendall, a Louisiana officer. Horses, too, were slaughtered and eaten, but the men insisted that the larger beasts were "not equal to mule." So, from that time on, the demand for the dark, coarse, mule meat increased, adding to the number of them killed each day, and dwindling the number left. But despite the preference for mule over no meat at all, some of the men simply refused to eat it. "We have no meat but mule and horse flesh," wrote Colonel Steedman in a letter to his uncle. "Many are eating it, but many prefer to live entirely upon peas, bread and molasses." "Rats," remembered Kendall, "of which there were plenty ... were also caught by many officers and men, and their flesh was found to be a luxury." Soldiers who were sick or wounded in the hospitals had the good fortune to be served rat meat although they were misled into believing it was squirrel. By this point, the corn supply was almost gone, too. In fact, hardly anything was left except cowpeas, sugar and molasses. But the peas were so infested with weevils that they were considered unfit for human consumption. In the hope that the corn supply might be conserved a little longer, the peas were fed to the animals, and it was not surprising that a few of them died from eating them. "Starvation began to stare us in the face," recalled Crawford Jackson, an Alabama sergeant. "Many a time did I see a scuffle and a fight between the veterans for the possession of a rat," and such desperation was not limited to the private soldiers. No one, including the commanding general, escaped the emptiness of the famine. In those last days, remembered Jackson, "All that was seen on Gen. Gardner's table were a few broiled rats, sugar and weevilly [sic] peas." Soon there would be nothing. Diarist R. L. McClung admitted that before it was over he and his comrades had eaten "all the beef—all the mules—all the dogs—and all the rats."[9]

Indeed, the Rebel soldiers at Port Hudson could not have consumed much of what they did without an appetite inflated by intense hunger and stomachs hardened by continuous abuse. Upriver, at Vicksburg, the lack of food was also severe, and hungry men were known to eat just about any living creature, big or small, having a pulse. Nothing was safe. One regiment of Missourians at Vicksburg had supposedly acquired a camel that had been used as an army transport animal before the war, and adopted him as their mascot. He was described as a "quiet, peaceful fellow, and a general favorite." Unfortunately—or fortunately, depending on their perspective and hunger—he was killed one day by a Yankee sniper and quickly carved up, cooked and eaten. Although the troops at Vicksburg endured much deprivation, their experience with starvation did not rise to the level of that at Port Hudson. In fact, it was not until July 3 that the butchering of mules was officially ordered at Vicksburg. Unofficially, however, the men did partake of dogs, horses, rats and mules prior to that time. The threat of starvation prodded hungry Confederates everywhere to innovate, adapt, and experiment. Many would at least try to consume things that, before the war, they would have never considered ingesting. Private Sam Watkins, who was nowhere near Port Hudson or Vicksburg, heard about the men at Vicksburg subsisting on rats and, like Rebel soldiers elsewhere in the South, he was hungry. Watkins and his mess mates decided they would go "rat hunting." They succeeded in finding one that was "old and gray" residing in an outhouse, and proceeded to chase him. "We were determined to have that rat," remembered Watkins. "After hard work we caught him. We skinned him, and washed and salted him, buttered and peppered him, and fried him. He actually looked nice. The delicate aroma of the frying rat came to our hungry nostrils. We were keen to eat a piece of rat; our teeth were on edge; yea even our mouth watered to eat a piece of rat." But when it was done and Watkins "raised the piece of rat to my mouth," he began to think about the rat—the tail especially—and his mind overcame his hunger. "I had lost my appetite," he confessed. "It was my first and last effort to eat dead rats."[10]

For those at Port Hudson who could not stomach the thought of mules, dogs and rats, they had little choice but to subsist on a diet of peas. However, besides being infested with weevils, there were, in the opinion of Daniel Smith, an Alabama artilleryman, other serious impediments to consider before resorting to that vegetable. "The peas were stored in bulk on the floor of the church, and the concussion of the bombardment had broken in every pane of glass in the building. This in comminuted form, was mingled with the peas; and it was no unusual incident to be made painfully aware of its presence in masticating the peas." Other times, chicanery was necessary to tempt the starving soldiers into eating what they ordinarily could not swallow. Smith told of one such incident when "an unexpected discovery was made of sixty barrels of corned beef. Some wonder was expressed as to this windfall, but it was accepted, eaten in good faith and pronounced excellent. It was not until after the surrender that those who ate it knew that it was carefully corned mule."[11]

Beyond the gnawing emptiness of being hungry, the men continued living their lives smothered in the thick, humid air of South Louisiana and baking under its brutal sun. More and more of the Southerners became sick, suffering through the effects of various stages of sunstroke, dysentery, malaria and other fevers. However, fewer of them reported to the camp hospitals, since there was little the doctors could do for them. Effective cures for the killer fevers were still unknown, and the supply of medicines within Port Hudson, such as quinine, had long since been exhausted. Moreover, because there were no reserves to take their places on the line, the sick, like everyone else, had to remain at their posts in a constant state of vigilance. If they needed rest and recuperation, they were forced to find it within the filthy ditches. Those suffering from wounds that required surgery, such as an amputation, were compelled to endure it without an anesthetic. Remembering the conditions that he and his comrades endured during the siege, a compassionate soldier recalled their ordeal with these words: "With no shoes, bareheaded, a ragged shirt or jacket, pants in patches, and nothing to eat except sugar, weevilly [sic] peas, mule meat and rats, they lay at their post, unprotected from the rays of a June and July sun."[12]

Taken together—the sickness, the lack of food, medicine, clothing, the heat, the insects (especially lice), the filth, the hard labor, and the constant perils of war—it was no small wonder that anyone continued to endure, day after day. It took a hard man to survive such deprivations and hardships. Within the confines of Port Hudson, such men clearly existed. They were not the sons of affluent planters. These were the private soldiers, the rank and file. For the most part, they came from agrarian backgrounds and rural communities, and had led hardscrabble lives before the war. They came off small farms where they had followed a mule and plow, forcing the dirt to pay with their sweat. Others were backwoodsmen, hunters, fishermen, millers or mechanics. Whatever their backgrounds, most were proficient with a weapon, as they were practically born with a shotgun or pistol in their hands. Although many were illiterate or semi-literate, they were adept at milking cows, slopping hogs, tracking wild game and combing the woods for edible plants. In short, they knew how to live off the land and scrounge the barest essentials from it. As a self-sufficient, independent breed of men, these Southerners had naturally developed a sort of inner strength, an indomitable spirit that gave them the will to persevere.

When the War Between the States broke out, they found themselves in the Confederate army. Many of them, seeking a daring adventure, had enlisted for the duration of the war, and were already veterans of many bloody battlefields, such as Shiloh and Stones River. Others, whose families depended on them for survival, remained home until they were forced into the service of the Confederacy by the Conscription Act of 1862. In either case, however, the loyalties of these men were mainly to their people, their particular communities, and each other. They had little, if any, interests in political abstracts such as state's rights or the various differences that might arise in a democratic government. Very few of them owned slaves, nor did they especially care anything about the plight of the black man. Thus, like their poor Yankee cousins, they had little interest in fighting and dying for or against that institution. Yet within the Southern psyche there was a certain inclination towards violence and fighting. That, of course, was inculcated in them as a by-product or result of their personal hardships. They were a people who were raised to survive, and instilled with the aggressiveness to do so. While it may have seemed an odd characteristic for such an impoverished people, most harbored a deep sense of honor, pride and self-respect. Southerners seemed to have also shared an inherent do-or-die kind of creed where no affront was to be left unanswered. And it was only natural that their differences were usually settled with fists, knives, or more often, guns. Thus, when something as traumatic as a national insurrection broke out, they fought. But rarely did they fight for those causes explained within the covers of the history books. For most of them, the reasons to fight were simple and uncomplicated: to bond with their people, to protect the man beside them. And perhaps there was an even less pretentious reason: there were soldiers from another place, strangers, tearing down their fences, trespassing on their land, stomping down their corn, and stealing their chickens and pigs. That was a provocation they could not and would not abide without a fight.[13]

Otherwise, the character of the Southerners was much the same as that of their Northern brothers. Qualities ranged from the very righteous to the wicked, but the vast majority of them could only be thought of as decent men. Yet, crowding them together in the awful conditions that were typical in wartime, especially a siege, brought out sides of their nature which had heretofore never been revealed. Deprived of whatever civilization they had known or been accustomed to, the true characters of the men—good, bad, brave or cowardly—were suddenly exposed. What's more, men discovered hidden traits in each other, sometimes virtuous, sometimes villainous, which they could have never imagined. At times those traits were magnified. Good men became better men and the mean became meaner. But whatever their natures, every man, whether from the North or South, shared many of the same miseries. For the besieged Southerners, those miseries were at least mitigated with the hope that the Yankee legions surrounding them would somehow be turned back, and they would be free from the suffering internment of Port Hudson. Yet they knew it would require a miracle to drive Banks away from the confines of Port Hudson. For the siege to be lifted there were only two remote and unlikely possibilities. Either Joe Johnston's army had to come from Jackson and relieve them, or—an even more unlikely chance—that Richard Taylor's small force might begin threatening New Orleans, compelling Banks to draw off his army and defend that city.[14]

As the days passed, hopes of a rescue continued to diminish. By June 27, the Rebels within Port Hudson had finally abandoned all hope of receiving any help. Such hope was lost the night before when the valiant Robert Pruyn, who Gardner had sent to General Johnston in Jackson with a plea for help, returned with the despairing reply that no aid would be forthcoming. Yet, the fact that Pruyn returned to the garrison at all was incredible since he was the first of Gardner's messengers to safely get back from Jackson with word from Johnston. Pruyn's return trip was every bit as exciting and courageous as the first one to Jackson on June 11. After retrieving the dozen canteens he had hidden and left behind after his initial trip, Pruyn once again tied them together, creating a life preserver to float himself down the river. Landing on the west side opposite Port Hudson, he crawled a quarter mile on his hands and knees through the enemy lines. At one point he was seen by a group of Federal officers on horseback. Even though he was carrying two pistols with him, he had the "presence of mind" to immediately sit down on a log and begin whittling on a stick. At that moment the officers thought he was only a teamster or maybe one of their own from camp, and paid no further attention to him. At dusk, the resourceful Pruyn spotted a group of Federal soldiers going to the river for water and began walking alongside them. Pruyn then lingered at the riverbank until the soldiers returned to camp. Then he stripped off his civilian clothes, dove into the river, and swam against a strong current to the Confederate side of the Mississippi. Rebel soldiers, who later heard the remarkable tale of his journey, were amazed, but saddened by the news that they would have to brace themselves for what they were afraid might be their last stand.[15]

Despite the depressing realization that any practical chance of rescue had come to an end, the Southerners vowed to fight on with grim determination. With the Union saps at both the Priest Cap and the Citadel drawing dangerously close to the fortifications of Port Hudson, the Rebels continued to attempt to burn down the cotton bales being used to protect the Yankee work parties. Skirmishes and sneak attacks were still conducted by both sides. Nothing really changed. Desperate men, blue and gray, tormented each other by lobbing hand grenades, or artillery shells attached to burning fuses, into each other's ditches. At times, Yankee raiding parties even managed to scale the parapets and get inside the Rebel works, only to be slaughtered by rifle fire or in hand-to-hand combat.[16]

After three days of constantly shelling the Citadel, General William Dwight once again decided to assault the Rebel works and establish his place in history as the hero of the Port Hudson siege. The plan of attack was made by Dwight and his staff on the night of June 28, during a roaring midnight drunk. As in the previous failures, the tactic called for a huge artillery barrage, followed by an early morning onslaught of the Rebel fortifications by the One Hundred and Sixty-fifth Regiment of New York Zouaves and the Sixth Michigan Regiment. Dwight named General Franklin Nickerson, a prewar lawyer from Maine with the U.S. Customs Department, to command the attack. Unfortunately, the Sixth Michigan had to go into battle without their disillusioned commander, Lieutenant Colonel Edward Bacon, who along with the commander of the Fourteenth Maine, had been put under house arrest by Dwight for "speaking in a discouraging manner of the prospects of this army." It was obvious, by now, that any officer with the temerity to question Dwight about the sanity of his decision to launch another of the ill-fated attacks which had already failed twice would be punished.[17]

Yet the morning of June 29 came and went without an order from General Dwight to commence the attack. It seemed that following the revelry of the drunken planning session, Dwight, had continued to consume still more copious amounts of whiskey, and had somehow lost track of time. Thus it was five o'clock in the afternoon before he regained enough conscious sobriety to actually order the assault to begin. It was no surprise that the assault came to be known throughout Dwight's command as the infamous "Whisky Charge." "Charge, and keep on charging as long as you have a corporal's guard left," he told Nickerson, who, according to one account, "had prepared himself for it by imbibing at the safe [Dwight's bunker or command post] large quantities of the spirit of command." Soon, the two regiments began moving through a long, deep sap leading to the foot of the hill below the Citadel. Their ranks had been depleted because of battle losses and sickness, and they only numbered about three hundred men. Waiting for their charge, the Rebels had seven hundred men defending the Citadel and, according to a participant, Nickerson was informed of this disparity by a Rebel deserter, but being fortified with the "spirit of command," chose to ignore it. So it came as no surprise that as soon as the Michigan men and New York Zouaves started up the hill, the fire from the Rebel rifles was so devastating that they began hugging the ground for cover. One of the Michigan lieutenants remembered that "whoever rose up was shot. No orders of any kind, and no reinforcements came." Lying among the dead and wounded, they clung to the awful hillside throughout the night while Dwight, who was drunk again, cowered in his bunker, peering out for some sign of success, and Nickerson, in the same condition, remained hidden in a trench.[18]

Just before dawn on June 30, with no orders from their generals, the Federal soldiers realized they must get off the hillside or be killed. Even though there were no orders granting them permission to retreat, they began leaving one at a time. Some, however, stayed, "lying among the dead bodies and pools of blood" until the middle of the day when the last of them, driven by desperation, fled from the hill. In the afternoon, Dwight, who had retired to his quarters to sleep it off, reappeared at the bunker accompanied by "his jug-bearers," and gave orders for the same two regiments to charge the Citadel again. And once again, the remnants of the Sixth Michigan and the New York Zouaves rushed up the hill. Just as before, they were mowed down in the advance, but this time some of the Federals actually managed to get over the Rebel fortifications and into their trenches. "A hand-to-hand encounter ensued," recalled a Rebel officer, as both sides were "shouting and using their guns as clubs. Federals and Confederates were killed there within six feet of each other." Soon, the defending Rebels were joined by Louisiana and Arkansas reinforcements, who caught the Federals in a cross fire and drove them back. Of those blue-coats who managed to get into the Confederate trenches, none survived, and according to Lieutenant John Kendall of the Fourth Louisiana Regiment, "Fully half the assailants fell in the few minutes during which the attack lasted." For the Southerners, the attack did not rise to the level of a serious threat. In fact, O.P. Lyles, the colonel commanding the Confederate right wing, told Gardner afterwards, "I can repulse him [the enemy] every time, and will do it." For the Federal soldiers who survived and managed to return, they were met by a bitter and cursing Dwight, who immediately accused them of disobeying his orders to take the Citadel.[19]

Dwight then retreated into his bunker with his personal staff for another inebriated council of war. Hours passed before he emerged, sending orderlies scurrying with messages that ordered all officers of every regiment to assemble before him at his bunker. As they arrived, one officer recalled: "Dwight sat full of whisky in his safe [bunker], like an ugly little heathen god in his pagoda." He then proceeded with his prepared speech, the highlights of which follow: "The Citadel is no longer tenable by the enemy. To take the Citadel is nothing ... you will have to take it with a rush. It is to be done immediately. Never stop until you get orders from me, for I am going to take Port Hudson by storm this very night. I order you to pay no attention to any fire that may be opened upon you. No, you are to rush forward with a shout, and carry those interior works at the point of the bayonet. The enemy will think there is a perfect earthquake, and will fly in all directions before you." Dwight then admonished the officers with the caveat "Let no man forget he is under my eye. I am the only general in this army who knows how to enforce discipline." Execution, he warned, awaited "every man who retreats without my permission." That said, Dwight dismissed them, "Go execute my orders, and in the morning Port Hudson surrenders to me."[20]

The remnants of Dwight's battered regiments once again filed into the trenches. Morose expressions appeared on the faces of the demoralized men as they prepared for what they knew would be another defeat and waste of lives. "Every man felt as if he was under sentence of death," said one officer, "and the whole affair was only a military execution in disguise." But suddenly some of the officers began calling a halt to the operation. It then became apparent that General Banks had somehow learned of the bloody debacle which had been going on for the last two days, and had sent orders for Dwight to cease the pointless attacks. Only then did Dwight end his quest to be the hero of Port Hudson and earn a promotion to major general. Among the spared troops of the debacle, a lieutenant gave a summary of the feelings of the men in evaluating their ordeal: "'*The Whisky Charge*,'" he snapped in disgust, "a name likely to be remembered by those who know what quantities of the fire-water were consumed at the safe. I think that recent events ... tend to prove our General's greatest merit, namely, that his absurdities are likely to defeat his wickedness."[21]

CHAPTER TEN

Submission

As the month of July began, Nathaniel Banks's quandaries persisted. Morale of his troops—especially the nine-month volunteers—continued to worsen. Grumbling soldiers refused to perform any duty involving danger, while others spurned duty of any kind. Such conduct, in Banks's words, caused "great embarrassment and trouble." Open mutiny finally broke out in the Fourth Massachusetts Regiment, forcing Banks to disarm those soldiers, court-martial the ringleaders, and threaten the rest with hard labor or death. Though most of them did return to duty, the regiments made up of nine-month volunteers remained dissatisfied and demanded to go home as soon as their time was up. But without the twenty-two regiments of these volunteers, Banks's strength would be reduced to less than 10,000 men. Worse still, he knew that by the end of August all of the enlistments of those regiments would be expired. He also knew that if that loss of men were to spell defeat for him at Port Hudson it would mean the end of his political aspirations. It troubled him to think that those aspirations may have already suffered irreparable harm, considering how long the siege had lasted, together with the horrific loss of lives the campaign had cost. To this point, the butcher's bill was appalling, with the latest casualty count climbing to more than 4,000 men.[1]

Banks confessed most of these problems to his superiors in Washington. In a letter to Henry Halleck he explained; "the reduction of Port Hudson has required a longer time than at first supposed." The underlying source for most of his problems, of course, was mired in the fact that Banks had completely failed to appreciate the difficulties in taking a strongly fortified position. This he admitted. But there were other troubles which Halleck and others would not understand or even care about. His generals, especially the West Point graduates, had not always been cooperative. Many of them resented him because he did not have a military education, and most of them disliked the idea of taking orders from a politician. Others, such as William Dwight, were not only incompetent, but their principal interest was in personal enrichment through confiscating Confederate

Chapter Ten. Submission 133

cotton, or in gaining fame by landing an undeserved promotion. That aside, after two major defeats on May 27 and June 14, followed by a dozen or so smaller losses, the rank-and-file soldiers, especially those with short enlistments, had lost confidence in him, something he sensed but could never admit. On top of all that, Banks could never seem to solve the problem of the Confederate cavalry, a scourge that continued to haunt his army. Since the siege had begun, the gray horsemen had disrupted his supply lines, killed or captured many of his soldiers, stolen his ammunition and provisions, and even kidnapped one of his generals, an embarrassing incident even though the loss of Neal Dow was welcomed by his own men. Now Banks could only hope that Port Hudson would fall before the Rebel riders could strike again.[2]

But they did strike again. On the morning of July 2 at daylight, Rebel cavalry from Colonel Frank Powers's command suddenly appeared on the Springfield Road, galloping towards the river landing and the main Union supply depot, which was located about seven miles south of Port Hudson. The riders numbered about two hundred and were divided into three groups of men. To protect this important depot Banks had assigned an entire regiment, the 162nd New York, and a detachment of the 16th New Hampshire. Although they knew the enemy horsemen were nearby, they were totally surprised. With no warning, the first group of Rebel cavalry, numbering about fifty, thundered into a squad of thirty armed Colored troops, supposedly on guard duty, but who were still in their tents. The Rebel horseman, carrying bottles of turpentine, began setting them afire and tossing them. Within a few seconds of the commotion, piles of quartermaster and commissary stores were burning in flames. The buildings housing the records were then torched, and total bedlam ensued as frantic officers and men, seeking safety, dashed aboard the steamer *Suffolk*, which churned off into the river for safety. At the same time, raiders from the second party tore through the crude huts that housed the contraband slaves who worked at the landing. In a wild panic, black men, women and children began running into the woods or jumping into the river, where some of them drowned. A Rebel cavalryman described the chaotic sight in his memoirs: "In the glare of the flames men and horses took unnatural shapes, as they dashed to and fro, back and forth under an intense excitement, adding still more to the demon-like scene."[3]

The third and largest party of Rebel raiders attacked the commissary. By this time, however, the New York regiment had rallied, and moved at the double quick towards the levee. Fire from those infantrymen, together with the shells from a gunboat in the river, emptied some Southerners' saddles and forced them to withdraw. But on the road out they still managed to capture a number of the pickets as prisoners. By eleven o'clock the raiders were gone. Sadly, though, the damage was done. It was estimated that over a million dollars in provisions and equipment from the commissary and quartermaster's stores had been destroyed, including a hundred wagons. In terms of human losses, Logan reported killing or wounding 140 Union men, and taking 35 prisoners, while he claimed to have suffered only 15 losses. The next afternoon Richard Irwin, the adjutant general, visited the sight and reported the entire ordeal to Banks, while at the same time imputing the blame as he saw it. "I attribute the surprise entirely to the negligence of the picket in allowing itself to be taken without a shot by an enemy who could not approach within 100 yards without being in sight." Nevertheless, for Banks, the culpability issue was only an afterthought. For him, the raid was just another curse added to an ever-increasing heap of troubles.[4]

The next day was a Saturday, the Fourth of July. Inside Port Hudson, Confederate soldiers, instead of celebrating, passed the day wondering how much longer they could hold out. Most of them, including General Gardner, were not optimistic. However, there was one group of officers, which included Louisianan John Kendall, who were actually having a celebration dinner. A young Negro boy named Charlie who cooked for them had appeared at mealtime with a huge steak, covering a large fine china dish one of the officers had furnished. Looking "juicy and tender," they asked where it had come from since the supply of beef had been exhausted for days. A great smile then stretched across Charlie's face, and he proudly replied: "It was cut from a black pony belonging to General Miles." Although one man abruptly excused himself from the table, Kendall admitted, "The rest of us ate without any qualms."[5]

Across the long line of ditches, behind the Union lines, Henry Gardner penned a letter to his parents on the Fourth of July: "We are still *before* Port Hudson instead of *in* Port Hudson, and General Banks's promise of a dinner within the works [by the Fourth of July] has turned out to be an idle one." What's more, within the ranks there was the dreaded realization that Banks was about to order another attack. "We imagined the 4th of July would be the day, but it was not," recalled Corporal James Hosmer, who had, by now, accepted the grim truth: "There is no going home for us till the place falls." Henry Johns, a Massachusetts soldier, felt that Banks had delayed the attack for a good reason: "We conclude that he [Banks] believes the enemy has eaten nearly all his mules, and that he can safely wait a few days for starvation to do the work of an assault. I hope he is right." Then, reflecting on the bloody attacks they had already made, he said: "There are full enough precious graves here, full enough loyal hearts whose saddest recollection will twine about these graves." Indeed, most of the troops would have agreed with that opinion. They all shared an impatience for the Rebel garrison to surrender and a discontent that it had not, but there was still a holiday spirit among them on this the eighty-seventh anniversary of Independence Day. The fact that all military operations were suspended on this day and liquor was distributed to the men probably accounted for a great many lifted spirits. Johns, too, was inspired by a patriotic feeling as expressed in a letter home dated July 6: "We wanted to connect the surrender of this place with the hallowed memories of the 4th of July." He went on to relate how a battery of "unshotted" [sic] guns had been fired as a salute announcing the National Anniversary to the Rebels across the way, and reminding them that this was a fight for the Union: "The thirty-four guns rang out to them our proud assertion that every state was yet in the Union, and while we had a cannon or a man left, all should stay there."[6]

Banks spent that Independence Day planning, much like he had spent every other day. Taking Port Hudson had become his obsession and now he was preparing for what he believed would be the final death blow to the Confederates within that bastion. The subterranean tunnels under the Citadel and Priest Cap were quickly nearing completion. Within a few days they would be finished, and explosives would be loaded into the mines. Corporal Hosmer remembered walking through one of the zigzagging saps and encountering one of the mines, which he described in his memoirs: "A hole about four feet square, where a party of men were burrowing under the enemy's earthwork. I stooped and looked in at the mouth. Negroes, on their knees, were working there by candlelight excavating a place in which are to be put kegs of powder. It was a perilous place." Hundreds of pounds of powder would soon be placed into the two mines and exploded on command, signaling the men of the "Forlorn Hope" to charge into the ruptured Rebel lines, followed by the rest of Banks's army. Although he experienced a couple of delays, Banks finally succeeded in scheduling a third grand attack, which was planned to take place on July 9.[7]

But for Banks and his weary soldiers, that attack would fortunately never take place. On the Fourth of July, 135 winding miles up the Mississippi River, another event beyond their control had taken place at the town of Vicksburg. Although Banks and his men did not know because they could not know, at ten o'clock on the morning of the Fourth long gray lines of ragged Rebels began a sullen march out of their fortifications under white flags, surrendering that all-important river city. John Pemberton and his Confederate army had fought with a grim determination but, like their compatriots in Port Hudson, they had endured too much death, suffering and starvation. Pemberton, supported by his generals, felt that further resistance was hopeless and, for them, no other recourse but capitulation existed. After the surrender, Ulysses Grant, a man who had never been given to melodramatic prose, sat down and wrote a bland dispatch to Banks. It was vintage Grant, beginning with the lucid, pithy seven-word announcement: "The garrison of Vicksburg surrendered this morning." The dispatch was given to Colonel Kilby Smith of Grant's staff, who boarded the Union gunboat *General Price* with orders to personally deliver the news to Banks. On the morning of July 7, shortly before eleven o'clock, Smith arrived at Port Hudson and handed the welcomed news to Banks.[8]

Soon the telegraph wires were buzzing, and all the division commanders were notified of the good news. They in turn sent their staff officers rushing off to the ditches where the word was spread. Wild cheering and howls bellowed forth from the throats of Union soldiers, and laughter was heard from men who had almost forgotten the sound of it. Out on the river, gunboats began firing salutes, and up and down the Union lines regimental bands that had rarely played a tune broke out in patriotic songs. Looking back on the moment, Richard Irwin of Banks's staff wrote: "From man to man, from company to company, from regiment to regiment, the word passed, and as it passed, once more the cheers of the soldiers of the Union rang out, and again the forest echoed with the strains of "The Star-Spangled Banner" from the long-silent bands. Many a rough cheek, unused to tears, was wet that morning, and the sound of laughter was heard from many lips that had long been set in silence; but when the first thrill was spent, it gave way to a deep-drawn sigh of relief." A New England sergeant's joy was evident in his diary entry of July 8: "It was told to us that Port Hudson had unconditionally surrendered. Imagine all the enthusiasm of thousands of men, who had been watching and waiting for weeks and months for this moment; imagine anything and everything, but the reality can never be described." Over the dirty banks of the parapets and ditches, jubilant Yankee soldiers shouted the news out to the Rebels across the way. The nine-month soldiers knew they would soon be heading for home, and one Massachusetts man recalled his joy: "Home! Can any outside the army imagine what this word means to us who have lain so many weary weeks in the swamps of Louisiana watching the lines of the enemy with the eyes of hungry wolves, dying by hundreds, by bullet, and shell, and disease?" Some of the Union officers wrapped their dispatches around dirt clods or sticks and slung them into the enemy ditches. At first, the Southerners were incredulous, and could not or would not believe it. One suspicious Arkansas officer, who was handed a scrap of paper bearing the news of Vicksburg's surrender, hollered for everyone to hear: "This is another damned Yankee lie."[9]

Throughout the day on Tuesday, July 7, Confederate soldiers listened to the constant sounds of the Yankee celebration. After a while, they began to come to grips with the reality that there might be truth in the hateful news. "As the darkness of night approached, no sound could be heard within our lines," remembered Crawford Jackson, an officer on Gardner's staff, "silence and sadness reigned supreme." Every defender realized that with the fall of Vicksburg Grant would now be left free to join Banks in an overwhelming attack against them. They also suspected that there was no military reason to continue trying to defend Port Hudson if Vicksburg had indeed fallen, especially with a garrison of men who were facing starvation. Perhaps no one appreciated this predicament as much as their commander, General Franklin Gardner, who according to Crawford Jackson, spent the early evening hours sitting with members of his staff on the portico of the house that served as the general's headquarters. Smoking a pipe, Gardner was deep in thought, pondering the situation. "About 12 o'clock he came into my room," recalled Jackson, "and gently laying his hands on me to get up and come into his office." The general then instructed Jackson to sit down and write the unit commanders with a summons: "I wish to see them at headquarters immediately." As soon as they arrived the meeting began, and it lasted only a few minutes. About two o'clock in the morning of July 8, Gardner dispatched a messenger under a flag of truce, asking Banks for an official statement from Grant, which would confirm the surrender of Vicksburg. Banks, of course, quickly complied, providing him with a copy of the letter from Grant that Kilby Smith had delivered.[10]

After receiving the confirmation, Gardner sent another dispatch to Banks asking for a "cessation of hostilities" and proposing a meeting between a commission of three officers chosen from each side to discuss and draw up the terms of surrender. At nine o'clock on the morning of July 8, the commissioners met in a tent between the lines under a shady grove of magnolia trees. Banks was represented by Colonel Henry Birge, commander of the "Forlorn Hope," and Generals Charles Stone and William Dwight. Gardner appointed three of his colonels, Isaiah Steedman, William Miles and Marshall Smith, as his commissioners. By two o'clock in the afternoon, the paperwork for an unconditional surrender was complete. Gardner would be compelled to turn over the garrison of Port Hudson, together with all its weapons and other materials of war. The Officers and men were to be treated as prisoners of war, although the enlisted men would soon be paroled and sent to their homes. After the articles of surrender were signed and approved, a long wagon train loaded with food, medicine and supplies for the starving Rebels began rumbling down the Plains Store Road and into Port Hudson. Because it was so late in the day, the formal ceremony was postponed until seven a.m. on July 9, when the Southerners were to line up, stack their arms, and surrender their colors.[11]

On this same day, Wednesday, July 8, Gardner reluctantly issued his last order to his troops. The following memorandum was circulated among the men that defended Port Hudson:

General Orders No. 61

I. Nobly have the troops performed their duty in the defence of this position, continued from the 21st of May to the present date. The cheerfulness, bravery and zeal displayed by the troops during the hardships and suffering of this long siege has never been surpassed, and every man can feel the proud satisfaction that he has done his part in the heroic defence of Port Hudson. This place is surrendered at the last moment it is proper to hold it and after a most gallant defence in several severe attacks in of which the enemy have been signally repulsed. Let all continue, during the duties that still remain to be performed, to show that cheerful obedience which has distinguished them as soldiers up to this time.

II. The troops will be paraded at 6 o'clock a.m. tomorrow, for surrender, in line of battle in the same order as they are now at the breastworks, with the heavy artillery on the right. In the edge of the prairie, in rear of the railroad depot; the left extending towards the town of Port Hudson. All officers and men will be in their places under arms.

By command of Major Gen. Frank Gardner.[12]

Between the time of the commissioners' meeting on July 8, and the official surrender on July 9, a few of the officers managed to escape. A getaway from a place as heavily surrounded as Port Hudson was a dangerous venture. But the officers that attempted it believed it was worth the chance to avoid the horror of a Northern prison camp such as that at Johnson's Island, Ohio, where many of them would probably be sent. Among those who successfully escaped was the daring Captain Robert Pruyn, who had already proven his skill at escaping when he delivered the dispatch from Gardner to Johnston. Joining Pruyn this time was Captain Ben Burnett. Just as Pruyn had done in his earlier venture, the men swam the Mississippi River on the night of July 8 and made their way to Mobile, Alabama. Another daring escape was accomplished by Sergeant Crawford Jackson of Gardner's staff, who masqueraded as a Union officer and galloped his horse through line after line of Yankee sentries, deceiving all of them with his bold charade. Others, too, made it out by slowly crawling through the darkness of night to the cover of the woods and swamps and eventually finding their way to the safety of the Confederate cavalry.[13]

On the morning of July 9, precisely at seven o'clock, a long column of blue coated soldiers marched up the Jackson Road and into the fortifications of Port Hudson. Riding at the head of that formation was the distinguished George Andrews, Banks's chief of staff, followed by Colonel Henry Birge and his storm troopers of the "Forlorn Hope." Behind them paraded a number of honored regiments representing the four divisions of the Nineteenth Corps. The Confederate troops were grimly standing in a long line with General Gardner in front. At Gardner's command to "ground arms," every soldier bowed his head and placed his rifle on the ground in a "token of submission." As was the custom, Gardner then attempted to surrender his sword to Andrews, who declined to accept it, saying: "I return your sword as a proper compliment to the gallant commander of such gallant troops—conduct that would be heroic in another cause." Gardner simply returned his sword to its scabbard and curtly replied: "This is neither the time nor place to discuss the cause." Then a long silence settled over the scene as the Federal troops had previously been instructed not to cheer. Albert Plummer, a soldier in one of the honored Massachusetts regiments, remembered, "The rebels were drawn up in line with General Gardner at their head, the right resting near the railroad station.... It was a very affecting sight, and there was no man in the victorious army who did not experience a feeling of pity go out to the brave men who had been compelled to surrender after so long and so brilliant a defense." Sometime during the next hour the Stars and Bars flying over Port Hudson was hauled down, and the Stars and Stripes of the United States was hoisted up the flagstaff, followed by a booming salute from a nearby Yankee battery. Finally, the entire Rebel garrison slowly filed away as prisoners of war, ending the ceremony.[14]

Following the formal ritual of surrender, the Rebel enlisted men returned to Port Hudson to await their paroles. Although the Southern officers generally maintained a proud attitude of reserved hostility, the private Rebel soldiers began fraternizing with their counterparts in blue. They swapped stories about their ordeals during the siege, and even did a

Artist's illustration depicting the formal surrender at Port Hudson, as the two lines faced each other and the Confederate soldiers ground arms. Port Hudson State Historic Site Photograph Collection, from *Harper's Weekly*.

little trading, although the Rebels had very little to trade except corn beer and buttons off their uniforms, which the Union soldiers took as tokens and souvenirs. But even though they had nothing of value, the Southerners' spirits continued to improve as medical care was given to the sick and wounded, and food was provided to the starving men. It was, in fact, the first time in days when they had been able to satisfy their hunger with a decent meal.[15]

With the surrender of Port Hudson, there was little left for the Yankee soldiers to do except to satisfy their curiosity over the people and place they had spent so much time fighting. A week following the surrender of the garrison, the Third Massachusetts Cavalry was allowed to tour the interior of the fort. "The men looked about with great interest," according to James Ewer, who was appalled at the wretched sights. "Scenes of desolation and ruin were on every hand. Dead horses and mules remained unburied or only partially covered. Broken bits of shell were seen scattered over the ground. Great guns disabled, and gun carriages broken, were found at every angle of the fort; while the buildings were torn by shot and shell; with many in ruins. Little ammunition was found; but many rifles. They lay in huge piles like those of cordwood. They were well worn and rusty." Ewer, who would spend his postwar years in the ministry as a reverend, felt compassion for the five hundred sick and wounded Confederate they discovered during their excursion. "In the hospitals were poor, emaciated soldiers, sadly needing the comforts of home and the blessings of peace. Gardner's men had put up a stubborn fight, and had suffered heavily. Food was furnished to them, and kind nurses ministered to their wants." In the face of the cruel slaughter he had witnessed during the siege, Ewer was moved by the kindness of his compatriots and said so: "The men of the North were not only as *brave as a lion;* they could also be as *gentle as a lamb.*"[16]

Among the first men to walk through the fortifications of the bastion was Lieutenant Colonel Edward Bacon, who was supposedly still under house arrest by General Dwight. Once he began walking the ground the first thing that struck Bacon was the damage done to the trees within Port Hudson, as every one of them had been hit by shot and shell, tearing away the bark, and leaving nearly all of them dead or dying. Walking over the ground the Union men had advanced across, he saw many "blue caps, relics of accoutrements, cartridges, arms" and other traces of the battles that lay scattered over the ground. When he entered the Rebel breastworks he marveled at the damage: "I find broken and the earthen dens and shelters where the Rebels had lived and fought. Here was their home," he sadly reflected, "Here the unpaid, half-clothed and undisciplined starving rebels lived, every man at his post, ready to rise up and fight on an instant's warning." As he continued his tour, he reported: "I find dismounted guns and shattered carriages and caissons here, as everywhere along the line. I find, also, traces of the rations of unground corn and molasses issued to the rebel soldiers." Bacon soon discovered the absence of medical care: "Here sick and well generally remained together. Only the badly wounded men and those who were very sick, were sent to the general hospital in a great ravine."[17]

Bacon was only one of many Union men to take an excursion through the Rebels' works. Corporal James Hosmer and a few of his comrades also made a journey to visit what had heretofore not been seen. Unlike that of the officer, Bacon, Hosmer's perspective was that of an enlisted man. Walking behind the parapets, Hosmer found it strange to accustom himself to walking upright, and pointed out: "For it had become second nature to us to crawl and stoop." They soon came upon a large group of Rebels under guard and gathered in a shady hollow. "Here they were," recalled Hosmer, "the real truculent and unmitigated reb, in butternut of every shade— butternut mixed with a dull characterless gray. I am bound to say, they seemed like pleasant men. All were good natured and met our advances cordially. They were brown and dusty; though no more so than we, who, like them, had lived in burrows, on our backs and stomachs for a month." Like Hosmer, Colonel Bacon also reported the Rebels to be quite cordial, good-natured and seemed relieved that their misery had come to an end. "Proud old Southerners and their fiery sons, wild Texans and tawny Creoles are here," said Bacon, and he was pleasantly surprised at their willingness to fraternize with him: "These Southerners appear glad to see me, and want to delay me with conversation."[18]

Not all Southerners, however, would have been glad to see Bacon or any other Yankee soldier. And for good reason. With the fall of Vicksburg and Port Hudson, the Union had now taken complete control of the great Mississippi River, the "Father of Waters," from Minnesota to the Gulf of Mexico, news of which was received with grief and despair throughout the South. Confederate Secretary of War James Seddon, who more than anything wanted to bring the president some piece of good news, was compelled to submit the tragic report to the attention of Jefferson Davis on July 7, prefaced with his sincerest apology: "With the deepest regret at being compelled to inflict the pain of such disastrous intelligence." Soon, a storm of indignation swept through the Confederate congress and the usual finger-pointing began. Most of the blame for the loss of the river and its bastions was cast upon either Davis, Johnston or Pemberton, depending upon the political alliances of the Richmond politicians who were doing the condemning. Finally, on top of this, more bad news hit. On July 9, Davis received official word from General Lee written five days earlier that validated his defeat at Gettysburg, prompting the beaten president to refer to the twin disasters as "the darkest hour of our political existence." All of this was simply too much of an oppressive burden for Davis, a man whose health was already in jeopardy, and a serious concern for his doctors.[19]

Like Davis, citizens throughout the South were in shock and disbelief at the realization that the Mississippi River had been lost. Josiah Gorgas, a government official in Richmond, privately confided to his journal: "One brief month ago we were apparently at the point of success. Lee was in Pennsylvania threatening Harrisburg, and even Philadelphia. Vicksburg seemed to laugh at all Grant's efforts to scorn. All looked bright. Yesterday we rode on the pinnacle of success—today absolute ruin seems to be our portion. The Confederacy totters to its destruction." From Columbia, South Carolina, Mary Chesnut, who learned of the loss from a newspaper, wrote to her diary: "I felt a hard blow struck on the top of my head, and my heart took one of its queer turns." Sarah Morgan, the Louisiana diarist, reacted in much the same way: "Shall I cry, faint, scream or go off in hysterics?" While living at a nearby plantation, she had listened to the first sounds of the obstinate guns of Port Hudson during Farragut's naval battle back in March. Now, in New Orleans, Sarah found herself reading of Port Hudson's surrender from *The Era*, a Federal newspaper. But as she considered the source, she had second thoughts, and began doubting the veracity of the news: "I'll never believe this is true until it is confirmed by a stronger authority than that of these Yankees.... I don't, can't, won't believe it." Yet, that same afternoon, her fears were confirmed by her brother, who was a Southern soldier and had reliable information. "It seems so hard," she penned in her diary, "How the mighty are fallen! Port Hudson gone!" Finally, though, Sarah's shock and grief began melting away, replaced instead by compassion for the Southern soldiers. "Port Hudson does not matter so much, but those brave noble creatures. May the Lord look down in pity on us."[20]

Yet there were other Southerners, Union sympathizers, who were grateful and jubilant over the news of the surrender. The next night, a Saturday, July 11, from an upper balcony in New Orleans, Sarah Morgan along with some of her family watched a celebration taking place in the street below and her anger returned: "What a scene I have just witnessed," she wrote in her diary the morning after. "A motley crew of thousands of low people of all colors parading the streets with flags, torches, music and all other accompaniments, shouting, screaming, exulting over the fall of Port Hudson and Vicksburg.... We saw crowds of soldiers mixed up with the lowest rabble of the town, working men in dirty clothes, newsboys, ragged children, negroes, and even women walking in the procession, while swarms of negroes and low white women elbowed each other in a dense mass on the pavement. To see such creatures exulting over our misfortune was enough to make one scream with rage." As the raucous parade passed their house, they could hear the loud yells: *Down with the Rebels!* "That made us gnash our teeth in silence." At that moment, Sarah admitted, "The devil possessed me." In frustration, she whispered a prayer "that their flag may burn" as the torches danced around it. It was an earnest prayer, but then she realized that "it must have been a wicked prayer, for it was not answered."[21]

Because Port Hudson and Vicksburg had been totally isolated during the long siege, no one really knew the extent of the suffering which had taken place within those confines until the paroled or exchanged prisoners from the two bastions began recounting their stories. Kate Cumming, a Confederate nurse, heard of the horrors the men endured when they came to the Confederate hospital in Georgia where she worked to ask for treatment. "Poor fellows!" she entered in her journal on July 27, "The suffering of our men, both there [Vicksburg] and at Port Hudson was terrible." Soon, the Southern press began picking up some accounts of the siege, which were retold for the readers to memorialize the awful event. The Mobile *Advertiser and Register*, for example, quoted the words of Colonel Isaiah Steedman in a poignant letter to his son in which he told the boy, "The gallantry, heroism, endurance and sufferings of our little garrison of about five thousand men all told, against overwhelming odds of army and navy, can never be realized except by participants."[22]

Epilogue

The news of the surrender of Vicksburg resolved the question of Port Hudson's survival. Its fate was sealed since it was inextricably bonded with that city's destiny. Somehow, though, it seems pathetically unjustifiable that so many men had to suffer and die for an outcome which could have been decided without firing a shot. When the butcher's bill was finally tallied, the Nineteenth Corps of the Union army had lost, during the period of the siege alone, 663 men and 45 officers killed, 3,145 men and 191 officers wounded and another 319 officers and men reported as captured or missing. But because the Confederates had taken so few prisoners it can be assumed that most of this last category surely perished during one of the fights. In any event, the bloody total came to 4,363 men. In a comparison of casualties, the Confederates fared much better, and if numbers alone determined the victor, they would have won the contest. Although no complete statement of losses was ever made, the chief surgeon reported total losses of 623 of which 176 were killed and 447 wounded, or roughly one Confederate lost for every seven Union men.

Yet when it was over, 6,340 men marched out of the place as prisoners of war. This number, represented 405 officers and 5,935 enlisted men. However, there were others, like laborers and some civilians from within Port Hudson, who were most likely included in that total. Of the effective soldiers fit for duty, Gardner's assistant Inspector General, estimated that number to be only about twenty-five hundred, which would not equal half of those who were taken as prisoners. As in many campaigns of the Civil War, there were puzzling discrepancies and unreported losses. Inexplicably, neither side, Union or Confederate, provided an accurate account of the men who were hospitalized with sickness and disease and subsequently died, a figure which was undoubtedly high during an extended siege, and one which took place in a hostile climate such as Port Hudson. Nor do the Union numbers include the seamen who had fallen during the naval battle in March, or the subsequent losses from the gunboats during the siege. Missing, too, are the casualties from the minor operations leading up to the investment. Finally, there was not even an estimate of how many slaves and contrabands were killed or wounded while working on the trenches of both armies, nor how many of the black teamsters, cooks, and servants who served both sides perished during the siege.[1]

But numbers do not tell the whole story. Neither do they bleed, suffer, or find themselves psychologically scared and traumatized for life. The wounded soldiers of both sides were often left crippled or badly maimed, returning to their homes without an eye, an arm or a leg. Perhaps though, none were so dramatically affected as the 405 Confederate officers who were imprisoned after the surrender. Unlike the enlisted men who were released to their homes on parole, these officers were either sent to New Orleans or Memphis, and then on to permanent prisoner of war camps. About half the officers—the most unfortunate of the lot—found themselves at the Ohio camp known as Johnson's Island, where most of them remained for the duration of the war. By some accounts, the place was considered one of the worst of the Union prison camps, and living conditions there were more inferior and unhealthy than the squalid depths of Port Hudson. For that reason, many of the Rebel officers attempted to escape. An example of the fate of those officers who surrendered and were incarcerated at Johnson's Island can be found in the records of the two Alabama regiments, the First and the Forty-ninth. Of the twenty-three officers taken, five successfully escaped, and three were killed by prison guards, presumably while trying to escape. Others died of disease or sickness while there, and the remainder were never exchanged and had to endure the misery of their internment until the Confederacy surrendered.[2]

Although the Union soldiers were spared the horrors of spending time in a Confederate prison, they were, nevertheless, exposed to a nightmare of suffering and death during the campaign for Port Hudson. The Northern troops, especially those from New England, were not accustomed to the steamy climate of Louisiana, and far more of them lost their lives to disease and exposure than the Southerners. It's estimated that over 4,000 Union men were hospitalized from sickness during the course of the siege. But, still, combat losses accounted for most of the Federal losses, and compared to the Southern casualties the seven-to-one ratio was possibly the most disproportionate one of any other Civil War campaign. What's more, for the Union soldiers at Port Hudson, there was a serious and growing loss of confidence in the leadership of Banks and his generals as the siege went on. Such despair continued to mount until mutiny was threatening to erupt in some units. Thus, the New Englanders whose enlistment expired as the siege ended were so demoralized that many of them refused to reenlist.[3]

In spite of the fact that the Union achieved a victory at Port Hudson, it was clearly a pyrrhic one. In other words, the victory came at too great a cost in blood to be considered a success. Besides, the same result would have eventually been achieved by simply laying siege to the place and waiting for one of two things to happen: yielding to the imminent starvation within Port Hudson or the surrender of Vicksburg. Either would have resulted in the submission of the Rebel bastion. As commander of the Union forces, Nathaniel P. Banks must ultimately accept the responsibility for the costly assaults at Port Hudson. After the failure of the first assault on May 27, he blamed his subordinates with comments such as "General Sherman has failed utterly and criminally to bring his men into the field." It was a typical ploy of a politician such as Banks, who had mastered the art of pointing out scapegoats. Yet, even before the attack of May 27 was made, that same general, Thomas Sherman, had made it clear that it would be too costly, prompting Banks to reply, "The people of the North demand blood, sir." Such a remark clearly confirms a lack of understanding of military matters, rejecting the advice of others and, still worse, validates a willingness to abandon humane principles in favor of political expediency.

But Banks's most glaring weakness was his failure to learn from his own mistakes. Hardly had the bodies all been buried from the first assault when Banks aggressively announced plans for another attack on June 14, which bore similar tactics and similar results. Even though his tactics were sound, they were much too daring to succeed against a prepared fortification without the benefit of well-timed and coordinated attacks, which he obviously did not have the military experience to execute. Neither did he appreciate the importance of reconnoitering the ground over which the attacks would take place. For the most part, Banks's choice of subordinate generals also proved to be disappointing, if not disastrous. But here again, many of them were chosen because they were either politically connected or offered the promise of support in his future public endeavors, the grandest of which was to one day become president of the United States. Having a good war record would certainly benefit him in achieving such a lofty goal as the presidency. Grant, for example, had already become the toast of the North and was being lauded as a likely president. Thus Banks maximized the importance of his victory at Port Hudson—if a surrender without winning a fight could be considered a victory—and minimized the significance of his losses. "There are but few sieges in the history of the war," he bragged in a later report to the War Department, "[which had] difficulties to be encountered more numerous, the victory more decided, or the result more important."[4]

But the victory at Port Hudson, such as it was, was Banks's only one in his brief military career, and, of course, he tried to embellish it as much as he could. Unfortunately, Grant's capture of Vicksburg and Meade's victory at Gettysburg, both occurring about the same time, left it buried on the back page of the war news of 1863. Following the Port Hudson surrender, Banks led the Union army in the Red River Campaign in 1864, another ill-fated disaster and embarrassing defeat, which proved once and for all that an opportunistic politician almost never makes for a good general. After the war Banks resigned his commission and returned to New England to pursue his political career. He was quickly elected to Congress, first as a Republican and later as a Democrat. In his ten terms as a congressman, he chaired the important Foreign Affairs Committee. But, for the most part, the postwar years were not much better than those he experienced during the war. Just as he had done most of his days, Banks waffled between the two parties and divided his loyalty between those who were politically radical and those of the conservative faction, trying to please both. Hence, he lost the support and respect of both sides, which dashed any hopes he had for the presidency. Nevertheless, Banks had a long and distinguished record as an American statesman, serving in Congress until 1893. Then, with his health failing—deteriorating with a condition his biographer believed to be what we know today as Alzheimer's disease—he returned to his home in Waltham, Massachusetts, where he died September 1, 1894, at the age of seventy-eight. Nathaniel Banks, despite his failings and flaws, was a loyal patriot and an honorable man. To his credit, there is no evidence that he was involved in the widespread corruption and theft that took place in Louisiana during the time of his command. In fact, he turned down bribes from men seeking illicit gains, and did what he could to stop the corruption. Even today, a statue stands in his home state of Massachusetts bearing the inscription: "N.P. Banks, soldier and statesman."[5]

To be fair, Banks inherited some of his military problems from Benjamin Franklin Butler, his predecessor in command of the Department of the Gulf. Butler during his reign had ruled the civilian population with an iron hand, but neglected the military, which was disorganized and untrained. He assigned his best officers to civil jobs, and many of them became involved in the widespread corruption and theft that was typically rampant in Butler's regime. Those officers who were not involved in the dishonest conduct were, however, aware of it and demoralized by it, and all of them, the corrupt and the disenchanted, later became Banks's problem. Although Butler was never convicted of anything dishonest, historian Bruce Catton said it best when he wrote: "There always seemed to be a dead rat behind the wainscoting somewhere." After his removal from command, Butler was given command of the Army of the James in 1863. In that position, he proved his ineptness once again when he was outwitted and "bottled up" by General P.G.T. Beauregard in Grant's campaign of 1864. Thus the bald, meaty-faced general who had earned the name of "Beast Butler" in New Orleans was embarrassed and became known as "Bottled-Up Butler."

Grant, having seen enough of Butler, ordered him to go home in January of 1865, and then asked Lincoln to make sure he was never given another command. After the war, Butler, who apparently still had a loyal following in Massachusetts, was elected to Congress in 1866 as a Republican and served until 1875. During that time, Butler emerged as a ringleader in the effort to impeach President Andrew Johnson. Joining the Radical Republicans, he condemned Johnson for his lax Reconstruction policies, accusing him of promoting white supremacy and opposing civil rights. "The war did not end with the surrender of Lee," railed Butler in an impeachment speech in New York. Then the man never known for his virtuous morals added: "The moral victory of every war depends upon the moral gain that is obtained after its close." Butler came to be hated by conservative Democrats and Republicans alike. In 1878, he reappeared on the political scene when he was once again elected to Congress, this time as a member of the short-lived Greenback Party. That was the third of his political parties, and he ran unsuccessfully as their presidential candidate in 1884. Nine years later, in January of 1893, Benjamin Butler died in Washington, D.C., and was buried in his wife's family cemetery in Massachusetts.[6]

Unlike Banks, David Glasgow Farragut's performance in the campaign for the Mississippi River propelled him into the spotlight, and he was hailed as one of America's great naval heroes. A New York newspaper praised him with the title "American Viking." Indeed the government thought so, too, awarding him with the promotion of rear admiral after he took New Orleans. Following the fall of Vicksburg and Port Hudson, Farragut went on to claim his greatest victory at the Battle of Mobile Bay, the capstone of his career. It was there that he called out his famous order, "Damn the torpedoes, full speed ahead." Again, a grateful government promoted him to vice admiral, and after the war to full admiral. In the wake of his victory at Mobile, Farragut was exhausted. The "old sea dog" was in desperate need of a rest, and he said so: "Six months constantly watching day and night for an enemy; to know him to be brave, as skillful, and as determined as myself, who pledged to his government and the South to drive me away and raise the blockade and free the Mississippi from our rule. While I was equally pledged to my government that I would capture or destroy the rebel." Although he could not participate in the war's final campaigns, Farragut recovered and commanded the European Squadron after the war until his retirement. He passed away in New Hampshire in 1870 at the age of sixty-nine.[7]

Many of the commanding officers who served under Banks were incompetent, and contributed to the poor military performance at Port Hudson. But, ironically, quite a few of these same ones had been appointed by Banks and, for reasons known only to him, were never disciplined or replaced. Like Banks, a number of them had no military experience. Others were unfit for duty and in a constant state of drunkenness. Some were glory seekers who refused to cooperate with each other. Generals who had attended West Point were resentful of those who didn't, which unfortunately included their commander, Banks. And, in the tradition of Benjamin Butler, far too many of them devoted their time to their own agendas, such as stealing cotton and sugar from Southern plantations and selling it on the black market. Without a doubt, the general who exemplified the most unscrupulous characteristics was none other than the odious William Dwight. But even after his disgraceful performance at Port Hudson, he continued to retain his command. Following the siege of Port Hudson, he acted as Banks's chief of staff during the Red River Campaign, where he continued to engage in a corrupt cotton trade. In July of 1864, Dwight was transferred back to Virginia and served in the Shenandoah Valley Campaign. There, during the battle at Winchester, he was discovered cowering out of the gunfire and subsequently arrested. The charges, however, were never acted on and apparently forgotten. Finally mustered out of the army in 1866, Dwight surfaced again in Cincinnati, Ohio, where he joined his brothers in the railroad business. In time, he returned to his home state of Massachusetts, where he died in Boston in the year 1888, still without penalty for his wartime behavior.[8]

Another example of a commander of dubious character within Banks's Corps was the sanctimonious Neal Dow, a general who created severe morale problems within the ranks of an army already demoralized by poor leadership. At first glance, he appeared to be the very antithesis of the boozer Dwight, mainly because of his militant stance and preoccupation with the evils of liquor. That aside, Dow, like Dwight, was one of the "worst pillagers" in the Nineteenth Corps. He also spent much valuable time punishing his troops for temperance violations, and for some unknown reason prohibited them from indulging in small pleasures, such as reading newspapers and eating candy. Such petty restrictions naturally earned him the hearty hatred of his troops. As a result, when the sanctimonious Dow was captured by the Confederate cavalry it was a most welcomed event for his men. Following his eight-month imprisonment in Richmond, Dow's health had diminished to the point where he was compelled to resign from the army. After recovering, he resumed his lifelong crusade against alcohol and was appropriately dubbed the "Napoleon of Temperance." Originally a Republican who hated slavery, whiskey, and for some unknown reason, Irish immigrants, he later joined the Prohibition Party and ran for president on their ticket in 1880. In 1897, at the ripe old age of ninety-three, Dow died in Portland, Maine.[9]

There were, of course, other men under Banks's charge who were just as guilty of misbehavior and conduct unbecoming an officer. Colonel Thomas S. Clark and General Franklin Nickerson would certainly bear mentioning. Clark, who commanded the Sixth Michigan, had a long list of despicable charges filed against him during the Teche Campaign, and was again accused of cowardly behavior on May 27 at Port Hudson when he feigned a wound and hid during the battle. Then there was Nickerson, who was drunk when he led from behind in the safe confines of a ditch during Dwight's "Whisky Charge" in the final days of the Port Hudson siege. He, too, should have been charged with neglect of duty and court-martialed. Neither man, for some unfortunate reason, was ever disciplined or punished.[10]

By no means should the citing of these officers be meant to imply there were no competent and brave leaders among Banks's command. Clearly there were. General officers such as Christopher Augur, Cuvier Grover, Halbert Paine and Thomas Sherman were capable infantry commanders and all were promoted or cited for gallant service during their military careers. Banks was also fortunate to have a cavalry commander of the caliber of Benjamin Grierson, who returned to Grant's command following the Port Hudson Campaign, and soon thereafter promoted to major general. In the case of Paine and Sherman they were unquestionably brave, as both men lost a leg leading assaults at Port Hudson. Banks, unfortunately, often blamed these qualified officers for his own mistakes. His authority was further weakened by the fact that he surrounded himself with a number of incompetent, inexperienced commanders, which seemed to indicate that he was incapable of telling the difference between experienced competent officers and those who were inept at military command. Those choices only confirmed the belief that Nathaniel Banks was not a good judge of men.[11]

Notwithstanding the tribulations caused by shortages in food, supplies and medicine that the Confederate soldiers experienced during the siege of Port Hudson, they fared much better under their leadership than their Northern counterparts. Although there were a number of hunger-driven desertions, the morale of the Southerners remained generally good. After all they had been through, that was particularly surprising. During the prolonged siege the supply of food continued to diminish until mule meat became the last cuisine of choice. Yet, the soldiers did not blame their officers for the shortages, mainly because the officers, to their credit, never hoarded rations for themselves, but humbly shared in the scant scraps that were available. Neither did they blame their officers for being desperately outnumbered and outgunned. For the most part, the Confederate officers did a remarkable job, and worked well with their troops in building a formidable network of defensive strongholds and then fighting tenaciously to hold them. Despite the overwhelming odds against them, the Southerners could rightfully claim victory in each of the major Union attacks, especially if victory had been measured by the number of casualties recorded.

Much of the credit for the excellent performance of the officers and men within Port Hudson must be attributed to General Franklin Gardner. Using all his energy and skill, he clearly met or exceeded any reasonable expectation for the defense of Port Hudson. No one except a man with an engineer's mind and a military education could have accomplished all that Gardner did in holding a line over four miles long for so many days against a much larger and better equipped force. He did this by having his engineers create strong interior lines of defense with redoubts placed in strategic positions. Equally impressive were the shelters and tunnels that were dug to offer his troops some protection from the constant artillery barrages of the Federal guns. Being a man ahead of his time, he employed methods of warfare which would not be refined until the First World War. They included protecting his works with rows of wire and sharpened stakes known as *abatis* or *cheval de frise,* and planting land mines in front of those positions. Gardner was not only creative but also resourceful, using whatever he had to make the most of what he didn't have. For example, he only had a limited supply of ammunition. But Gardner was an innovator and he overcame the shortage by ordering their canister to be made out of all sorts of scrap metal, like nails, nuts and bolts, ball-bearings, railroad spikes, horseshoes, and anything else they could find to ram down the muzzles of the cannons, transforming them into huge shotguns.[12]

Because he was greatly outgunned, about ten to one, the Rebel general could not afford to lose any of his cannons. Thus Gardner constantly instructed his chief of artillery, Colonel Marshall Smith, to keep moving the batteries from place to place where they could do the most damage but, more importantly, to prevent the Federal artillery batteries from pinpointing their positions. Gardner also made the most of keeping one of his enormous ten-inch Columbiad siege guns out of their sights by having it mounted on a flatbed railcar and moving it up and down the track, firing on various Yankee positions. When the load from the big cannon passed over them in route to its target, it made a horrifying sound, causing the Union soldiers to baptize the mighty gun the "Demoralizer." On those occasions when the Union artillery succeeded in hitting a Rebel cannon and blowing it off its carriage, he did all he could to keep it in service by ordering it propped up with braces of sandbags and blocks.[13]

Perhaps Gardner's greatest strength, though, was the management of his troops. Always outnumbered, he made the best use of them during the best opportunities. The uncoordinated and ill-timed attacks made by Banks gave Gardner more freedom to maneuver his men from point to point, thus forcing the Union commander to pay dearly for those mistakes. And the Rebels gave much better than they got. He also made sure his troops were well supplied with plenty of weapons. Each man was usually armed with at least two guns, some of which were shotguns and deadly at close range. Because the Union assaults were continually turned back in devastating slaughters, the *espirit de corps* of the Confederate soldiers was maintained throughout the siege. And Gardner was careful to keep it that way by encouraging them, and sharing in all of the miseries his men faced, a fact which didn't escape their attention. Such an instance occurred when the meat supply was exhausted, and he joined them in dining on rats and mules, and never complained.

Franklin Gardner, like his counterpart, John Pemberton, the Confederate commander at Vicksburg, was born in the North and married into a Southern family. Both of them were West Point graduates and career army officers. Both men left the Union army at the beginning of the war, and both remained loyal to the Confederacy throughout the war. Because their families continued to be devoted to the Union, some Southerners were naturally suspicious of them, and as a consequence, they were hesitant to accept their services. Yet, during the war years, Gardner somehow seemed to escape the extent of scrutiny and criticism that Pemberton experienced, although, like Pemberton, he was never fully accepted into the Southern brotherhood. When it was over, and both strongholds, Vicksburg and Port Hudson, had surrendered, Gardner was spared much of the harsh criticism that Pemberton suffered.

So it came as no surprise that after the fall of Vicksburg Pemberton became the chief scapegoat for disgruntled Southerners. Some went so far as to falsely accuse him of intentionally surrendering the city on the Fourth of July to promote the morale of the enemy. Independence Day, thereafter, became a day of shame and dishonor for Vicksburg, and was not officially recognized again by the city until 1945. Before long Pemberton was vilified in both the North and the South as a traitor. Disowned by his family in the North and without a family in the South, he became a man without a country. After the war, he settled on a small farm in Virginia and tried to scratch out a meager living for his wife and five children. The work was hard and the economy during Reconstruction was poor. For Pemberton, life was far from the pastoral picture of antebellum moonlight and magnolias, and rarely did he hear the sound of a kind Southern voice. Finally, he gave up and returned to Philadelphia, where he died in 1881 at the age of sixty-seven. Though the question is not a significant one, some might wonder if, had the roles of Gardner and Pemberton been reversed and Gardner been in command of Vicksburg, would he have conducted its defense any differently? Could he have saved it? If not, after the surrender, would he have been as despised in the South as his counterpart Pemberton? But such questions are only *what-ifs,* and really do not matter since there are so many different contingencies in the outcomes of history's cause and effect that one change among many causes would not necessarily lead to a different result.[14]

Even though Gardner was never lauded as a war hero in the postwar years, he was clearly a competent general. If there is fault to be found in his performance at Port Hudson, it might be his failure to take any real offensive measures to lift the siege. However, given the numerical superiority of Banks, lifting the siege could never have been a realistic expectation without the aid of Joe Johnston's small army in Jackson. And that would have required a coordinated effort, which would have been difficult if not impossible without some means for the two generals to effectively communicate. Port Hudson, like Vicksburg, was so tightly sealed that the only message between Gardner and Johnston ever delivered was through the extraordinary efforts of Captain Robert Pruyn. What's more, Johnston's primary concern was supposedly to save Vicksburg, or at least free Pemberton's army from Grant's clutches. Johnston, though, was a wary general, indecisive and more likely to withdraw than attack, and as early as the middle of June he had already warned the War Department in Richmond: "I consider saving Vicksburg hopeless." Even though his army reached a strength of 32,000, Johnston was unwilling to come to the aid of Pemberton and Vicksburg. He wanted no part of the responsibility for surrendering the most important garrison on the Mississippi. If a head was going to roll because of its loss, let it be Pemberton's. Thus, any hope for Port Hudson and Gardner's little army was never really a serious possibility.[15]

Following the surrender of Port Hudson, Gardner found himself a prisoner of war but was exchanged and released in August of 1864. The Confederacy then assigned him to duty in Mississippi, under the command of Richard Taylor, under whom he served until the end of the war. After the war, the New York–born Gardner returned to his adopted home of Louisiana and resumed the quiet life of a planter on his father-in-law's plantation in the area of Lafayette. There he remained for the rest of his life, which ended in his fiftieth year in April of 1873.[16]

Gardner's officers, especially the engineers and senior officers, did an excellent job in aiding him in the defense of Port Hudson. The only general officer assisting Gardner was Brigadier General William Beall, a West Point–educated Kentuckian who commanded the center of the Confederate line. Although Beall had very little prior combat experience, he proved himself an excellent leader. To his misfortune, he was imprisoned at Johnson's Island after the surrender. But the general was released on parole in 1864 in order to act as the Confederate agent to supply blankets and clothing to Confederate prisoners in Northern prison camps. Released in 1865, he became a merchant in Tennessee, and died there in 1883. Banks's other two senior field officers, Colonels Isaiah Steedman and William Miles, also played a commendable role in holding the left and right sides of the Rebel line. Both men were imprisoned when the garrison surrendered. After he was released, Steedman, a physician before the war, went to St. Louis, where he practiced medicine, and died there in 1917. Miles also continued his prewar career as a Mississippi lawyer and planter in Yazoo City, where he died on New Year's Day 1900. John Logan, the cavalry commander at Port Hudson, was captured later in the war. After his parole, he moved to New Orleans and made his living as a merchant, but died in a yellow fever epidemic in 1871. Logan's counterpart, the daring Frank Powers, who led the audacious cavalry raid against the regiment of New York Swedes, was said to have owned a hotel in Jackson, Louisiana, after the war, and was a violent opponent of Reconstruction. Possibly a Klansman, Powers, a man given to violence, led an armed band of men against any assembly where the newly freed Negroes were gathered. He was alive in 1886, but subsequently disappeared from the records and was believed to have died in Mississippi.[17]

But Gardner's most important asset in his defense of Port Hudson was the little band of ordinary men who held the place for forty-eight of the most trying days in Civil War history. Although they were outnumbered and weakened by fighting, disease and starvation, most of them somehow managed to survive the siege, and practically all of them went on to fight with the Confederate army through the final years of the war. Yet, when it was over, those who lived through it and returned home hardly received a hero's welcome. Instead, they faced the almost impossible task of rebuilding a land vanquished by war. They had the misfortune of living through an epic time when they were forced to witness unimaginable horrors and destruction, leaving countless numbers of them with mental scars. Thousands of them who returned home with battle wounds died from complications, or lived their lives in constant pain. In time, they all vanished. Sarah Morgan, the insightful diarist who chronicled the defense and surrender of Port Hudson as well as all the remaining days of the doomed Confederacy, perhaps best described the feelings of those men and every other Southerner when she quoted the British poet Tennyson in her entry of April 19, 1865: "All things are taken from us, and become portions and parcels of the dreadful past."[18]

Appendix A
The Port Hudson Garrison: Organizations Paroled at Port Hudson, July 10, 1863

(Statement taken from 26 OR 1: 143)

First Alabama Regiment, Colonel I.G.W. Steedman.
Forty-ninth Alabama Regiment, Major T.A. Street.
Maury (Tennessee) Artillery, attached to Twelfth Louisiana Heavy Artillery.
First [Eighth] Arkansas Battalion, Lieutenant Colonel B. Jones.
Tenth Arkansas Regiment, Major C.M. Cargile.
Eleventh and Seventeenth Arkansas (detachments).
Twelfth Arkansas Regiment, Colonel T.J. Reid, Jr.
Fourteenth Arkansas Regiment, Lieutenant Colonel Pleasant Fowler.
Fifteenth Arkansas Regiment, Colonel Ben W. Johnson.
Sixteenth Arkansas Regiment, Colonel David Provence.
Eighteenth Arkansas Regiment, Lieutenant Colonel W.N. Parish.
Twenty-third Arkansas Regiment, Colonel O.P. Lyles.
Fourth Louisiana (detachment), Captain Charles T. Whitman
Ninth Louisiana Battalion (Infantry), Captain T.B.R. Chinn.
Ninth Louisiana Battalion (Partisan Rangers), Major J. De Baun.
Twelfth Louisiana Heavy Artillery Battalion, Lieutenant Colonel P.F. De Gournay.
Thirtieth Louisiana (detachment), Captain T.K. Porter.
Miles's Louisiana Legion, Colonel W.R. Miles.
Boone's Louisiana Battery, Captain S.M. Thomas.
Watson's Louisiana Battery, Lieutenant E.A. Toledano.
First Mississippi Regiment, Colonel A.S. Hamilton.
Thirtieth Mississippi Regiment, Colonel W.B. Shelby.
Claiborne Mississippi Light Infantry, Captain A.J. Lewis.
First Mississippi Light Artillery (Abbay's, Bradford's and Herod's Batteries).
English's Mississippi Battery, Lieutenant P.J. Noland.
Seven Stars Mississippi Artillery, Lieutenant F.G.W. Coleman.

First Tennessee Heavy Artillery, Company G, Captain James A. Fisher (attached to Twelfth Louisiana Heavy Artillery).

First Tennessee Light Artillery, Company B, Lieutenant Oswald Tilghman (attached to Twelfth Louisiana Heavy Artillery).

Improvised Tennessee Battalion composed of details from the Forty-first, Forty-second, Forty-eighth, Forty-ninth, Fifty-third, and Fifty-fifth Tennessee Regiments, Captain S. A. Whiteside.

Appendix B
Organization of the Union Troops at Port Hudson (Nineteenth Army Corps), as of May 31, 1863, Major General Nathaniel P. Banks, Commanding

(Statement of Organization taken from 26 OR 1:529–531)

First Division: Major General Christopher C. Augur

First Brigade, Colonel Charles J. Paine

Second Louisiana Regiment (Union), Lieutenant Colonel Charles Everett.
Twenty-first Maine Regiment, Colonel Elijah F. Stone.
Forty-eighth Massachusetts Regiment, Colonel Eben F. Stone.
Forty-ninth Massachusetts Regiment, Major Charles T. Plunkett.
One Hundred Sixteenth New York Regiment, Captain John Higgins.

Second Brigade, Brigadier General Godfrey Weitzel

On May 14 Weitzel was assigned to command a provisional division consisting of his brigade and Dwight's Brigade from the Fourth Division.

Twelfth Connecticut Regiment, Lieutenant Colonel Frank H. Peck.
Seventy-fifth New York Regiment, Colonel Robert B. Merritt.
One Hundred Fourteenth New York Regiment, Colonel Elisha B. Smith.
One Hundred Sixtieth New York Regiment, Lieutenant Colonel John B. Van Petten.
Eighth Vermont Regiment, Lieutenant Colonel Charles Dillingham.

Third Brigade, Colonel Nathan A. M. Dudley

Thirtieth Massachusetts Regiment, Lieutenant Colonel William W. Bullock.
Fiftieth Massachusetts, Colonel Carlos Messer.
One Hundred Sixty-first New York Regiment, Colonel Gabriel T. Harrower.
One Hundred Seventy-fourth New York Regiment, Major George Keating.

Artillery

First Indiana Heavy Artillery, Colonel John A. Keith.
First Maine Battery, Lieutenant John E. Morton.
Sixth Massachusetts Battery, Lieutenant John F. Phelps.
Twelfth Massachusetts Battery, Lieutenant Edwin M. Chamberlin.
Eighteenth New York Battery, Captain Albert G. Mack.
First United States, Battery A, Captain Edmund C. Bainbridge.
Fifth United States, Battery G, Lieutenant Jacob B. Rawles.

Miscellaneous

First Louisiana Engineers, Corp d'Afrique, Colonel Justin Hodge.
First Louisiana Native Guards, Lieutenant Colonel Chauncey J. Bassett.
Third Louisiana Native Guards, Colonel John A. Nelson
First Louisiana Cavalry, Major Harai Robinson.
Second Rhode Island Cavalry, Lieutenant Colonel Augustus W. Corliss.

Second Division: Brigadier General William Dwight (replaced Thomas W. Sherman, who was wounded May 27)

First Brigade, Colonel Thomas S. Clark

Twenty-sixth Connecticut Regiment, Lieutenant Colonel J. Selden.
Sixth Michigan Regimen, Lieutenant Colonel Edward Bacon.
Fifteenth New Hampshire Regiment, Colonel John W. Kingman.
One Hundred Twenty-eighth New York Regiment, Lieutenant Colonel James Smith.
One Hundred Sixty-second New York Regiment, Lieutenant Colonel Justus W. Blanchard.

Third Brigade, Brigadier General Frank S. Nickerson

Fourteenth Maine Regiment, Colonel Thomas W. Porter.
Twenty-fourth Maine Regiment, Colonel George M. Atwood.
Twenty-eighth Maine (detachment), Colonel Ephraim W. Woodman.
One Hundred Sixty-fifth New York Regiment, Captain Felix Agnus.
One Hundred Seventy-fifth New York Regiment, Major John Gray.
One Hundred Seventy-seventh New York Regiment, Colonel Ira W. Ainsworth.

Artillery, Captain William Roy

First Indiana Heavy Artillery (one company), Captain William Roy.
Twenty-first New York Battery, Captain James Barnes.
First Vermont Battery, Captain George T. Hebard.

Third Division: Brigadier General Halbert E. Paine

First Brigade, Colonel Timothy Ingraham

Fourth Massachusetts Regiment, Colonel Henry Walker.
Sixteenth New Hampshire Regiment, Colonel James Pike.
One Hundred-tenth New York Regiment, Colonel Clinton H. Sage.

Second Brigade, Colonel Hawkes Fearing, Jr.

Eighth New Hampshire Regiment, Captain William M. Barrett.
One Hundred Thirty-third New York Regiment, Colonel Leonard D.H. Currie.
One Hundred Seventy-third New York Regiment, Captain George W. Rogers.
Fourth Wisconsin Regiment, Colonel Sidney A. Bean.

Third Brigade, Colonel Oliver P. Gooding

Thirty-first Massachusetts Regiment, Lieutenant Colonel W.S.B. Hopkins.
Thirty-eighth Massachusetts Regiment, Major James P. Richardson.
Fifty-third Massachusetts Regiment, Colonel John W. Kimball.
One Hundred Fifty-sixth New York Regiment, Lieutenant Colonel Jacob Sharpe.

Artillery, Captain Richard C. Duryea

Fourth Massachusetts Battery, Lieutenant Fred W. Reinhard.
First United States, Battery F, Captain Richard C. Duryea.
Second Vermont Battery, Captain Pythagoras E. Holcomb.

Fourth Division: Brigadier General Cuvier Grover

First Brigade, Colonel Joseph S. Morgan

First Louisiana (Union) Regiment, Colonel Richard E. Holcomb.
Twenty-second Maine Regiment, Colonel Simon G. Jerrard.
Ninetieth New York Regiment, Major Nelson Shaurman.
Ninety-first New York Regiment, Colonel Jacob Van Zandt.
One Hundred Thirty-first New York Regiment, Lieutenant Colonel Nicholas W. Day.

Second Brigade, Colonel William K. Kimball

Twenty-fourth Connecticut Regiment, Colonel Samuel M. Mansfield.
Twelfth Maine Regiment, Lieutenant Colonel Edward Ilsley.

Forty-first Massachusetts Regiment, Lieutenant Colonel Lorenzo D. Sargent.
Fifty-second Massachusetts Regiment, Colonel Halbert S. Greenleaf.

Third Brigade, Colonel Henry W. Birge

Thirteenth Connecticut Regiment, Captain Apollos Comstock.
Twenty-fifth Connecticut Regiment, Lieutenant Colonel Mason C. Weld.
Twenty-sixth Maine Regiment, Colonel Nathaniel H. Hubbard.
One Hundred Fifty-ninth New York Regiment, Lieutenant Colonel Charles A. Burt.

Artillery, Captain Henry W. Closson

Second Massachusetts Battery, Captain Ormand F. Nims.
First United States, Battery L, Captain Henry W. Closson.
Second United States, Battery C, Lieutenant Theodore Bradley.

Cavalry: Colonel Benjamin H. Grierson

Sixth Illinois Cavalry, Lieutenant Colonel Reuben Loomis.
Seventh Illinois Cavalry, Colonel Edward Prince.
First Louisiana (Union detachment) Cavalry,
Fourteenth New York Cavalry (one company attached to Fourth Division).
Second Massachusetts Battalion.

Corps D'Afrique

Sixth, Seventh, Eighth, Ninth and Tenth Infantry Regiments.

Chapter Notes

Chapter One

1. James G. Hollandsworth, *Pretense of Glory: The Life of General Nathaniel P. Banks* (Baton Rouge: Louisiana State University Press, 1998) 19, 50. The Zouave uniforms mentioned were sometimes adopted by both Union and Confederate troops during the Civil War. They were especially popular in some of the New York regiments as well as a couple of the Louisiana regiments, and were modeled after the Zouave battalion of the French army.
2. Ibid. David P. Porter, *Incidents and Anecdotes of the Civil War* (New York, 1885), 218–19.
3. Ibid., 1–4; Ezra Warner, *Generals in Blue: Lives of the Union Commanders* (Baton Rouge: Louisiana State University Press, 1964), 18–19.
4. U.S. War Department, *The War of the Rebellion: A Compilation of the Official Records of the Union and Confederate Armies* (Washington, DC: Government Printing Office, 1880–1901), ser. 1, 15:590. Hereafter, this source will be cited as OR, with all references being to series 1. Whenever a volume consists of two or more parts, the volume number will precede the OR, followed by the part number and page(s) citations; David Herbert Donald, *Lincoln* (New York: Simon & Schuster, 1995), 485–86.
5. John D. Winters, *The Civil War in Louisiana* (Baton Rouge: Louisiana State University Press, 1963), 146–48; Thomas Ewing Dabney, "The Butler Regime in Louisiana," *The Louisiana Historical Quarterly*, vol. 27, no. 1 (April 1944), 495–505; Warner, *Generals in Blue*, 60–61; *Daily Picayune*, May 3, 1862; Howard Palmer Johnson, "New Orleans under General Butler," *Louisiana Historical Quarterly*, vol. 24 (January–October 1941), 525–32; OR 15:426, 482.
6. Dabney, "The Butler Regime in Louisiana," 496, 502–3, Butler's letter to a friend quoted 502 and printed in the *Daily Picayune*, July 31, 1862; Charles East, ed., *Sarah Morgan: The Civil War Diary of a Southern Woman* (1991; rprt., New York: Simon & Schuster, Inc., 1992), 146.
7. Dennis J. Dufrene, *Civil War Baton Rouge, Port Hudson and Bayou Sara: Capturing the Mississippi* (Charleston, SC: The History Press, 2012), Davis's proclamation quoted 38.
8. Winters, *The Civil War in Louisiana*, 125–148, passim; Donald, *Lincoln*, 485; Winston Groom, *Vicksburg, 1863* (New York: Alfred A. Knopf, 2009), 135–36.
9. OR 15:639; Banks to Mary Banks, January 3 and 15, 1863, Nathaniel Banks Collection, Library of Congress, Washington, DC; Hollandsworth, *Pretense of Glory*, 88–89; Shelby Foote, *The Civil War, a Narrative: Fredericksburg to Meridian* (New York: Random House, 1963), note from Smith and response to wife 55.
10. OR 15:615, 619–21, 623–24; Butler's farewell speech quoted in Johnson, "New Orleans under General Butler," 526–27; Hollandsworth, *Pretense of Glory*, 92–98; Winters, *The Civil War in Louisiana*, 147–48.
11. Robert Underwood Johnson and Clarence Clough Buel, eds., *Battles and Leaders of the Civil War* (1887; rpt. Edison, NJ: Castle), vol. 3, 586–87; Edward Cunningham, *The Port Hudson Campaign, 1862–1863* (Baton Rouge: Louisiana State University Press, 1963), 17; Lawrence Lee Hewitt, *Port Hudson, Confederate Bastion on the Mississippi* (Baton Rouge: Louisiana State University Press, 1987), 38; Winters,

The Civil War in Louisiana, 167, 206; OR 15:627, 640.

12. Groom, *Vicksburg, 1863,* 231.

13. OR 15:627; Warner, *Generals in Blue,* 12, 142, 193–4, 440–441; Hollandsworth, *Pretense of Glory,* 91; Winters, *The Civil War in Louisiana,* 147; Cunningham, *The Port Hudson Campaign,* 4–5; Groom, *Vicksburg, 1863,* 231.

14. Cunningham, *The Port Hudson Campaign,* 19; Hewitt, *Port Hudson,* 41; Ezra J. Warner, *Generals in Gray: Lives of the Confederate Commanders* (1959; rpt. Baton Rouge: Louisiana State University Press, 1987), 21–22, 97; Jon L. Wakelyn, *Biographical Dictionary of the Confederacy* (Westport, CT: Greenwood Press, 1977), 196.

15. John S. Sledge, *The Gulf of Mexico: A Maritime History* (Columbia: University of South Carolina Press, 2019), 111, Jefferson quoted 89; John Williamson Crary, *Reminiscences of the Old South 1834–1866,* vol. 1 of *Southern History and Genealogy Series* (Pensacola, FL: The Perdido Bay Press, 1984), 43; Winters, *The Civil War in Louisiana,* 46.

16. Groom, *Vicksburg, 1863,* 107–19; Cunningham, *The Port Hudson Campaign,* 4–6; Davis quoted in William C. Davis, *Jefferson Davis: The Man and His Hour* (Baton Rouge: Louisiana State University Press, 1991), 407.

17. C. Vann Woodward, ed., *Mary Chesnut's Civil War* (New Haven, CT: Yale University Press, 1981), 330; Richard Barksdale Harwell, ed., *Kate: The Journal of a Confederate Nurse* (1959; rpt. Baton Rouge: Louisiana State University Press, 1987) 26, 29; East, ed., *Sarah Morgan: The Civil War Diary of a Southern Woman,* 47.

18. Clement Eaton, *Jefferson Davis* (New York: The Free Press, 1977), 3–4, 33–35; Davis, *Jefferson Davis,* 73.

19. Davis, *Jefferson Davis,* 408, 482–85; Eaton, *Jefferson Davis,* 248, 272.

20. Davis, *Jefferson Davis,* 485–88; Warner, *Generals in Gray,* 232–33.

21. Davis, *Jefferson Davis,* 486–487, Jefferson Davis quoted 487.

22. Ibid., 488; Shelby Foote, *The Civil War, a Narrative: Fredericksburg to Meridian,* 13–16, Davis quoted 16.

Chapter Two

1. Association of Defenders of Port Hudson (hereafter, "Association of Defenders), "Fortification and Siege of Port Hudson," *Southern Historical Society Papers,* vol. 14 (January–December 1886), 305–6; Lawrence E. Estaville, Jr., "A Small Contribution: Louisiana's Short Rural Railroads in the Civil War," *Louisiana History,* vol. 18 (Winter 1977), 95–97. Cunningham, *The Port Hudson Campaign,* 5–8; Hewitt, *Port Hudson, Confederate Bastion on the Mississippi,* 3–5; Pedro Garcia, *Port Hudson: Last Bastion on the Mississippi* (Orange, CA: The Paragon Agency, Publishers, 2005), 11–15; Harris H. Beecher, *Record of the 114th Regiment New York State Volunteers, Where it went, What it saw, and What it did* (Norwich, NY: J. F. Hubbard, Jr., 1866), 198.

2. Hewitt, *Port Hudson,* 41–43; Noel Crowson and John V. Brogden, eds., *Bloody Banners and Barefoot Boys: The Civil War Memoirs and Diary Entries of J.P. Cannon* (Shippensburg, PA: Burd Street Press, 1997), 19.

3. Crowson and Brogden, eds., *Bloody Banners and Barefoot Boys,* 19; Cunningham, *The Port Hudson Campaign,* 15.

4. Hewitt, *Port Hudson,* 42–43; F. Jay Taylor, ed., *Reluctant Rebel: The Secret Diary of Robert Patrick 1861–1865* (Baton Rouge: Louisiana State University Press, 1959, 1987), 71; East, ed., *Sarah Morgan,* 274.

5. Hewitt, *Port Hudson,* 47–52; Crowson and Brogden, eds., *Bloody Banners and Barefoot Boys,* 20; Taylor, ed., *Reluctant Rebel,* 88–89, 91.

6. Warner, *Generals in Gray,* 118–119, 216; 24 OR 3:613; OR 15:934–935, 948–949. These command dispositions are taken from returns date January 31, 1863, and will change from time to time as troop transfers take place.

7. Howard C. Wright, *Port Hudson: Its History from an Interior Point of View* (St. Francisville, LA: The Eagle Press, 1978), 10–11.

8. Hewitt, *Port Hudson,* 50, 52, 57; Wright, *Port Hudson,* 5 ("Slaughter's field"); Taylor, ed., *Reluctant Rebel,* 71.

9. OR 15:656, 671, 690; Foote, *The Civil War, a Narrative: Fredericksburg to Meridian,* 212; Groom, *Vicksburg,* 231, 266–67.

10. James P. Duffy, *Lincoln's Admiral: The Civil War Campaigns of David Farragut* (New York: John Wiley & Sons, 1997), 104; Shelby Foote, *The Civil War, a Narrative: Fort Sumter to Perryville* (New York: Random House, 1963), 357–58; Jack Friend,

West Wind Flood Tide: The Battle of Mobile Bay (Annapolis: Naval Institute Press, 2004); Sledge, *The Gulf of Mexico*, 141.
   11. Foote, *The Civil War, a Narrative: Fredericksburg to Meridian*, 213; Farragut quoted in Cunningham, *The Port Hudson Campaign*, 24; United States Department, *Official Records of the Union and Confederate Navies in the War of the Rebellion* (Washington, DC: U.S. Government Printing Office, 1905), 19:644. Hereafter, this source will be cited as ORN, followed by the volume number.
   12. Groom, *Vicksburg*, 268; Cunningham, *The Port Hudson Campaign*, 36; Hewitt, *Port Hudson*, 60–61.
   13. Hewitt, *Port Hudson*, 72–73; Foote, *The Civil War, a Narrative: Fredericksburg to Meridian*, 213.
   14. Groom, *Vicksburg*, 266–68, Farragut's speech to Banks quoted 267.
   15. OR 15:253; Frank M. Flinn, *Campaigning with Banks in Louisiana '63 and '64 and with Sheridan in the Shenandoah Valley in '64 and '65* (Lynn, MA: Press of Thomas P. Nichols, 1887), 21.
   16. OR 15:251–53; ORN 14:768; George W. Powers, *The Story of the Thirty-eighth Regiment of Massachusetts Volunteers* (Cambridge, MA: Dakin and Metcalf, 1866), 53; Hewitt, *Port Hudson*, 65–71, 75 ("He had as well been in New Orleans"); Duffy, *Lincoln's Admiral*, 182.
   17. Hewitt, *Port Hudson*, 57–58; Taylor, ed., *Reluctant Rebel*, 103; Robert Partin, "Report of a Corporal of the Alabama First Infantry on Talk and Fighting Along the Mississippi, 1862–63," *Alabama Historical Quarterly*, vol. 20 (Spring 1958), 587; East, ed., *Sarah Morgan*, 430.

Chapter Three

   1. Duffy, *Lincoln's Admiral*, 169, 182. Some sources identify Profit Island as Prophet or Prophet's Island.
   2. Ibid., 181–82; ORN 19:668–69 (Farragut's instructions quoted).
   3. ORN 19:670; Duffy, *Lincoln's Admiral*, 183–84; J. P. Cannon quoted in Crowson and Brogden, eds., *Bloody Banners and Barefoot Boys*, 23–24; Patrick quoted in Taylor, ed., *Reluctant Rebel*, 104; East, ed., *Sarah Morgan*, 439–40.
   4. Wright, *Port Hudson*, 18; Hewitt, *Port Hudson*, 15, 76; Cunningham, *The Port Hudson Campaign*, 10, 26.
   5. Groom, *Vicksburg*, 270; Duffy, *Lincoln's Admiral*, 184–87; ORN 19:671.
   6. Duffy, *Lincoln's Admiral*, 187; ORN 19:672–73, Alden quoted 677.
   7. ORN 19:672–73, 677–79; "The Fight at Port Hudson," *Memphis Appeal*, reprinted as Doc. 138 in Frank Moore, ed., *Rebellion Record, A Diary of American Events*, vol. 6 (New York: Arno Press, 1977), 458; Groom, *Vicksburg*, 270–71; Cunningham, *The Port Hudson Campaign*, 28–29.
   8. ORN 19:686–91; Duffy, *Lincoln's Admiral*, 189–91; Cunningham, *The Port Hudson Campaign*, 29–30.
   9. ORN 19:680–82; Cunningham, *The Port Hudson Campaign*, 30; Duffy, *Lincoln's Admiral*, 191.
   10. ORN 19:680–82; Smith and Dewey quoted in Hewitt, *Port Hudson*, 88–89, and Duffy, *Lincoln's Admiral*, 191–93; Reuben Gold Thwaites, *Rear Admiral Melancton Smith, U.S.N.—A Memoir* (Madison: State Historical Society of Wisconsin, 1893), 9.
   11. ORN 19:681–82 (Report of Melancton Smith), 694; Dewey quoted in Hewitt, *Port Hudson*, 90.
   12. Patrick quoted in Taylor, ed., *Reluctant Rebel*, 104; Cannon quoted in Crowson and Brogden, eds., *Bloody Banners and Barefoot Boys*, 24; Hewitt, *Port Hudson*, 90–95; Dewey quoted in Groom, *Vicksburg, 1863*, 271.
   13. "The Fight at Port Hudson," *New York "World,"* March 15, 1863, reprinted in Moore, ed., *Rebellion Record*, vol. 6, 456; Hewitt, *Port Hudson*, 92–93. Numbers of Union casualties reported vary from source to source. Figures given here for Union losses are from Winters, *The Civil War in Louisiana*, 217. Confederate losses are taken from "Returns of casualties in picket engagement and during bombardment of Port Hudson, La. on the evening and night of March 14," in OR 15:278.
   14. Powers, *The Story of the Thirty-eighth Regiment of Massachusetts Volunteers*, 54.
   15. ORN 19:665–668; OR 15:251–256.
   16. Powers, *The Story of the Thirty-eighth Regiment of Massachusetts Volunteers*, 55. James K. Hosmer, *The Color-Guard: A Corporal's Notes of Military Service in the Nineteenth Army Corps* (Boston: Walker, Wise and Company, 1864), 100; Hollandsworth, *Pretense of Glory*, 106–7.

17. Hosmer, *The Color-Guard*, 100–104; Flinn, *Campaigning*, 25; Hewitt, *Port Hudson*, 100–101.

Chapter Four

1. Hollandsworth, *Pretense of Glory*, 18–19, 46, 50, 108–9;
2. Donald S. Frazier, "Texans on the Teche, The Texas Brigade at the Battles of Bisland and Irish Bend, April 12–14, 1863," *Louisiana History*, vol. 32, no. 1 (Winter 1991), 418.
3. Winters, *The Civil War in Louisiana*, 222; Warner, *Generals in Gray*, 299–300; S. C. Gwynne, *Rebel Yell: The Violence, Passion, and Redemption of Stonewall Jackson* (New York: Scribner, 2014), 293–94; For Taylor's description of Stonewall Jackson's reaction to cursing, see, Richard Taylor, *Destruction and Reconstruction: Personal Experiences of the Late War* (New York: D. Appleton and Co., 1879), 58.
4. 26 OR 1:43–45; OR 15:296–297; Winters, *The Civil War in Louisiana*, 222–223.
5. Jackson Beauregard Davis, "The Life of Richard Taylor," *The Louisiana Historical Quarterly*, vol. 24 (January–October 1941), 72–73; Donald S. Frazier, "Texans on the Teche: The Texas Brigade at the Battles of Bisland and Irish Bend, April 12–14, 1863," *Louisiana History*, vol. 32, no. 1 (Winter 1991), 418–19; For Richard Taylor's quotes, see, Taylor, *Destruction and Reconstruction*, 132; Powers, *The Story of the Thirty-eighth Regiment of Massachusetts Volunteers*, 71; Flinn, *Campaigning*, 56.
6. OR 15:296–97, OR 15:388–36; Davis, "The Life of Richard Taylor," 72–73; Taylor, *Destruction and Reconstruction*, 136.
7. Powers, *The Story of the Thirty-eighth Regiment of Massachusetts Volunteers*, 72; Flinn, *Campaigning*, 26.
8. Hollandsworth, *Pretense of Glory*, 117; Winters, *The Civil War in Louisiana*, 232–33; 26 OR 1:494–45, 500–501.
9. 24 OR 3:814–15, 828, 842, 845; OR 15:1080.
10. 26 OR 2:9; Joseph E. Johnston, *Narrative of Military Operations during the Civil War* (New York: Da Capo Press, Inc. 1874, 1959), 189–91.
11. Dufrene, *Civil War Baton Rouge, Port Hudson and Bayou Sara*, 81; Cunningham, *The Port Hudson Campaign*, 41–42;

Hollandsworth, *Pretense of Glory*, 120–21.
12. Association of Defenders, "Fortification and Siege of Port Hudson," 312–13; Cunningham, *The Port Hudson Campaign*, 36–38; Hewitt, *Port Hudson*, 123.
13. Cunningham, *The Port Hudson Campaign*, 38–39; Association of Defenders, "Fortification and Siege of Port Hudson," 313; Wright, *Port Hudson*, 21–23.
14. Wright, *Port Hudson*, 24–25, 28–29; Cunningham, *The Port Hudson Campaign*, 39.
15. Hewitt, *Port Hudson*, 128–130; Cunningham, *The Port Hudson Campaign*, 43–44; Dufrene, *Civil War Baton Rouge, Port Hudson and Bayou Sara*, 84–88; Wright, *Port Hudson*, 24–25. Although some historians contend that the Battle of Plains Store was significant in that it closed the last escape route from Port Hudson, the position of Union forces at this time would have probably foreclosed any possibility for the outnumbered Confederates to break out of Port Hudson.
16. Association of Defenders, "Fortification and Siege of Port Hudson," 312; Gardner quoted in Hewitt, *Port Hudson,*, 131; Wright, *Port Hudson*, 13.
17. 26 OR 1:504, 526–27; Hewitt, *Port Hudson*, 131, 138; Cunningham, *The Port Hudson Campaign*, 47. The 1959 movie *The Horse Soldiers*, starring John Wayne, is based on "Grierson's Raid."
18. Hewitt, *Port Hudson*, 132–33; "Official Report of Colonel J. G. W. Steedman, First Regiment Alabama Volunteers," in "Fortification and Siege of Port Hudson," *Southern Historical Society Papers*, vol. 14, (January–December 1886), 315–22.
19. Hollandsworth, *Pretense of Glory*, 122; Edward Bacon, *Among the Cotton Thieves* (Detroit: The Free Press Steam Book and Job Printing House, 1867), 130.
20. 26 OR 1:504, 508–9; Banks quoted in Hollandsworth, *Pretense of Glory*, 122–23.

Chapter Five

1. Pedro Garcia, *Port Hudson: Last Bastion on the Mississippi* (Orange, CA: The Paragon Agency, 2005), 59, 61; Hewitt, *Port Hudson*, 137–38; Cunningham, *The Port Hudson Campaign*, 49; 26 OR 1:506–7, 508–9.

2. Bacon, *Among the Cotton Thieves*, 146; Willoughby M. Babcock, Jr., *Selections From the Letters and Diaries of Brevet-Brigadier General Willoughby Brabcock, The Seventy-Fifth New York Volunteers, A Study of Camp Life in the Union Armies During the Civil War* (New York: University of the State of New York, 1922), 30; L. Carroll Root, ed., "The Experiences of a Federal Soldier in Louisiana in 1863: Private Journal of William H. Root, Second Lieutenant, Seventy Fifth New York Volunteers, April 1—June 14, 1863," "Private Journal of William H. Root, Second Lieutenant, Seventy-Fifth New York Volunteers, April 1-June 14, 1863," *The Louisiana Historical Quarterly*, vol. 19 (January –October 1936), 658–59; Warner, *Generals in Blue*, 548–49; Winters, *The Civil War in Louisiana*, 250–51; Cunningham, *The Port Hudson Campaign*, 50.

3. 26 OR 1:163; Hewitt, *Port Hudson*, 142–44; John A. Kennedy, "Diary of a Rebel Soldier," in *Rebellion Record: A Diary of American Events*, vol. 6 (New York: Arno Press, 1977), 268.

4. 26 OR 1:128, 163; Hewitt, *Port Hudson*, 145; Kennedy, "Diary of a Rebel Soldier," 268; Root, "The Experiences of a Federal Soldier in Louisiana in 1863," 658–59; Cunningham, *The Port Hudson Campaign*, 50–52; Garcia, *Port Hudson*, 61–62; Wright, *Port Hudson*, 34; Warner, *Generals in Blue*, 356–57.

5. Garcia, *Port Hudson*, 51–52; Warner, *Generals in Blue*, 193–94; Cunningham, *The Port Hudson Campaign*, 52; Hewitt, *Port Hudson*, 151–52.

6. John G. Hollandsworth, Jr., *The Louisiana Native Guards: The Black Military Experience during the Civil War* (Baton Rouge: Louisiana State University Press, 1995), 51–52; Mary F. Berry, "Negro Troops in Blue and Gray: The Louisiana Native Guards, 1861–1863," *Louisiana History*, vol. 8, no. 1 (Winter 1967), 184–87;Benjamin Butler's remarks regarding the capabilities of black soldiers, quoted in Noah Andre Trudeau, *Like Men of War: Black Troops in the Civil War, 1862–1865* (Edison, NJ: Castle Books, 1998), 26.

7. Hollandsworth, *The Louisiana Native Guards*, 52; Bacon, *Among the Cotton Thieves*, 158–60, 166. Bacon's inspiration to title his book *Among the Cotton Thieves* undoubtedly came about because of Unionists such as Dwight who used their authority in the war to exploit the cotton crop of Southern planters for their own enrichment. Most historians agree with Ezra Warner, who in *Generals in Blue*, maintains, "Dwight's principal interest was flushing out stores of Confederate cotton for shipment to Massachusetts mills" (134–35).

8. Bacon, *Among the Cotton Thieves*, 159; William Dwight's letter to his mother quoted in Hollandsworth, *The Louisiana Native Guards*, 53.

9. Bacon, *Among the Cotton Thieves*, 159–60; Hollandsworth, *The Louisiana Native Guards*, 54–56; Trudeau, *Like Men of War*, 38–43; Moore, ed., "Siege of Port Hudson, a Rebel Narrative," *Rebellion Record*, vol. 7, 336.

10. Bacon, *Among the Cotton Thieves*, 160–61.

11. 26 OR 1:68; Winters, *The Civil War in Louisiana*, 253–54; Berry, "Negro Troops in Blue and Gray," 189–90; Commentary from the *New York Times* quoted in Hewitt, *Port Hudson*, 177; Wright, *Port Hudson*, 35–36. There were some unverified reports that retreating black soldiers were shot by a line of white Yankee troops that followed behind them. In "Siege of Port Hudson, a Rebel Narrative " (Moore, ed., *Rebellion Record*, vol. 7, 336), a participant wrote: "The enemy themselves report that six hundred of them perished. If this be so, they must have been shot down by the Yankees in the rear, for the execution we did upon them did not exceed two hundred and fifty; and indeed volleys of musketry were heard in the direction of their flight." A similar account by Lieutenant Daniel P. Smith appears in his *Company K First Alabama Regiment, Three Years in the Confederate Service* (Pratville, AL: Published by the Survivors, 1885), 63.

12. Richard B. Irwin, *History of the Nineteenth Army Corps* (New York: G. P. Putnam's Sons, 1893), 176–77; 26 OR 1:509.

13. Ibid.; Warner, *Generals in Blue*, 9.`

14. Cunningham, *The Port Hudson Campaign*, 58–59; Hewitt, *Port Hudson*, 157–59; Wright, *Port Hudson*, , 5, 33; Winters, *The Civil War in Louisiana*, 254–55.

15. John Smith Kendall, ed., "Recollections of a Confederate Officer," *The Louisiana Historical Quarterly*, vol. 29, no. 1 (January 1946), 1114; Association of

Defenders, "Fortification and Siege of Port Hudson," 325.
16. Smith, *Company K First Alabama Regiment*, 62–64. Quaker guns mentioned here refer to the simulated guns the Confederates placed at the river batteries. They were often nothing more than logs made to appear as heavy artillery from a distance.
17. Winters, *The Civil War in Louisiana*, 255–57; Hewitt, *Port Hudson*, 159–62, Sherman quoted 159; Cunningham, *The Port Hudson Campaign*, 59–62; Warner, *Generals in Blue*, 130; Wright, *Port Hudson*, 33 ("The gay colors"). Thomas Sherman was transported to New Orleans where his leg was amputated at Sisters Hospital (see Cunningham, *The Port Hudson Campaign*, 60). Neal Dow, before recovering from his wounds, was taken prisoner by the Confederates and remained in prison in Richmond and Mobile until March of 1864, when he was exchanged and released (see Warner, *Generals in Blue*, 131, and W. H Pascoe, "Confederate Cavalry around Port Hudson: A Thrilling Story of Southern Dash and Valor Told by an Orleanian Who Was One of the Heroic Horsemen," *Southern Historical Society Papers*, vol. 33 (1905).
18. Hollandsworth, *Pretense of Glory*, 124; Warner, *Generals in Blue*, 12; Albert Plummer, *History of the Forty-eighth Regiment Massachusetts Volunteer Militia During the Civil War* (Boston: Press of the New England Druggist Publishing Company, 1907), 37; Henry T. Johns, *Life with the Forty-ninth Massachusetts Volunteers* (1864; Washington, DC: Ramsey and Bisbee, 1890), 252–25.
19. Johns, *Life with the Forty-ninth Massachusetts Volunteers*, 253–54, 256, 261; Irwin, *History of the Nineteenth Army Corps*, 180–81; Plummer, *History of the Forty-eighth Regiment Massachusetts Volunteer Militia*, 38; Warner, *Generals in Blue*, 79.

Chapter Six

1. Hosmer, *The Color-Guard*, 174, 178; Johns, *Life with the Forty-ninth Massachusetts Volunteers*, 268; Irwin, *History of the Nineteenth Army Corps*, 181–82.
2. 26 OR 1:46–47, 67–70, 511, 520, 536; Moore, ed. (Augur's headquarters), "Siege of Port Hudson, a Rebel Narrative," *Rebellion Record*, vol. 7, 43; Bacon, *Among the Cotton Thieves*, 132.
3. 26 OR 1:513–15; Irwin, *History of the Nineteenth Army Corps*, 181, 185; Winters, *The Civil War in Louisiana*, 260; Cunningham, *The Port Hudson Campaign*, 69–70; Wright, *Port Hudson*, 37.
4. Irwin, *History of the Nineteenth Army Corps*, 185; Bacon, *Among the Cotton Thieves*, 129, 131.
5. Irwin, *History of the Nineteenth Army Corps*, 186–87; Winters, *The Civil War in Louisiana*, 261.
6. Irwin, *History of the Nineteenth Army Corps*, 187–88. Prior to the Port Hudson Campaign, several officers had brought formal charges against Colonel Clark, charging him with several nefarious acts, including "neglect of duty, misbehavior before the enemy, drunk and unfit for duty, and cowardice." An official hearing, however, was apparently never held. During the May 27 attack, Bacon contends that Clark feigned being wounded, but was found hiding in a ravine behind the lines, claiming he was blown there from the concussion of a gun. (See Winters, *The Civil War in Louisiana*, 220, and Bacon, *Among the Cotton Thieves*, 123–24, 126.)
7. Cunningham, *The Port Hudson Campaign*, 70–77; William F. Tiemann, *The 159th Regiment Infantry New York State Volunteers in the War of Rebellion* (Brooklyn, NY: William F. Tiemann, 1891), 43.
8. John A Kennedy, "Operations at Port Hudson: Diary of a Rebel Soldier," Moore, ed., *Rebellion Record*, vol. 7, 267; Wright, *Port Hudson*, 38; Root, ed., "The Experiences of a Federal Soldier in Louisiana in 1863," 664; Kendall, ed., "Recollections of a Confederate Officer," 1124.
9. Bell Irvin Wiley, *The Life of Johnny Reb: The Common Soldier of the Confederacy* (Baton Rouge: Louisiana State University Press, 1943), 250–51; Tiemann, *The 159th Regiment Infantry New York State Volunteers*, 43–44.
10. J. W. DeForest, *A Volunteer's Adventures: A Union Captain's Record of the Civil War* (New Haven, CT: Yale University Press, 1946), 116–18; Kendall, ed., "Recollections of a Confederate Officer," 1117–18, 1123–24; Wright, *Port Hudson*, 38.
11. George H. Hepworth, *The Whip, Hoe, and Sword, The Gulf-Department in '63* (Boston: Walker, Wise and Company, 1864), 293–94.

12. 26 OR 1:180; Bruce S. Allardice, *Confederate Colonels: A Biographical Register* (Columbia: University of Missouri Press, 2008), 242, 312; Bruce Catton, *Grant Moves South* (1960; rpt. Edison, NJ: Castle Books, 2000), 422; Hepworth, *The Whip, Hoe, and Sword*, 288–89; Emerson quoted in John Bowers, *Chickamauga and Chattanooga: The Battles That Doomed the Confederacy* (New York: Avon Books, Inc., 1994), 73.
13. 26 OR 1:134–45, 180; W. H. Pascoe, "Confederate Cavalry around Port Hudson: A Thrilling Story of Southern Dash and Valor Told by an Orleanian Who Was One of the Heroic Horsemen," *Southern Historical Society Papers*, vol. 33 (1905), 91–93.
14. 26 OR 1:134–137, 180–81.
15. Irwin, *History of the Nineteenth Army Corps*, 192.
16. Winters, *The Civil War in Louisiana*, 265–66; Cunningham, *The Port Hudson Campaign*, 77–78; 26 OR 1:14, 131–32, 157–58; L. Carroll Root, ed., "The Experiences of a Federal Soldier in Louisiana in 1863," 665.
17. 26 OR 1:14, 552–53; Winters, *The Civil War in Louisiana*, 266–67.
18. Irwin, *History of the Nineteenth Army Corps*, 193; Wright, *Port Hudson*, 39; 26 OR 1:155–56.
19. Irwin, *History of the Nineteenth Army Corps*, 193; Bacon, *Among the Cotton Thieves*, 148; 26 OR 1:552–3.
20. Crawford M. Jackson, "An Account of the occupation of Port Hudson, La.," *Alabama Historical Quarterly*, vol. 18, no. 1 (Spring 1956), 475; 26 OR 1:553.
21. Bacon, *Among the Cotton Thieves*, 148–49.
22. 26 OR 1:548–49, 554–55; Irwin, *History of the Nineteenth Army Corps*, 194–95; Garcia, *Port Hudson*, 95; Cunningham, *The Port Hudson Campaign*, 80–81.

Chapter Seven

1. Irwin, *History of the Nineteenth Army Corps*, 196; Hosmer, *The Color-Guard*, 188; Garcia, *Port Hudson*, 95; Winters, *The Civil War in Louisiana*, 266; Homer B. Sprague, *History of the 13th Infantry Regiment of Connecticut Volunteers During the Great Rebellion* (Hartford: Case, Lockwood & Co., 1867), 148.
2. 26 OR 1:158; Hollandsworth, *Pretense of Glory*, 127; Cunningham, *The Port Hudson Campaign*, 82–83; Daniel P. Smith, *Company K First Alabama Regiment*, 65.
3. 26 OR 1:873; Kendall, ed., "Recollections of a Confederate Officer," 1124–25. In his account, Kendall believes that Gardner had already sent as many as fifteen couriers to Johnston, and that Pruyn was probably number sixteen.
4. Irwin, *History of the Nineteenth Army Corps*, 196.
5. Ibid., 197; Winters, *The Civil War in Louisiana*, 268.
6. Ibid.; Garcia, *Port Hudson*, 96–97; Association of Defenders, "Fortification and Siege of Port Hudson," 328–29.
7. Irwin, *History of the Nineteenth Army Corps*, 197; Powers, *The Story of the Thirty-eighth Regiment of Massachusetts Volunteers*, 108.
8. Winters, *The Civil War in Louisiana*, 269–71; 26 OR 1:129–30, 133; Association of Defenders, "Fortification and Siege of Port Hudson," 332; Cunningham, *The Port Hudson Campaign*, 85–89; Jerrard quoted in Sprague, *History of the 13th Infantry Regiment of Connecticut Volunteers*, 157. For his insubordination, Jerrard was dishonorably discharged from the U.S. army, 26 OR 1:589–90; Harris H. Beecher, *Record of the 114th Regiment New York State Volunteers*, 207–8; Irwin, *History of the Nineteenth Army Corps*, 199; Garcia, *Port Hudson*, 102.
9. Sprague, *History of the 13th Infantry Regiment of Connecticut Volunteers*, 154–55; Tiemann, *The 159th Regiment Infantry New York State Volunteers*, 47.
10. Cunningham, *The Port Hudson Campaign*, 90; Winters, *The Civil War in Louisiana*, 271; Johns, *Life with the Forty-ninth Massachusetts Volunteers*, 321.
11. 26 OR 1:549; Garcia, *Port Hudson*, 102–3; Bacon, *Among the Cotton Thieves*, 155, 208.
12. Bacon, *Among the Cotton Thieves*, 153–75.
13. Ibid., 171–73; For a comprehensive listing of all the charges filed against Thomas Clark, see Winters, *The Civil War in Louisiana*, 220.
14. Bacon, *Among the Cotton Thieves*, 174–75;
15. Irwin, *History of the Nineteenth Army Corps*, 200; Plummer, *History of the Forty-eighth Regiment Massachusetts Volunteer Militia*, 43.

16. Bacon, *Among the Cotton Thieves*, 175–85; Cunningham, *The Port Hudson Campaign*, 91–93; Winters, *The Civil War in Louisiana*, 271–73.

17. 26 OR 1:14; Warner, *Generals in Blue*, 356–57; Moore, ed., *Rebellion Record*, vol. 7, 49; Irwin, *History of the Nineteenth Corps*, 197; George Carpenter, *History of the Eighth Regiment, Vermont Volunteers, 1861–1865*. (Boston: Press of Deland & Barta, 1886); 124; Hosmer, *The Color-Guard*, 194.

18. 26 OR 1:46–47; Winters, *The Civil War in Louisiana*, 273; Hosmer, *The Color-Guard*, 194; Beecher, *Record of the 114th Regiment New York State Volunteers*, 209–10.

Chapter Eight

1. 26 OR 1:57, 556, 557; Banks letter to his wife, Mary, quoted in Hollandsworth, *Pretense of Glory*, 129–30.

2. 26 OR1:557; Irwin, *History of the Nineteenth Army Corps*, 204; Groom, *Vicksburg, 1863*, 367–68.

3. Bacon, *Among the Cotton Thieves*, 185–86.

4. Cunningham, *The Port Hudson Campaign*, 96, Southern woman quoted 150n12; Association of Defenders, "Fortification and Siege of Port Hudson," 333; Hosmer, *The Color-Guard*, 198; Kenneth E. Shewmaker and Andrew K. Prinz, eds., "A Yankee in Louisiana: Selections from the Diary and Correspondence of Henry R. Gardner, 1862–1866." *Louisiana History*, vol. 5, no. 1 (Winter 1964), 282; Moore, ed., "Siege of Port Hudson, a Rebel Narrative," *Rebellion Record*, vol. 7, 338; Nelson diary quoted in William B. Stevens, *History of the Fiftieth Regiment of Infantry, Massachusetts Volunteer Militia in the Late War of the Rebellion* (Boston: Griffith-Stillings Press, 1907), 191.

5. Association of Defenders, "Fortification and Siege of Port Hudson," 334; Bacon, *Among the Cotton Thieves*, 209.

6. Wickham Hoffman, *Camp Court and Siege: A Narrative of Personal Adventures and Observations During Two Wars, 1861–1865, 1870–1871* (London: Sampson Lowe, Marston, Searle & Rivington, 1877), 72–73.

7. Irwin, *History of the Nineteenth Army Corps*, 212–213, 218; Banks speech quoted Hollandsworth, *Pretense of Glory*, 130; Moore, ed., "Account by a Participant, Bivouac of the 'Thousand Stormers' Before Port Hudson," *Rebellion Record*, vol. 7, 51.

8. Hollandsworth, *Pretense of Glory*, 131.

9. Winters, *The Civil War in Louisiana*, 274–76; Cunningham, *The Port Hudson Campaign*, 102–5; Irwin, *History of the Nineteenth Army Corps*, 221–23.

10. Johns, *Life with the Forty-ninth Massachusetts Volunteers*, 288–89.

11. Carpenter, *History of the Eighth Regiment Vermont Volunteers*, 120.

12. Stevens, *History of the Fiftieth Regiment of Infantry, Massachusetts Volunteer Militia*, 197.

13. Irwin, *History of the Nineteenth Army Corps*, 222–23. Later in the war as sieges became more common, especially in the Atlanta Campaign, many of these same techniques and methods continued to be used by both sides. By World War I, when trench warfare was prevalent, Europeans modeled and refined most of their tactics after those employed in sieges by soldiers in the U.S. Civil War.

14. Wright, *Port Hudson*, 38–39. "Ipecac," or ipecacuanha, the dried root of a South American shrub, was used as a nineteenth-century remedy.

15. Pascoe, "Confederate Cavalry around Port Hudson," 87–89.

16. Ibid.; Allardice, *Confederate Colonels*, 312.

17. Pascoe, "Confederate Cavalry around Port Hudson," 88–89.

18. Hosmer, *The Color-Guard*, 201–4; Cunningham, *The Port Hudson Campaign*, 114–15; Dufrene, *Civil War Baton Rouge, Port Hudson and Bayou Sara*, 94.

19. Neal Dow, *The Reminiscences of Neal Dow: Recollections of Eighty Years* (Portland, ME: The Evening Express Publishing Company, 1898), 699–700; Winters, *The Civil War in Louisiana*, 278

20. Dow, *Reminiscences of Neal Dow*, 699–702.

21. Ibid., 701–3. There are several versions of the capture of General Neal Dow, and as Dow admits, "No two of them alike" in the particulars of the story. I chose to use the version contained in Dow's *Reminiscences*, since it contained Dow's account and the account of John Simms, who claimed to have participated in the capture, and Dow's endorsement that the Simms account was "correct in all important particulars."

22. Ibid.; Winters, *The Civil War in Louisiana*, 278; Dennis Dufrene, *Civil War Baton Rouge, Port Hudson and Bayou Sara*, 102.
23. 26 OR 1:565; Cunningham, *The Port Hudson Campaign*, 111-13.; Stevens, *History of the Fiftieth Regiment of Infantry Massachusetts Volunteer Militia*, 191.

Chapter Nine

1. Bacon, *Among the Cotton Thieves*, 209, 221.
2. Ibid., 210, 227-28.
3. Ibid., 221-23, 225.
4. Ibid., 223-24.
5. Ibid., 224-26, 260. Colonel Bacon survived the war to write the account *Among the Cotton Thieves*, describing his experiences in the war. Although much of his narrative is scornful in its cynicism towards Dwight, Bailey and others, it offers not only an accurate account of the events, but an understanding of the morale problems within the Army of the Gulf, as well as some of the personalities responsible for those problems. Irwin, *History of the Nineteenth Army Corps*, 228; Winters, *The Civil War in Louisiana*, 277; Dufrene, *Civil War Baton Rouge, Port Hudson and Bayou Sara*, 95.
6. Hosmer, *The Color-Guard*, 211-12; Irwin, *History of the Nineteenth Army Corps*, 221-23.
7. Flinn, *Campaigning*, 84-85.
8. Wright, *Port Hudson*, 46; Cunningham, *The Port Hudson Campaign*, 102-3, 107.
9. Kendall, ed., "Recollections of a Confederate Officer," 1120-21; *Mobile Register and Advertiser*, August 9, 1863; Smith, *Company K First Alabama Regiment*, 77; Jackson, "An Account of the Occupation of Port Hudson, La.," 476-77; McClung quoted in Wiley, *The Life of Johnny Reb*, 94.
10. Wiley, *The Life of Johnny Reb*, 94; Groom, *Vicksburg, 1863*, 393-94 ("quiet, peaceable fellow"); Sam Watkins, *Company Aytch: Or a Side Show of the Big Show* (1882; rpt. New York: Plume, 1999), 75.
11. Smith, *Company K First Alabama Regiment*, 77.
12. Jackson, "An Account of the Occupation of Port Hudson, La.," 476; Winters, *The Civil War in Louisiana*, 275-76.
13. Wiley Sword, *Southern Invincibility: A History of the Confederate Heart* (New York: St. Martin's Press, 1999), 8-14
14. Ibid., passim; Cunningham, *The Port Hudson Campaign*, 106.
15. Kendall, ed., "Recollections of a Confederate Officer," 1125-26; Association of Defenders, "Fortification and Siege of Port Hudson," 336.
16. 26 OR 1:150-51; Winters, *The Civil War in Louisiana*, 276-77.
17. Bacon, *Among the Cotton Thieves*, 260; Warner, *Generals in Blue*, 345-46; 26 OR 1:599-600. Charges against the officers arrested by Dwight were never formally brought. Banks ordered their release and both men were later promoted.
18. Bacon, *Among the Cotton Thieves*, 260-62.
19. Ibid., 263-264; Kendall, ed., "Recollections of a Confederate Officer," 1128; 26 OR 1:151.
20. Bacon, *Among the Cotton Thieves*, 263-65.
21. Ibid., 266.

Chapter Ten

1. 26 OR 1:14; Winters, *The Civil War in Louisiana*, 278-79; Hollandsworth, *Pretense of Glory*, 128, 130; Irwin, *History of the Nineteenth Army Corps*, 216.
2. 26 OR 1:564-65; Cunningham, *The Port Hudson Campaign*, 114-15.
3. 26 OR 1:72-73, 182; Pascoe, "Confederate Cavalry around Port Hudson," 91; Cunningham, *The Port Hudson Campaign*, 115-16.
4. 26 OR 1:72-73, 182; Winters, *The Civil War in Louisiana*, 278; Irwin, *History of the Nineteenth Army Corps*, 216. There exist discrepancies within these sources as to the number of casualties, as well as which of the Confederate cavalry colonels, Logan or Powers, conducted the raid. Sources also vary as to whether the raid occurred during the morning or the night of July 2. I have generally followed the accounts of Logan and Irwin in the Official Records.
5. Kendall, ed., "Recollections of a Confederate Officer," 1120
6. Shewmaker and Prinz, eds., "A Yankee in Louisiana," 281; Hosmer, *The Color-Guard*, 214; Winters, *The Civil War in Louisiana*, 280-81.

7. Hosmer, *The Color-Guard*, 214; Winters, *The Civil War in Louisiana*, 281.
8. 24 OR 3:470; Irwin *History of the Nineteenth Army Corps*, 225-26; Ulysses S. Grant, *Personal Memoirs of U.S. Grant* (1885; rpt. New York: Penguin Books, 1999), 313.
9. Irwin, *History of the Nineteenth Corps*, 226-27; Stevens, *History of the Fiftieth Regiment of Infantry Massachusetts Volunteer Militia*, 200; Plummer, *History of the Forty-eighth Regiment Massachusetts Volunteer Militia*, 51.
10. Jackson "An Account of the Occupation of Port Hudson, La.," 477; Kendall, ed., "Recollections of a Confederate Officer," 1129.
11. 26 OR 1:52-54; Association of Defenders, "Fortification and Siege of Port Hudson," 341-42; Irwin, *History of the Nineteenth Corps*, 228-31. Irwin was originally appointed as a commissioner but, at his own request, was relieved of that duty and replaced by General Dwight. As to the enlisted Confederates who were paroled, most rejoined the army because of a technical error in the terms of the conditions established by the two governments. (See Cunningham, *The Port Hudson Campaign*, 120.)
12. Wright, *Port Hudson*, 56.
13. Kendall, ed., "Recollections of a Confederate Officer," 1132; Jackson, "An Account of the Occupation of Port Hudson, La.," 478-85; Cunningham, *The Port Hudson Campaign*, 118-19.
14. Irwin, *History of the Nineteenth Corps*, 231-32; Kendall, ed., "Recollections of a Confederate Officer, 1131-32; Plummer, *History of the Forty-eighth Regiment Massachusetts Volunteer Militia*, 50.
15. Wright, *Port Hudson*, 55-56
16. Rev. James K. Ewer, *The Third Massachusetts Cavalry in the War for the Union* (Maplewood, MA: Published by Direction of the Historical Committee of the Regimental Association, 1903), 109.
17. Bacon, *Among the Cotton Thieves*, 289-93.
18. Ibid., 289; James Hosmer, *The Color-Guard*, 218-19.
19. Davis, *Jefferson Davis*, 506-11, Seddon quoted 506; Davis quoted in Groom, *Vicksburg, 1863*, 422.
20. Gorgas quoted Groom, *Vicksburg, 1863*, 423; Woodward, ed., *Mary Chesnut's Civil War*, 459; East, ed., *Sarah Morgan*, 514-15.
21. East, ed., *Sarah Morgan*, 517.
22. Harwell, ed., *Kate*, 121; *Mobile Register and Advertiser*, August 9, 1863.

Epilogue

1. Irwin, *History of the Nineteenth Corps*, 233-34; 26 OR 1:144, 642; Winters, *The Civil War in Louisiana*, 283.
2. 26 OR 1:642; Willis Brewer, *Alabama: Her History, Resources, War Record and Public Men* (1872; rpt. Spartanburg, SC: Reprint Company Publishers, 1975), 589-91, 662-63; Cunningham, *The Port Hudson Campaign*, 120-21. Following the surrender, Banks suffered a great deal of criticism from Federal authorities, including Halleck and Benjamin Butler, because of a technical error he made in paroling the Confederate enlisted men. According to the terms of the cartel in place at the time, Gardner was the only officer available who was authorized to sign the approval of the paroles. But because he too was a prisoner of war, he was legally barred by the agreement from granting approval. Seeing the error, the Confederate government allowed the enlisted men released to be immediately reintegrated into other units and to continue in combat against Union forces. Ordinarily, under the agreement, they would have been required to either not to engage in military affairs during the war, or to be exchanged for Union prisoners of war before being allowed to take up arms again. Northerners were enraged that the Confederate government had violated the spirit of the agreement. Thus, after the summer of 1863, almost all exchanges were ceased until April of 1864 when General Grant forbade all exchanges. See E. Merton Coulter, *The Confederate States of America 1861-1865*, vol. 7 of *The History of the South* (Baton Rouge: Louisiana State University Press, 1950), 478-80; Hollandsworth, *Pretense of Glory*, 36n.
3. Hollandsworth, *Pretense of Glory*, 257; Cunningham, *The Port Hudson Campaign*, 123-24.
4. 26 OR 1:17, 509-10; Cunningham, *The Port Hudson Campaign*, 124-26; Hollandsworth, *Pretense of Glory*, 255-58, Banks quoted 122-23.
5. Hollandsworth, *Pretense of Glory*,

247–58; Warner, *Generals in Blue*, 17–18; Garcia, *Port Hudson*, 131.

6. Warner, *Generals in Blue*, 60–61; Brenda Wineapple, *The Impeachers: The Trial of Andrew Johnson and the Dream of a Just Nation* (New York: Random House, 2019), 168–71, Butler's impeachment speech quoted 170; Bruce Catton, *Terrible Swift Sword* (New York: Doubleday, 1963), 359.

7. Duffy, *Lincoln's Admiral*, 219–20; Groom, *Vicksburg, 1863*, 446; Friend, *West Wind Flood Tide*, 245, Farragut quoted 246.

8. Warner, *Generals in Blue*, 134–135.

9. Ibid., 130–131; Winters, *The Civil War in Louisiana*, 278.

10. Winters, *The Civil War in Louisiana*, 220.

11. Warner, *Generals in Blue*, 12, 189–90, 356, 440–41.

12. Garcia, *Port Hudson*, 127–28.

13. Cunningham, *The Port Hudson Campaign*, 71;

14. Groom, *Vicksburg, 1863*, 155n, 434–35; Warner, *Generals in Gray*, 232–33.

15. Craig L. Symonds, *Joseph E. Johnston: A Civil War Biography* (New York: W. W. Norton & Company, 1992), 212–18; 24 OR 1:227; Groom, *Vicksburg, 1863*, 402, 434–35; Joseph E. Johnston, *Narrative of Military Operations During the Civil War* (New York: Da Capo Press, 1959), 224–25.

16. Warner, *Generals in Gray*, 97; Garcia, *Port Hudson*, 128.

17. Warner, *Generals in Gray*, 21–22; Allardice, *Confederate Colonels*, 273, 243, 312, 355.

18. East, ed., *Sarah Morgan*, 605.

Bibliography

Primary Materials

Newspapers and Periodicals

Boston Traveler
Harper's Weekly
Memphis Appeal
Mobile Register and Advertiser
New Orleans *Daily Picayune*
New Orleans *Daily True Delta*
New Orleans *Era*
New Orleans *Times-Democrat*
New York Herald
New York World
Port Hudson *Evening Courier*

Books, Articles and Manuscripts

Association of Defenders of Port Hudson. "Fortification and Siege of Port Hudson." *Southern Historical Society Papers*, vol. 14 (January–December 1886).

Babcock, Willoughby M., Jr. *Selections from the Letters and Diaries of Brevet-Brigadier General Willoughby Babcock of the Seventy-Fifth New York Volunteers, A Study of Camp Life in the Union Armies During the Civil War*. New York: University of the State of New York, 1922.

Bacon, Edward. *Among the Cotton Thieves*. Detroit: The Free Press Steam Book and Job Printing House, 1867.

Banks, Nathaniel P. Collection and Papers. Library of Congress, Washington, DC.

Beecher, Harris H. *Record of the 114th Regiment New York State Volunteers, Where it Went, What it Saw, and What it Did*. Norwich, NY: J. F. Hubbard, Jr., 1866.

Carpenter, George N. *History of the Eighth Regiment, Vermont Volunteers, 1861–1865*. Boston: Press of Deland & Barta, 1886.

Crary, John Williamson, Sr. *Reminiscences of the Old South 1834–1866*. Vol. 1, *Southern History and Genealogy Series*. Pensacola, FL: The Perdido Bay Press, 1984.

Crowson, Noel, and John V. Brogden, eds. *Bloody Banners and Barefoot Boys: The Civil War Memoirs and Diary Entries of J. P. Cannon*. Shippensburg, PA: Burd Street Press, 1997.

DeForest, J.W. *A Volunteer's Adventures: A Union Captain's Record of the Civil War*. New Haven, CT: Yale University Press, 1946.

Dimitry, John. *Louisiana*. Vol. XIII of Clement Evans, ed. *Confederate Military History Extended Edition*. Reprint, Wilmington, NC: Broadfoot Publishing Company, 1988.

Dow, Neal. *The Reminiscences of Neal Dow: Recollections of Eighty Years*. Portland, ME: The Evening Express Publishing Company, 1898.

East, Charles, ed. *Sarah Morgan: The Civil War Diary of a Southern Woman*. 1991. Reprint, New York: Simon & Shuster, 1992.
Evans, Clement, ed. *Confederate Military History Extended Edition*. Atlanta: 1899. Reprint, Wilmington, NC: Broadfoot Publishing Company, 1988.
Ewer, Rev. James K. *The Third Massachusetts Cavalry in the War for the Union*. Maplewood, MA: Published by Direction of the Historical Committee of the Regimental Association, 1903.
Flinn, Frank M. *Campaigning with Banks in Louisiana in '63 and '64 and with Sheridan in the Shenandoah in '64 and '65*. Lynn, MA: Press of Thomas P. Nichols, 1887.
Grant, Ulysses S. *Personal Memoirs of U. S. Grant*. 1885. Reprint, New York: Penguin Books, 1999.
Harrell, John M., ed. *Arkansas*. Vol. XIV of Clement Evans, ed. *Confederate Military History Extended Edition*. Atlanta: 1899, Reprint, Wilmington, NC: Broadfoot Publishing Company, 1988.
Harwell, Richard Barksdale. *Kate: The Journal of a Confederate Nurse*. 1959. Reprint, Baton Rouge: Louisiana State University Press, 1959, 1987.
Hepworth, George H. *The Whip, Hoe, and Sword: The Gulf Department of '63*. Boston: Walker, Wise and Company, 1864.
Hoffman, Wickham. *Camp Court and Siege: A Narrative of Personal Adventures and Observations During Two Wars, 1861–1865, 1870–1871*. London: Sampson Low, Marston, Searle & Rivington, 1877.
Hosmer, James K. *The Color-Guard: A Corporal's Notes of Military Service in the Nineteenth Corps*. Boston: Walker, Wise and Company, 1864.
Hughes, Nathaniel Cheairs, Jr., ed. *Liddell's Record: St. John Richardson Liddell*. Baton Rouge: Louisiana State University Press, 1985.
Irwin, Richard B. "The Capture of Port Hudson." In *Battles and Leaders of the Civil War*. Vol. 3. New York: The Century Company, 1887.
_____. *History of the Nineteenth Army Corps*. New York: G. P. Putnam's Sons, 1893.
Jackson, Crawford M. "An Account of the Occupation of Port Hudson, La." *Alabama Historical Quarterly*, vol. 18 (Spring 1956).
Johns, Henry T. *Life with the Forty-ninth Massachusetts Volunteers*. Washington, DC: Ramsey and Bisbee, 1890.
Johnson, Robert U., and Clarence B. Buel, eds. *Battles and Leaders of the Civil War. Being for the Most Part Contributions by Union and Confederate Officers*. 4 vols. New York: The Century Co., 1887.
Johnston, Joseph E. *Narrative of Military Operations During the Civil War*. 1874. Reprint, New York: Da Capo Press, 1959.
Kendall, John Smith, ed. "The Diary of Surgeon Craig, Fourth Louisiana Regiment, C.S.A., 1864–65." *The Louisiana Historical Quarterly*, vol. 8 (January–October 1925).
_____. "Recollections of a Confederate Officer." *The Louisiana Historical Quarterly*, vol. 29 (January 1946).
Kennedy, John A. "Operations at Fort Hudson: Diary of a Rebel Soldier." In Doc. 48, vol.7 of Frank Moore, ed. *Rebellion Record: A Diary of American Events*. New York: Arno Press, 1977.
McMorries, Edward Young. *History of the First Regiment Alabama Volunteer Infantry, C.S.A.* Montgomery: The Brown Printing Company, 1904.
Moore, Frank, ed. *Rebellion Record: A Diary of American Events*. 12 vols. New York: Arno Press, 1977.
Partin, Robert. "Report of a Corporal of the Alabama First Infantry on Talk and Fighting Along the Mississippi, 1862–63." *Alabama Historical Quarterly*, vol. 20 (Spring 1958).
Pascoe, W. H. "Confederate Cavalry around Port Hudson: A Thrilling Story of Southern Dash and Valor Told by an Orleanian Who Was One of the Heroic Horsemen." *Southern Historical Society Papers*, vol. 33 (1905).
Plummer, Albert W. *History of the Forty-eighth Regiment Massachusetts Volunteer Militia During the Civil War*. Boston: Press of the New England Druggist Publishing Company, 1907.
Porter, David P. *Incidents and Anecdotes of the Civil War*. New York, 1885.
Powers, George W. *The Story of the Thirty-eighth Regiment of Massachusetts Volunteers*. Cambridge, MA: Dakin and Metcalf, 1866.

Read, C.W. "Reminiscences of the Confederate Navy." *Southern Historical Society Papers*, vol. 1 (January–June 1876).
Root, L. Carroll, ed. "The Experiences of a Federal Soldier in Louisiana in 1863: Private Journal of William H. Root, Second Lieutenant, Seventy Fifth New York Volunteers, April 1— June 14, 1863." *Louisiana Historical Quarterly*, vol. 19 (October 1936).
Shewmaker, Kenneth E., and Andrew K. Prinz, eds. "A Yankee in Louisiana: Selections from the Diary and Correspondence of Henry R. Gardner, 1862–1866." *Louisiana History*, vol.5 (Winter 1964).
Smith, Daniel P. *Company K First Alabama Regiment, Three Years in the Confederate Service*. Pratville, AL: Published by the Survivors, 1885.
Sprague, Homer B. *History of the 13th Infantry of Connecticut Volunteers During the Great Rebellion*. Hartford: Case, Lockwood & Company, 1867.
Stevens, William B. *History of the Fiftieth Regiment of Infantry, Massachusetts Volunteer Militia in the Late War of the Rebellion*. Boston: Griffith-Stillings Press, 1907.
Taylor, F. Jay, ed. *Reluctant Rebel: The Secret Diary of Robert Patrick 1861–1865*. Baton Rouge: Louisiana State University Press, 1959, 1987.
Taylor, Richard. *Destruction and Reconstruction: Personal Experiences of the Late War*. New York: D. Appleton and Co., 1879.
Thwaites, Reuben Gold. *Rear Admiral Melancton Smith, U.S.N.—A Memoir*. Madison: State Historical Society of Wisconsin, 1893.
Tiemann, William F. *The 159th Regiment Infantry New York State Volunteers in the War of the Rebellion*. Brooklyn: William F. Tiemann, 1891.
U.S. Navy Department. *The War of the Rebellion: Official Records of the Union and Confederate Navies*. 30 vols. Washington, DC, 1894–1922.
U.S. War Department. *The War of the Rebellion: A Compilation of the Official Records of the Union and Confederate Armies*. 128 vols. Washington, DC, 1880–1901.
Watkins, Sam. *Company Aytch: Or a Side Show of the Big Show*. 1882. Rprt. New York: Plume, 1999.
Woodward, C. Vann, ed. *Mary Chesnut's Civil War*. New Haven, CT: Yale University Press, 1981.
Wright, Howard C. *Port Hudson: Its History from an Interior Point of View*. St. Francisville, LA: 1937. Reprint, Baton Rouge: The Eagle Press, 1978.

Secondary Materials

Books and Articles

Allardice, Bruce S. *Confederate Colonels: A Biographical Register*. Columbia: University of Missouri Press, 2008.
Berry, Mary F. "Negro Troops in Blue and Gray: The Louisiana Native Guards, 1861–1863." *Louisiana History*, vol. 8 (Winter 1967).
Bowers, John. *Chickamauga and Chattanooga: The Battles That Doomed the Confederacy*. New York: Avon Books, Inc., 1994.
Brewer, Willis. *Alabama: Her History, Resources, War Record and Public Men*. 1872. Reprint, Spartanburg, SC: Reprint Company Publishers, 1975.
Catton, Bruce. *Grant Moves South*. 1960. Reprint, Edison, NJ: Castle Books, 2000.
_____. *Terrible Swift Sword*. New York: Doubleday, 1963.
Coulter, E. Merton. *The Confederate States of America 1861–1865*. Vol. 7 of *The History of the South*. Baton Rouge: Louisiana State University Press, 1950.
Cunningham, Edward. *The Port Hudson Campaign, 1862–1863*. Baton Rouge: Louisiana State University Press, 1963.
Dabney, Thomas Ewing. "The Butler Regime in Louisiana." *The Louisiana Historical Quarterly*, vol. 27, no. (April 1944).
Davis, Jackson Beauregard. "The Life of Richard Taylor." *The Louisiana Historical Quarterly*, vol. 24 (January–October, 1941).

Davis, William C. *Jefferson Davis: The Man and His Hour.* Baton Rouge: Louisiana State University Press, 1991.
Donald, David Herbert. *Lincoln.* New York: Simon & Schuster, 1995.
Duffy, James P. *Lincoln's Admiral: The Civil War Campaigns of David Farragut.* New York: John Wiley & Sons, 1997.
Dufrene, Dennis J. *Civil War Baton Rouge, Port Hudson and Bayou Sara: Capturing the Mississippi.* Charleston, SC: The History Press, 2012.
Eaton, Clement. *Jefferson Davis.* New York: The Free Press, 1977.
Estaville, Lawrence E., Jr. "A Small Contribution: Louisiana's Short Rural Railroads in the Civil War." *Louisiana History,* vol. 18 (Winter 1977).
Evans, Clement, ed. *Confederate Military History Extended Addition* 17 Vols. Atlanta, 1899. Reprint Wilmington: Broadfoot Publishing Company, 1988.
Foote, Shelby. *The Civil War, a Narrative: Fort Sumter to Perryville.* New York: Random House, 1958.
_____. *The Civil War, a Narrative: Fredericksburg to Meridian.* New York: Random House, 1963.
Frazier, Donald S. "Texans on the Teche: The Texas Brigade at the Battles of Bisland and Irish Bend, April 12–14, 1863." *Louisiana History,* vol. 32, no. 1 (Winter 1991).
Friend, Jack. *West Wind Flood Tide.* Annapolis, MD: Naval Institute Press, 2004.
Gallman J. Matthew. *The North Fights the Civil War: The Home Front.* Chicago: Ivan R. Dee, Inc., 1994.
Garcia, Pedro. *Port Hudson: Last Bastion on the Mississippi.* Orange, CA: The Paragon Publishing Agency, 2005
Groom, Winston. *Vicksburg, 1863.* New York: Albert A Knopf, 2009.
Gwynne, S. C. *Rebel Yell: The Violence, Passion, and Redemption of Stonewall Jackson.* New York: Scriber, 2004.
Harwell, Richard B., ed. *The Civil War Reader.* New York: The Mallard Press, 1957.
Hewitt, Lawrence Lee. *Port Hudson, Confederate Bastion on the Mississippi.* Baton Rouge: Louisiana State University Press, 1987.
_____. "'... There is no use in trying to dodge God Almighty': Farragut Runs the Port Hudson Batteries." *Louisiana History,* vol. 26 (Winter 1985).
Hollandsworth, James G. *The Louisiana Native Guards: The Black Experience during the Civil War.* Baton Rouge: Louisiana State University Press, 1995.
_____. *Pretense of Glory: The Life of General Nathaniel P. Banks.* Baton Rouge: Louisiana State University Press, 1998.
Horn, Stanley F. *The Army of Tennessee.* Norman: University of Oklahoma Press 1952.
Johnson, Howard Palmer. "New Orleans under General Butler." *The Louisiana Historical Quarterly,* vol. 24 (January–October 1941).
Josephy, Alvin M., Jr. *The Civil War in the American West.* New York: Alfred A. Knopf, 1991.
Keegan, John. *The American Civil War: A Military History.* New York: Alfred A. Knopf, 2009.
Padgett, James A. "Some Letters of George Stanton Denison, 1854–1866: Observations of a Yankee on Conditions in Louisiana and Texas," *The Louisiana Historical Quarterly,* vol. 23 (January–October), 1940.
Sledge, John S. *The Gulf of Mexico: A Maritime History.* Columbia: The University of South Carolina Press, 2019.
Sword, Wiley. *Southern Invincibility: A History of the Confederate Heart.* New York: St. Martin's Press, 1999.
Symonds, Craig L. *Joseph E. Johnston: A Civil War Biography.* New York: W. W. Norton & Company, 1994.
Trudeau, Noah Andre. *Like Men of War: Black Troops in the Civil War, 1862–1865.* Edison, NJ: Castle Books, 1998.
Wakelyn, Jon L. *Biographical Dictionary of the Confederacy.* Westport, CT: Greenwood Press, 1977.
Warner, Ezra. *Generals in Blue: Lives of the Union Commanders.* Baton Rouge: Louisiana State University Press, 1964.

_____. *Generals in Gray: Lives of the Confederate Commanders*. Baton Rouge: Louisiana State University Press, 1959.

Wiley, Bell Irvin. *The Life of Billy Yank*. Indianapolis: The Bobbs-Merrill Company, 1955.

_____. *The Life of Johnny Reb: The Common Soldier of the Confederacy*. Baton Rouge: Louisiana State University Press, 1943.

Wineapple, Brenda. *The Impeachers: The Trial of Andrew Johnson and the Dream of a Just Nation*. New York: Random House, 2019.

Winters, John D. *The Civil War in Louisiana*. Baton Rouge: Louisiana State University Press, 1963.

Index

Abbay, George 71
Alabama Regiments: First Infantry 61–62, 95, 146; Forty-ninth Infantry 97, 146
Albatross U.S.S. 34, 37–38, 41
Alden, James 38–39
Alexandria, LA 50
Andrews, George 58, 69–70, 138–139
Augur, Christopher 15, 32, 49, 54–59, 69, 73–74, 77, 79, 92, 101, 109, 151
Arkansas Regiments: Fifteenth Infantry 63; Seventeenth Mounted Infantry 117
Atchafalaya River Basin 28, 55

Babcock, Willoughby 61
Bacon, Edward 79, 102, 122, 129, 140–141
Bacon, Thomas 30
Bailey, Joseph (Joe) 119–122
Banks, Nathaniel P.: analysis of command performance 147–151; appearance, personal characteristics and background 7–8, 48, 60; appoints commission to accept surrender 137–139; assumes command in New Orleans 8–9, 13–15; cooperates with Farragut in naval assault 30–33, 45–47; orders May 27 attack 58–60; plans and orders attack of June 14, 89–93; plans for making final attack 107, 110–111, 135; postwar years 148; reassigns commands 79–80; receives word of surrender at Vicksburg 137–139; in Teche Campaign 48–52
Baton Rouge, LA 14, 23
Battle of Shiloh 18
Bayou Sara 23, 32, 57, 93
Bayou Teche 50–51
Bealle, William N.R. 16–17, 26, 52, 58, 71, 108, 154–155
Birge, Henry W. 110, 137–138
Brashear City, LA 49–50
Bull Pen 63
Burnett, Ben 138
Butler, Andrew 11
Butler, Benjamin 8–11, 14, 65, 148–149

Caillioux, Andre 67
Cannon, J.P. 24, 26, 35, 43

Carpenter, George 106, 112
Carrell, Thomas 37
Catherwood, Charles 39
Chapin, Edward 73–74, 80
Chesnut, Mary 18, 142
Citadel 92, 102, 104–105, 111, 121–122, 129
Clark, Thomas 80, 103–104, 151
Clinton, LA 22–23, 53, 86–87
Clinton and Port Hudson Railroad 22, 80, 87
Coleman, James 56
Cordon, John 103–104
Crary, John 17–18
Cumming, Kate 18, 143
Cummings, A. Boyd 38

Dabney, Fred 123
Davis, Jefferson 9–11, 18–20, 49, 53, 141–142
Dawson, Sarah Morgan *see* Morgan, Sarah
DeForest, John 83
De Gournay, Paul Francis 37, 55, 80, 122
Department of the Gulf 8, 12
Dewey, George 42–44
C.S.S. *Diana* 48
Dow, Neal 70, 72, 80, 116–118, 133, 150
Donaldsonville, LA 49
Dwight, William 57, 65–68, 79–80, 92, 101–104, 108, 119–121, 123, 129–132, 137, 140, 150

Emory, William 15, 32, 50
U.S.S. *Essex* 29, 34, 43–44
Ewer, James K. 140

Farragut, David G.: analysis of performance 147–151; attacks Port Hudson 34–45; begins siege operations 55–56; blames Banks for failed attack 45; meets with Banks aboard *Hartford* 31–32; personal characteristics and background 28–29; postwar years 148; proposes joint army-navy attack 29–30
Fearing, Hawkes 63, 96
Ferris, Samuel 96
"Forlorn Hope" 70, 72–74, 93, 107, 110–111, 113, 135, 138
Fort Bisland 48, 50
Fort Desperate 64, 111, 114, 122

Index

Freeman's Plantation 114
Franklin, LA. 50

Gardner, Franklin : analysis of command performance 152–154; appearance, personal characteristics and background 15–16; assumes command 16; fortifies Port Hudson 24; issues final order and surrenders garrison 137–139; learns of Vicksburg's surrender 137; makes final preparations against attack of May 27, 57–58; postwar years 154; refuses to surrender 91; requests help from Johnston 95–96
Gardner, Henry 109, 134
U.S.S. *Genesee* 34, 38–39, 41
U.S.S. *General Price* 136
Gooding, Oliver 63, 96
Gorgas, Josiah 142
Grant, Ulysses S. 8, 12, 48, 52, 135–137, 147
Greenleaf, Halbert 116
Gregg, John 26
Grierson, Benjamin 57, 85–87, 105, 115–116, 151
Grover, Cuvier 14–15, 32, 50, 57–58, 63–64, 68–69, 79, 91–93, 100–101, 151

Halleck, Henry W. 8, 12, 52, 118, 132
Harper's Weekly 68
Hart, John 34
U.S.S. *Hartford* 30–31, 34–35, 37–38, 41, 55
Hepworth, George 83–85
Hoffman, Wickham 109–110
Holcomb, Richard 100–101
Hosmer, James 46, 76–77, 94, 106, 108, 116, 122, 134–135, 141
Howard, John 39

U.S.S. *Indianola* 29
Irwin, Richard 58–59, 69–70, 77, 88, 90, 97, 134, 136

Jackson, Crawford 91, 124, 136–138
Jackson, Stonewall 8, 48–49
Jackson, MS 21, 23, 96
Jackson Road 57, 71–72, 116
Jerrard, Simon 100
Johns, Henry 73–74, 101, 111–112, 134–135
Johnson, Andrew 9, 149
Johnson, Ben 63
Johnston, Joseph 53–54, 87, 95–96, 128, 141, 154
Johnson's Island 138, 146

Kendall, John 71, 82, 124, 130, 134
Kennedy, John 62
U.S.S. *Kineo* 34, 39–40
Knox, Samuel L. 62

Lee, Robert E. 37, 141
Lee, Rooney 171

Lincoln, Abraham 7–9, 12
Locke, M.B. 61–62
Logan, John 59, 85–87, 114, 116–118, 134, 155
Louisiana Native Guards 65–69, 110
Louisiana Regiment: Twentieth Infantry 82
Lovell, Mansfield 20
Lyles, O.P. 130

Macomb, W.H. 34, 39
Maine Regiments: Twelfth Infantry 88; Twenty-second Infantry 88
Maxey, Samuel Bell 26, 53
McKinstry, J.B. 40
McClung, R.L. 124
McKowen, John 117
Michigan Regiment: Sixth Infantry 79, 103, 129–130
Miles, William R. 56, 58, 71, 104, 137, 155
Miles's Legion 123
U.S.S. *Mississippi* 30, 34, 39, 41–45
Mississippi Regiments: First Infantry 71, 97, 123; Thirty-Ninth Infantry 66
Mississippi River 8, 141
Mobile, AL 138, 149
Mobile Register and Advertiser 143
U.S.S. *Monongahela* 30, 34, 39–40, 42
Morgan, Sarah 10, 18, 25, 33, 35, 142–143, 155
Mumford, William 10

Nelson, John 65, 67
Nelson, Solomon 109, 112–113, 118
New Iberia, LA 50–51
New Hampshire Regiments: Eighth 63; Sixteenth Infantry 133
New Orleans, LA 8–13, 15, 17–18, 128, 142–143
New Orleans Era 142
New York Regiments: Seventy Fifth Infantry 61, 82; One Hundred Fourteenth Infantry 99, 116; One Hundred Fifty-ninth Infantry 101; One Hundred Sixty-second Infantry 133; Fourteenth Cavalry 115; One Hundred Sixty Fifth Zouaves 61, 73, 82–83, 99, 101, 115–116, 129–130
New York Times 68
Nickerson, Franklin 70, 72–73, 129–130, 151
Nims, Ormand 96
U.S.S. *North Star* 7

O'Brien, James 73, 75

Paine, Halbert 57, 63, 79, 87, 94, 96–98, 106, 151
Patrick, Robert 25–26, 28, 33, 35, 43
Pemberton, John 20, 52–54, 57, 135, 141, 153–154
Plains Store 56–57
Plains Store Road 57, 137
Planciancois, Anselmas 67
Plummer, Albert 73, 104, 139
Porter, David Dixon 7, 29, 55

Index

Port Hudson, LA 15, 22
Port Hudson Chronicle 33
Port Hudson Courier 33
Powers, Frank 56, 85–86, 114–115, 133, 155
Powers, George 32, 98
Powers, John 33
Pretty Creek 86
Priest Cap 93, 96–99, 111, 113, 122
Pruyn, Robert 95–96, 128, 138, 154

Queen of the West, U.S.S. 29

Red River 17, 30, 35, 52
Red River Campaign 52, 148
U.S.S. *Richmond* 30, 34, 38–43, 55
Riley Plantation 58
Root, William 61–62, 82, 88–89

U.S.S. *Sachem* 34
Sandy Creek 58, 66
Seddon, James 141
Shelby, William 66
Shenandoah Valley 150
Sherman, Thomas W. 15, 54, 57–59, 69–70, 72–75, 147, 151
Simmesport, LA 52
Simms, John 117
Skelton, L.H. 124
Slaughter's Field 27, 70, 73
Smith, Daniel P. 72, 95, 125–126

Smith, Kilby 136–137
Smith, Marshall 26, 59, 80, 137, 152
Smith, Melancton 42–43
Sprague, Homer B. 100–101
Springfield Road 133
Stark, Henry 103–104
St. Charles Hotel 8
Steedman, Isaiah 58, 62–63, 78, 94, 123–124, 137, 143, 155
Stockdale, Thomas 85–86, 115–116
Stone, Charles 137
U.S.S. *Suffolk* 133

Taylor, Richard 28, 48–51, 128, 154
Taylor, Zachary 49
Teche Campaign 50–51, 151
Tiemann, William F. 81, 101
Thompson, John 39
Troth's landing 55

Vicksburg, MS 8, 12, 15, 17, 125, 135–136, 145
Washington Daily National Intelligencer 68
Watkins, Sam 125
Watters, John 34
Weitzel, Godfrey 50, 57–58, 60–64, 68–69, 79, 88, 91, 93–99
Whisky Charge 129, 151
Wright, Howard 27

Young Plantation 78–79

www.ingramcontent.com/pod-product-compliance
Ingram Content Group UK Ltd.
Pitfield, Milton Keynes, MK11 3LW, UK
UKHW042013140426
5217IPUK00015B/1144